European Business Studies

DAVID NEEDHAM

Darlington College of Technology

and

ROBERT DRANSFIELD

Nottingham Trent University

STANLEY
THORNES

First published in 1994 by
Stanley Thornes (Publishers) Ltd
Ellenborough House
Cheltenham
Glos. GL50 1YD
UK

A catalogue record for this book is available from The British Library.

ISBN 0 7487 1895 8

Typeset by Action Typesetting Ltd, Gloucester
Printed and bound in Great Britain at The Bath Press, Avon

Contents

Contents

Preface

The extensive media coverage of European affairs reaches daily into our homes and sometimes makes Europe feel more like a 'concept' or 'a way of thinking' than a group of different countries. However, no matter how you interpret this blanket of information, today it would be naive to ask: 'What has Europe got to do with me?' Have you ever thought about what you are looking for in life in 5, 10 or even 15 years? How can living in Europe and being part of a Union help you to achieve these ambitions? Europe offers us the opportunity for free trade, friendships between once hostile people, opportunities for swapping ideas and for working towards a sustainable future. But, perhaps more than anything else, by working together rather than against each other, Europe offers us peace and prosperity.

A European Union is not a modern concept. Hamish McRae (*The World in 2020*, HarperCollins, 1994) has argued that, in a number of ways, Europe was more integrated in medieval times than it is today: there was a common parallel currency in gold, a common religion in the form of the Roman Catholic Church, and a common language in Latin.

Today we are moving towards an enlarged European Union in a rapidly changing Europe. After 1995 the European Union may include 16 nations, including Finland, Sweden, Norway and Austria. The next step may involve central European countries such as Hungary, Poland and the Czech Republic and later still, perhaps, Ukraine, Armenia, Slovakia, Slovenia and even Russia itself.

At the same time, in various parts of the world huge trading blocs such as NAFTA, ASEAN and the EEA have been formed. In economic terms it is essential today that economies are competitive on a global scale involving hundreds of millions or even billions of consumers. Being able to compete in such markets involves having a competitive edge through either a cost advantage or being able to differentiate your products sufficiently to place them ahead of your rivals. Jacques Delors has set out ambitious new plans for the European Union to improve its infrastructure by developing advanced transport and other communication links, coupled with the modernization and restructuring of production facilities and bold moves towards a common currency by the beginning of the twenty-first century.

On the political front many member states would like to see the spread of democracy in the Union through the spread of Qualified Majority Voting to key decision-making areas such as the environment and social policy. Decisions are increasingly being made at a European level and the powers of both the European Parliament and the Council of Regions, which represent the interests of the EU's tapestry of regional cultures and local and economic groupings, are likely to be further developed.

Opinion polls have indicated that the UK remains the most anti-EU nation. For many the key issue is 'sovereignty'. The UK has opted out of the Social Chapter (see page 99) and dragged its heels on the move to Qualified Majority Voting.

Our aim in writing this book has been to reflect the dynamic nature of Europe as well as its institutions, its businesses and its peoples. The text is designed to appeal to both intermediate and advanced Business within Europe units offered by BTEC, RSA and City and Guilds.

The book has been widely researched from resources generously supplied by a range of organizations throughout the European Union. A lot of European source materials have been used and adapted in the compilation of this text, and although, at times, it has been extremely difficult to identify copyright holders, every attempt has been made to obtain the relevant permissions. In the maps that appear in many of the chapters in this book, the town and city names have been 'anglicized' where an English translation exists.

Europe is an important part of our lives, and we hope that this text will help you to develop opinions and improve your understanding of many of the messages you see in the media to enable you to become better informed.

David Needham

Robert Dransfield

Introduction—Towards a federal Europe?

Students of European affairs are constantly reminded that we are dealing with an ever-changing field. Every day changes are taking place in economic, political and social relations.

For example, a major change that has taken place is that today the word Union has replaced Community as the commonly used description of the close association of what will be 16 European states.

The Union Treaty signed at Maastricht on 7 February 1992 gave new powers to the European Parliament, and it became clear after the European elections in 1994 that the Parliament intended to use these new powers.

A major change in 1994 was the ending of Jacques Delors' term as President of the European Union (EU). Delors, one of the giants of European integration, was regarded as a thorn in the side of Conservative governments' intentions for Europe. Delors was associated with a centralizing tendency in the EU, with increasing powers for EU institutions at the expense of the powers of national governments. Delors was also associated with a Social Europe enshrined in the Social Chapter.

In July 1994 all members of the EU with the exception of the UK voted for the Belgian Jean-Luc Dehaene to take over the EU Presidency. However, the UK vetoed his appointment and the other countries had to back down. The UK Conservative government saw Dehaene as being a 'super European' who would be too closely associated with German and French centralizing tendencies.

A compromise candidate was put forward—Jacques Santer, the former Luxembourg Prime Minister. However, Santer soon distanced himself from UK Conservatives by pledging himself to wider EU powers. He argued that federalism involved greater delegation of powers to regional governments rather than centralization. (A federal model of government like the one that currently exists in Germany is one where individual states decide on local issues, leaving major federation-wide issues, e.g. defence policy, to the federal government.)

However, it was at this stage that the European Parliament flexed its muscles. The Union Treaty gave the European Parliament the right to approve EU Commissioners prior to appointment; the power of assent for major international agreements; and a greater role in enacting legislation. The aim of these measures is to create wider democracy in the Union. Of course, a major problem here is that in European elections people may vote for a different political party than they do in national elections. For example, in 1994, although there was a Conservative government in power in the UK, the vast majority of Members of the European Parliament (MEPs) chosen by the UK electorate were from the Labour Party. Indeed, in the Union as a whole the Socialists became the largest single grouping in the new 567-seat legislature. (It may also be worth pointing out that there is still tremendous apathy in the UK to voting in European elections—most people simply don't bother to vote. The electorate does not seem to be aware of the importance of European decision-making and its effects on many aspects of their lives.) Conservative or Christian Democratic governments are in power in most of the larger member states, including the UK, Germany, France and Italy, and in several smaller ones.

However, the results of the 1994 European elections suggest that another swing of the political pendulum impends, towards a very centrist form of social democracy, accelerated in the UK by the election of Tony Blair to lead the Labour Party.

Socialist MEPs from Germany, Belgium, the Netherlands, France and Britain were solidly against accepting Santer for the new European president, and in a vote in the European Parliament on 21 July Santer was only approved by the slimmest of majorities. The 62 British Labour MEPs provide the largest single national group of Socialists in the European Parliament. The MEPs felt that Santer was too weak, that he was not the giant that Delors had been. Furthermore, MEPs felt that they had not been consulted about the nomination of Santer. This was highly significant because it represented an increase in demand for powers from the European Parliament.

Currently the Parliament still ranks third among the three main institutions of the European Union. Broadly speaking, the Council of Ministers takes the decisions. The Commission has a near monopoly on the power to put forward policy proposals. Parliament's role has been largely consultative. But under the Single European Act of 1986, Parliament acquired powers to amend certain legislation; almost half of its proposals have been adopted. The Maastricht Treaty extended this power, adding the right to veto in certain fields. Maastricht also enabled MEPs to approve the new president of the Commission.

Clearly power relations within the European Union will change in time. Because the UK is a member of this Union, it is required to move with the majority view. In the short term, the UK government can drag its heels by opting out of some activities and vetoing other measures. However, in the longer term the development of an even greater Union puts pressure on the UK to move in step with other EU states. It seems likely that the European Parliament will increasingly take on more powers, and that there will be increased moves towards federalism.

Santer, the compromise candidate, was finally accepted as the new president of the European Union both by national governments and the European Parliament. He was chosen because of his high standing as a statesman and as a pro-European. It remains to be seen whether he can step into the Jacques Delors mould.

The new EU president takes responsibility for an increasingly wider Europe. The Austrian referendum surprisingly showed that 66 per cent of Austrians wanted to join the EU. This result put pressure on Scandinavian countries to join the Union.

At the same time the EU has devised a pre-accession strategy outlining ways of bringing eastern European states closer to the EU before they finally join. This includes allowing them to attend more of the EU's meetings; closing the gaps between their legal systems; and retargeting existing aid.

A major inter-governmental conference planned for 1996 will effectively alter the rules about entry into and membership of the European Union. The EU already has association agreements with six countries—Poland, Hungary, the Czech Republic, Slovakia, Romania and Bulgaria. These agreements hold out the prospect of eventual membership of the EU. It has also negotiated free-trade agreements with the three Baltic states—Estonia, Latvia and Lithuania.

Widening or deepening?

The UK government is currently in favour of a wider Europe. In particular, the UK is in favour of extending the economic ties created by free trade. It would like to see free markets extended to a larger group of countries. Within this area the UK wants to see less government interference rather than more, and flexible labour and product markets.

However, the UK is opposed to the creation of a deeper Europe in which decisions are increasingly made from the centre. The UK sees this as adding to bureaucracy and waste. A number of people see powers increasingly coming to be vested in European institutions. Added to this is a worry that the German/French axis will become the driving force behind Europe. Many decisions may increasingly come to be made by majority voting from the centre despite the development of new institutions such as the Council of the Regions.

Acknowledgements

We would like to thank George Antonouris and Brian Yeomans for their encouragement, support and help. We would also like to acknowledge the contribution of the following for providing us with information, permission to reproduce materials as well as help and advice:

Barclays Bank Economics Intelligence Unit; Department of Foreign Affairs, Ireland; DTI Business in Europe Service; European Union Directorate General for Regional Policies; Eurostat; France-Soir newspaper; London Business School; Portuguese National Statistical Institute; Shell Education Service; The Foreign Office of the Federal Republic of Germany; The Irish Embassy; The Luxembourg Embassy; The Office of Economic Development, Germany; The Royal Netherlands Embassy; Thuringer Landes-Wirtschaftsförderungs-Gesellschaft m.b.H., Erfurt; European Passenger Services for the photograph on page 180; Syndication International for the photographs on pages 205 and 208; and the teaching and library staff at Darlington College of Technology and Nottingham Trent University.

Finally, yet again (!), we would like to thank members of our families for their patience and understanding.

1

Living in the European Union

Europe

What does Europe mean to you?

To what extent do you consider yourselves to be European? Is this European identity important to you? Many people become interested in local and even national issues but often forget that the UK is an important partner in a wider European Union (EU) which influences many of the things we can or cannot do. Remember that European issues will in some way affect us all: your family, friends and neighbours. How important is it for us to understand these issues?

So where does Europe begin?

For a start, we are all in it? However, a lot of people feel that Europe begins at Dover or at any other place of embarkation they use when they go on holiday. We must not, however, forget Ireland. Some people argue that because there is a strip of water—the Channel—between ourselves and mainland Europe, it affects our way of thinking, and we see ourselves as somewhat less European than many of our neighbours. But, what about opportunities in Europe? Have you ever thought about living and working in another country because, at some time in the future, the organization you work for may ask you to do so? Will the ways in which many people think about Europe change with the advent of the Channel Tunnel, better European communications and the successes of the Single Market?

How much do you know about Europe?

You may have been on holiday to many of the countries in Europe—for example, Spain, Greece, Denmark or France—but what did you learn when you were there? Did you manage to use any of the language skills from school? In what ways was the country you visited similar or dissimilar to the UK? Have you any relatives in other parts of Europe? Have you or your friends ever been involved in exchanges? If you have, what did you learn?

Why should we learn about Europe?

Organizations today can trade freely throughout the European Union (EU). In many cases this may involve manufacturing in various parts of Europe or engaging in joint ventures with companies from other European companies. It might also mean supplying a service to different parts of Europe. At the same time, freedom of movement within the EU is also a right of its citizens. As an employee you could be expected to be more mobile and work in various parts of the EU. It might also mean that you could be competing for a job with someone from another part of the EU.

Another reason why we should learn about Europe is that many of the events taking place in Europe directly affect us. For example, EU legislation, the Common Agricultural Policy (CAP) and environmental policies. These events may affect you as an employee, as an individual, as a member of a community and as a voter. By learning about Europe you can develop more informed opinions upon such issues.

What is this book about?

In this book we hope to provide a mechanism which enables you to learn more about the wider European community in which you live. But this book is not just about the European Union, it is also about the whole of Europe. There are many countries in Europe outside the EU with whom we maintain very close links—for example, Switzerland, Finland and Iceland. There are also many countries within Europe with whom, because of their former membership of the 'Eastern Bloc' behind the 'Iron Curtain', we have never really developed close trading and cultural links—for example, Albania, Latvia and Slovenia.

The Europe of the mid-1990s is already very different from the Europe of the 1980s. The map of the former Eastern Bloc has changed significantly and, at the same time, as some countries within Europe develop closer links, many regions within Europe strive for their independence. This is a challenging time for many Europeans and there are countless issues involved, many of which will be discussed in this book.

 Task

Look at the map of Europe in 1992 (Fig. 1.1).

1. Which 11 countries are the closest to the UK?
2. Are these countries all members of the EU?
3. What are the four largest countries?
4. What are the four smallest countries?
5. Which countries have been formed over the last 10 years?
6. Are there any countries you have not heard of?

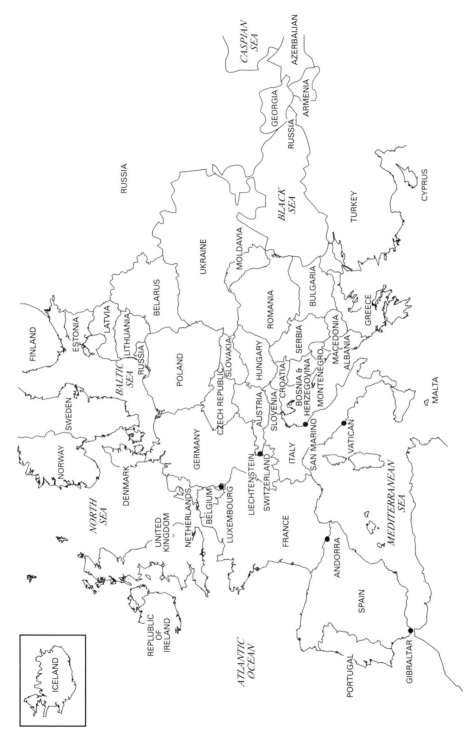

Figure 1.1   Europe in 1992

Healing divisions

At the end of the 1940s Europe was still reeling from the catastrophic consequences of the Second World War. Millions of people were literally wandering through countries homeless, cold and hungry. Food production was well below the levels required to meet everyone's needs and many of Europe's industries had been laid to waste. The Cold War was also beginning. Many believed that the divisions that had devastated Europe with two world wars had to be reversed and one important step to stop this happening again was the creation of closer co-operation between the countries of Europe.

The actions of two Frenchmen laid the foundations of the European Union we know today. John Monnet, a civil servant, and Robert Schuman, the foreign minister, argued that peace across Europe would only be possible if the former problems between France and Germany could be eliminated. They suggested joint action between the two countries. In 1950 France and Germany agreed upon the Schuman Plan which aimed to promote economic recovery by pooling the coal and steel industries of the two countries. By putting these key industries under a joint authority war would be impossible. Other countries were allowed to participate in this scheme and in 1951 the European Coal and Steel Community (ECSC) was established. As well as France and Germany, this included Italy, Belgium, the Netherlands and Luxembourg. In 1957 the same six countries, in Rome, signed two more treaties which set up the European Economic Community (EEC) and the European Atomic Energy Community (EAEC).

The EC or Common Market came into operation in 1958. This went further than just a simple trade agreement. It accepted that there should be closer economic co-operation and coordination between the participants. It formed a customs union, which meant that member countries could not stop or hinder producers from countries in the union from selling their goods. This effectively stopped governments protecting their own producers either with high customs taxes or through the use of subsidies to their own producers.

The UK did not join the EC in the 1950s. At the time the UK had strong trading links with the Commonwealth—which provided access to cheap food—as well as strong trading links with the USA. Many people felt that the UK was separate from the European mainland and were worried about joining a union that might lead to a loss of sovereignty.

Four years after the Treaty of Rome had been signed in 1961, the UK, Ireland and Denmark submitted applications to join the EC. This was followed by an application from Norway in 1962. In 1963 President De Gaulle of France vetoed the UK's application which caused negotiations with all of the applicants to be stopped. In 1967 the four countries applied again but the French refused to allow negotiations. Following further successful negotiations in 1973 the UK, Ireland and Denmark joined the EC. Norway did not join because the majority of its people had voted against it in a referendum. In 1981, Greece joined the EC, followed by Spain and Portugal in 1986.

The next group of new members of the European Union (EU) is likely to comprise members of the European Free Trade Association (EFTA), of which the UK was once a member. On 2 May 1992 the EFTA countries (except Switzerland) and the European Community signed an agreement to create a European Economic Area so that when the agreement came into force in 1993 a single market would operate between all these countries. Sweden, Austria, Finland and Switzerland, all members of EFTA, have also applied to become members of the EU, together with Turkey, Cyprus and Malta.

Though the former Communist countries of Central and Eastern Europe are not ready to join the EU at the moment, one important priority of the EU is to help such economies to develop so that they can become strong enough to cope with full membership of the EU in the future.

Some important dates in the development of the European Community are presented in Table 1.1, and Table 1.2 gives the population of member states in 1986.

Table 1.1 Some important dates in the European Community

Date	Event
1951	Signing of Treaty of Paris to create the European Coal and Steel Community (ECSC)
1957	Signing in Rome of treaties establishing the European Economic Community and the European Atomic Energy Community (EAEC): France, Germany, Italy, Belgium, the Netherlands and Luxembourg
1958	EC or Common Market came into operation
1973	UK, Ireland and Denmark join the EC
1981	Greece joins the EC
1986	Spain and Portugal join the EC

Table 1.2 The population of member states (in millions)

Country	Population	Country	Population
Germany	80	Belgium	10
Italy	58	Portugal	10
United Kingdom	57	Greece	10
France	56	Denmark	5
Spain	39	Ireland	3.5
Netherlands	15	Luxembourg	0.4

Total in European Community at 1986: 344 million

Towards a more unified Europe

As the European Union develops there are increasingly more arguments for stronger unification. Some of the reasons for this are:

- *Political stability.* The hope is that unity will help to create peace and harmony. The EU has played an important role in stabilizing economies and in acting as a European peace order.
- *Economic reasons.* No single state in Europe can compete on its own with the USA or Japan. Markets of hundreds of millions of consumers are today essential to enable companies to manufacture efficiently and offer goods and services at competitive prices.
- *Security reasons.* In order to preserve security Europe's continued membership of NATO is important however, as the Union develops Europe has to assume greater responsibility for its own security as well as for global peace.
- *Social reasons.* In Europe there are poor and rich regions. Common policies within a Union can help to narrow the gaps and overcome difficulties where real hardships exist.
- *Ecological reasons.* Pollution does not stop at national borders. Common environmental policies across Europe will help to diminish environmental damage.
- *Foreign policy reasons.* The combined policies of all of the European states will have more influence and can provide more help to solve disputes in other parts of the world.
- *Cultural reasons.* Life within Europe has become more varied and interesting and provided more choice since countries opened up their borders.

Case Study—The European Union and the Netherlands

The Dutch economy gained greatly from the establishment of the European Community (EC) in 1958. The first real benefit was that it made it easier for agricultural and industrial products to find their way to the other member states. In 1957 the EC countries, excluding the UK, Ireland, Denmark, Greece, Spain and Portugal, which were not then members, accounted for 41 per cent of Dutch exports. This figure has now risen to 61 per cent to the same countries and exports to the European Union (EU) as a whole now stand at 73 per cent.

The removal of trade barriers within the EC and the increased competition it encouraged did much to stimulate the Dutch economy during the 1960s. This led to more efficient techniques of production and economies of scale, both of which helped Dutch companies to remain efficient.

Another important benefit of joining the EC was that the Netherlands increased its importance as a transit country (Fig. 1.2) The ease of access from the North Sea helped Rotterdam to establish its Europort as the gateway to Europe and as a major centre of economic activity. The area became a key location for internationally oriented industry, such as petrochemicals.

Since joining the EC, the Netherlands has seen almost continuous expansion. For example, during the period 1959–1971, national income doubled in real terms.

Figure 1.2   The importance of the Netherlands as a transit country

The Netherlands wishes to see the EU contributing to the balanced expansion of world trade but also upholding the interests of developing countries. It would also like to see any remaining obstacles to free trade between member countries eliminated. The Netherlands considers that effective ways of coordinating the economic and financial policies of the member states must be found and its aim is to create an economic and monetary union in which powers will ultimately be transferred to a supranational European executive.

Questions

1. List the benefits the Dutch received from membership of the EC.
2. What sort of obstacles to free trade would have formerly have existed between European Union countries?
3. Comment briefly upon (a) the benefits and (b) the pitfalls of economic and monetary union.

Britain in Europe

It was no less a person than Winston Churchil who, in 1946, first spoke of the vision of 'a kind of United States of Europe'. However, since then British politicians of all parties have had differing views upon European unity. There have probably been many reasons for this; for example, some have argued that British foreign policy in the past was often against a strong European identity because a united Europe would have the political, economic and military strength to threaten Britain. In the early days it may have been felt that the countries forming the EC were weak; two had recently been enemies and had been defeated and four had experienced occupation. Surely, joining a union of six such weakened countries would not help the UK to become strong again! Another argument against Europeanization was the traditional indifference between the UK and France. As European integration in the 1950s had an unmistakable French slant, many British politicians of the time felt that joining the movement would be unacceptable.

Despite many of the above arguments the reluctance of Britain to join in with the movement towards European integration in the 1950s was due mainly to the reluctance to surrender any form of sovereignty (power to make laws) to any other authority. Today this argument is still cited by those against further European integration.

Though many politicians have a variety of different reasons either for or against European integration, the UK in the 1950s was heavily dependent upon foreign trade and an important element of this trade involved special arrangements between Britain and the Commonwealth. In 1950, 44.8 per cent of merchandise trade of the UK was from the Commonwealth. Commonwealth imports entered mostly duty-free and, in return, British exports received favourable treatment from Commonwealth partners. This compared with a mere 12 per cent with the six countries that proceeded to form the EC. The implication of this was serious. For Britain to become a member of the EC it would have to give preferential treatment to the six EC members and then positively discriminate against the Commonwealth.

The strategy of Britain was to outflank the EC with an alternative. A European Free Trade Area (EFTA) in industrial products was established in 1960 by seven countries: Austria, Denmark, Norway, Portugal, Sweden, Switzerland and the UK. These were later joined by Finland and Iceland.

Four years after the UK refused an invitation to join the EC, their policy changed. Harold Macmillan opened negotiations with a view to entry in 1961. Negotiations were vetoed in 1963 and in 1967 Harold Wilson repeated the attempt to negotiate. In 1973, under the leadership of Prime Minister Edward Heath, the UK became a full member of the EC.

An important question to be asked is why did British policy change so quickly? Over the 1950s and 1960s the British Empire changed into the Commonwealth and the position of the UK within the Commonwealth also changed as the UK lost its dominance. Another factor was the changing relationship with the United States and the declining status of the UK as a major world power. Economic factors also had a bearing and trade with the Commonwealth went into decline, so that by the 1980s less than 10 per cent of merchandise trade was with Commonwealth countries.

The UK, therefore, had to look for other markets and other partners. In the 1960s EC countries were achieving a rate of growth twice the UK average and as the UK did not want to become isolated politically and economically, it had to enter the Community and develop a profitable partnership with its members.

Though today few politicians in the UK doubt the importance of European Union (EU) membership, the extent of European integration has become an important issue with many members of the major parties. Margaret Thatcher, Norman Tebbit and Tony Benn are well known for their views on Europe, and their views contrast widely with those of John Major, Tony Blair and Paddy Ashdown. Contrasting views are not always a bad thing and no doubt arguments about the degree of European integration will continue for many years.

The European Union today

The Single European Market

The aim of completing one single 'common market' dates back to the thinking behind the European Community in 1957. A single market would create an area in which goods, capital, people and services could circulate freely without any restrictions imposed by frontiers. In 1986 the Single European Act set up the framework that would remove all internal barriers so that this truly 'common market' could be developed, and the completion of this phase occurred on 31 December 1992.

In the new Single Market of the 1990s members of the EU can work in any of the member states. There is mutual recognition of qualifications and the right for individuals to establish themselves and reside anywhere within the EU boundaries. No customs duties are charged within the Union and all the EU countries charge the same duty on imports from elsewhere in the world. Physical, technical and legal barriers between countries have been removed. The completion of these new measures involved the passing of nearly 300 new laws, with the hope that these measures would eventually lead to increased competition, lower prices and more choices for consumers.

Case Study—Freedom for professionals

Though the freedom to work anywhere in the EU was one of the basic rights laid down in the Treaty of Rome, it has taken nearly 35 years for this right to become a reality. One of the most important areas to be tackled in creating the Single Market was to look at the freedom of movement allowed to professional people. In the past, member states were not obliged to recognize professional qualifications obtained in member states. In 1991 the first general Directive for the mutual recognition of professional qualifications, was issued. Almost immediately 1200 professionals from other member states successfully applied to become members of UK professions. The most popular professions were teaching and law which, between them, attracted more than 75 per cent of applications.

Having looked at freedom of movement, the next move was to make it possible for professionals to set up and practise in cross-border organizations. Such organizations included vets, architects, doctors, lawyers, accountants and solicitors. The problems involved were often complex and required careful analysis of the differences between professions in different states.

Questions

1. Give *three* reasons why a professional, such as a doctor or a teacher, might want to practise in a different country.
2. Explain why rules and regulations for professionals such as lawyers might be different in various countries.
3. List the difficulties a professional might encounter when moving to another country.

Aims and objectives of the EC

The aims and objectives of the European Community (EC) were set out in the Treaty of Rome and the Single European Act. Against a background of a divided and war-torn Europe, the first aim was to achieve a closer relationship between the peoples of Europe in the hope that such events could not take place again. Doing so involved improving the living and working conditions of Europe's populations and reducing the deprivations that some suffered. Many would argue that this is potentially one of the important benefits of political union.

Another aim was to develop the EC within a framework of fair trade and competition. To do this required the elimination of customs duties and other restrictions as well as the abolition of obstacles to the free movement of persons, services and capital. By doing this the EC created a large domestic market which increased opportunities for organizations to benefit from substantial economies of scale. By coordinating and developing trade policy, the EC would also be able to exert greater collective influence upon world affairs than any of its individual members.

Other EC aims included the combining of resources to preserve and strengthen peace and harmony and to support developing nations. The effects of all of the measures generated by such aims were that there were few areas of economic life within member states that were not in some way influenced by EC policies.

Agriculture

The original aim of the Common Agricultural Policy (CAP) was to provide a stable supply of food at reasonable prices and, at the same time, to provide farmers with an adequate income. In the early years this was more of a priority because of food shortages. However, the high prices paid to farmers for food products under the CAP encouraged farmers to produce more, and by the late 1970s this led to large food surpluses. This created problems for the Community's budget and also complaints from other countries where agriculture is not subsidized. Reform of the CAP has been a priority and is leading to European Union (EU) prices being brought closer to those in the rest of the world.

European Monetary System

The European Monetary System (EMS) was set up in 1979 with the intention of establishing greater monetary stability in the European Community.

The EMS was used to introduce the European Currency Unit (ECU) which would be a measure of value for making loans between member states. Another measure was that member governments would deposit some of their foreign exchange reserves with the European Monetary Co-operation Fund and received ECUs in exchange. However, the most important part of the EMS was the setting up of the Exchange Rate Mechanism (ERM).

One of the main problems in trading overseas is one of uncertainty created by fluctuating exchange rates, and these may have a distinct bearing upon profit margins. The ERM attempted to reduce this uncertainty by getting members of the EC to make sure that their currencies did not change against each other by more than an agreed percentage. The pound sterling joined the ERM in October 1990 but was later forced to leave because it could not maintain the boundaries set for the pound. Since then some other currencies have also found it difficult to keep within their prescribed limits and many feel that these recent problems have made it more difficult to move towards further currency union.

Maastricht

In December 1991 the Heads of Government of the 12 EC countries met in Maastricht in the Netherlands to agree on a new treaty designed to lead to further political, economic and monetary union (Fig. 1.3)

Figure 1.3   Key areas of the Maastricht Treaty

So, what is Maastricht really about? In the treaty, member states build on and develop further existing co-operation on foreign and security policies. Though defence is still a matter for NATO, the European defence identity has been strengthened through an organization called the Western European Union, which acts as a bridge between the EU and NATO.

Another aspect of the treaty is that citizens of all EC countries are now 'Citizens of the Union', with the right to travel freely, work and live in other member states. However, the key feature of the Maastricht Treaty for most people is that it lays the foundations for economic and monetary union (EMU) within the EU. The objective is that eventually this will lead to a single currency between all member states. At this stage, though, to have a single European currency is very difficult because the policies and performances of member states vary so widely.

Another well-publicized issue from Maastricht was the Social Chapter (see page 99) which considered giving the EU wider powers to establish laws in areas of employment, social policy and working conditions. Though 11 states felt that the EU's powers should be increased to create more standards of employment protection, the UK opted out of this area. Other powers from Maastricht affected consumer protection, health, telecommunications, transport and energy.

Europe tomorrow

Since its beginnings in the 1950s, the European Union has doubled in size and today many other European states are enthusiastic to join. European countries have shown tremendous enthusiasm to work together on many economic, social and political areas which benefit further European union.

How, therefore, will Europe look in the year 2000? Since the walls separating the East and West crumbled there have been no limits to the imagination on how Europe could develop in the future. Europe in the year 2000 could well be frontierless from Dublin to Warsaw. There may be countless opportunities for travel, education, employment and retirement. Europe could be a harmonious union between different peoples, cultures, traditions and religions.

Freedom and democracy are going to be important in this new Europe. Achieving this 'common Europe' will require considerable co-operation between all the European states. Such co-operation will also help the business community to create jobs and expand prosperity to all regions of the 'new' Europe.

Another feature of this new Europe will be an increasing awareness of its identity. Symbols will become more important; for example, the European Union flag (a circle of 12 gold stars against a blue background; Fig. 1.4), its anthem (the *Ode to Joy* from Beethoven's Ninth Symphony), as well as a uniform passport and driving licence.

Despite all these changes it will be important to remember that the purpose of the EU is not to create a giant European state. Subsidiarity seeks to ensure that only those matters that can most efficiently be handled at a European level should be handed over to the EU. All other matters should be handled by national or local governments.

There will probably be around 65 million school children and students in the EU of the year 2000. They will be the first generation to understand and benefit from the many advantages of living in a large, frontierless, European internal market.

Centuries of disunity have divided Europe. The hope is that in the Europe of the future these divisions will have disappeared for ever.

Figure 1.4   The European Union flag

Studying Europe and thinking European

As citizens in this new Europe the organization you work for may well expect you to be more mobile than your parents or grandparents had to be. At the same time you are also more likely to find yourself working together with Europeans, both in your own country and overseas. You will need to be able to recognize opportunities as and when they arise, understand the values and cultures of other Europeans and appreciate each country's different lifestyles. This may well require you to learn other languages, eat different foods, visit far-away places and develop different skills.

By learning about Europe you are preparing yourself to meet the challenges of working and living in a wider and more integrated community.

2

An overview of Europe

A good starting point for understanding more about countries within Europe is to look at each of the countries in turn so that we can learn about their physical, economic, structural and demographic differences. Within a large community like the Single Market, which encompasses many different countries, it is important for us to recognize and have a basic appreciation of these differences.

In this chapter, as well as looking within the European Union (EU), we also look at other countries in the European Economic Area (EEA). The EEA came into existence on 1 January 1993, the same date as the completion of the Single Market. It extends the Single Market principles to the European Free Trade Association (EFTA) countries (Fig. 2.1) who have taken on much of the EC Single Market legislation. These countries include Austria, Finland, Iceland, Liechtenstein, Norway and Sweden. By doing this it enlarges the Single Market to comprise 19 countries with 375 million consumers. (In our analysis, and in Table 2.1, we also include Switzerland, the EFTA member which opted not to join the EEA.)

Figure 2.1   The link between the EU and EFTA

Figure 2.2 The 19 countries of the EEA, with EU countries shown in bold type

Table 2.1 The countries (including Switzerland) comprising the EU Single Market

Country	Population	Area (km²)	Capital	Language	Currency
Austria	7 500 000	83 848	Vienna	German	Schilling
Belgium	10 000 000	30 518	Brussels	Flemish/ French/German	Franc
Denmark	5 000 000	43 093	Copenhagen	Danish	Krone
Finland	5 000 000	338 145	Helsinki	Finnish/ Swedish	Markka
France	56 000 000	543 965	Paris	French/ Breton/Basque	Franc
Germany	80 000 000	356 961	Berlin	German	Deutschmark
Greece	10 000 000	131 957	Athens	Greek	Drachma
Iceland	255 800	103 600	Reykjavik	Icelandic	Krona
Ireland	3 500 000	70 285	Dublin	English/ Irish Gaelic	Irish Punt

Table 2.1 (*continued*)

Country	Population	Area (km²)	Capital	Language	Currency
Italy	58 000 000	301 286	Rome	Italian	Lira
Liechtenstein	28 000	158	Vaduz	German	Swiss Franc
Luxembourg	400 000	2 586	Luxembourg	French/German/ Letzeburgish	Franc
Netherlands	15 000 000	41 547	Amsterdam	Dutch	Guilder
Norway	4 250 000	323 878	Oslo	Norwegian	Krone
Portugal	10 000 000	91 985	Lisbon	Portuguese	Escudo
Spain	39 000 000	504 750	Madrid	Spanish/ Catalan/Basque/ Galician	Peseta
Sweden	8 600 000	410 929	Stockholm	Swedish/ Finnish/Lapp	Krona
Switzerland	6 800 000	41 293	Bern	German/French/ Italian/Romansch/ others	Franc
UK	57 000 000	244 100	London	English/Welsh/ Gaelic	Pound

Austria

Figure 2.3

Austria (Fig. 2.3) is a Federal Republic. The country is completely landlocked and is bordered by Switzerland, Germany, Bohemia, Slovakia, Hungary, Slovenia, Italy and Liechtenstein. Almost 70 per cent of Austria is mountainous and the Danube is the only navigable river which links Austria to other European countries.

Industrial development in Austria has been rapid over the last 25 years and the country enjoys considerable prosperity with high living standards. Austria's industry consists mainly of small to medium-sized businesses with only about 150 businesses employing more than 1000 people. In fact, the total number of industrial and trading companies is about 95 000, of which 95 per cent employ less than 50 people. Major exports from Austria are machinery, automative supplies, chemicals and semi-finished products.

Germany dominates the Austrian market and the European Union is by far the largest trading partner, accounting for about 70 per cent of its imports and exports. The Austrian economy looks set to grow well above the OECD average and predictions are good.

Belgium

Figure 2.4

Belgium (Fig 2.4) is a constitutional monarchy with a parliamentary democracy. It occupies a focal point in Europe with the Netherlands to the north, Germany and Luxembourg to the south-east and France to the south and south-west. Belgium has a 66 km North Sea coastline and is at the centre of an integrated network of European and intercontinental communications. As well as the North Sea ports of Antwerp, Bruges and Ostende, Belgium has many coastal and inland ports and 1500 km of navigable waterways. It also has the most concentrated railway system in the world. By virtue of its place at the heart of Europe 'where Europe meets', Brussels is the home of some of the EU's most important institutions such as the operational headquarters of the European Commission and Parliament as well as NATO.

Brussels is the seventh most important financial centre in the world and the fourth largest in Europe. It has many foreign banks and SWIFT (Society for Worldwide Interbank Financial Transactions) has its world centre in Brussels.

After the UK, Belgium was the first country in the world to be spurred on by industrialization. As a result, their steel, engineering, textile, chemical and glass industries account for a large proportion of their trade. Many of these traditional industries have specialized in making semi-finished products. For example, many companies, particularly in the automobile, aeronautical and electronics industries, make use of subcontract manufacture.

Denmark

Figure 2.5

Denmark (Fig 2.5) lies to the north of Germany and to the west of Sweden and has a coastline which borders the North Sea, Skagerrak, Kattegat and the Baltic. There are many islands, both inhabited and uninhabited. Denmark is a largely flat country, well known for its bacon and dairy products.

Denmark lies at the crossroads of three main markets, Scandinavia, the EC and Eastern Europe. Copenhagen airport is one of Europe's most modern airports and a network of bridges is currently under construction to link Denmark permanently with Sweden. Though only a small country, Denmark has one of Europe's strongest economies and the people of Denmark have one of the highest standards of living in the world. Denmark is well known for precision manufacturing in areas such as transport equipment and machinery.

Finland

Figure 2.6

Finland (Fig. 2.6) lies at the north-eastern edge of Europe, bordering Sweden, Norway and Russia. Finland is also to the north of Estonia, where many Finnish companies are involved in joint ventures. Finland became independent in 1917 after 600 years of Swedish rule, and this has left a lasting imprint upon Finnish life.

Finland is one of the most sparsely populated countries in Europe, the majority of the population being divided among the main towns. It was a highly industrialized economy which produces both capital and consumer goods. In terms of high income per capita, it ranks second only to Switzerland in Europe and so consequently there is demand for a wide range of consumer and luxury goods. Approximately 80 per cent of Finland's foreign trade is with Western Europe, the US and Japan.

France

Figure 2.7

France (Fig 2.7) is the largest country in Europe, has a coastline bordering the Channel, the Atlantic and the Mediterranean and has land borders with Spain to the south, Switzerland and Italy to the south-east as well as Germany, Belgium and Luxembourg to the west.

There are four principal rivers in France: the Seine, the Rhône, the Loire and the Garonne. There are also a number of mountain ranges including the Pyrenees and the Alps. Many agricultural crops are grown in France and it is the largest agricultural producer in the EU. It is particularly well known for its vines and is the second largest wine producer in Europe.

France is the EU's largest energy exporter and has a large industrial sector producing steel, motor cars, chemicals and other manufactured goods. French banks are among the largest in Europe.

Germany

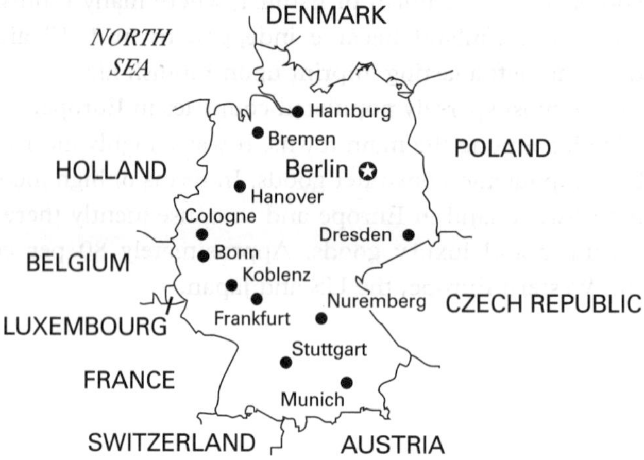

Figure 2.8

Germany (Fig. 2.8) has by far the largest population in Europe, particularly since reunification. Germany is bordered by the North Sea and the Baltic as well as Poland in the east, Bohemia and Austria in the south-east, Liechtenstein in the south, France, Belgium, Luxembourg and the Netherlands in the west and Denmark to the north.

Germany is the third largest country in Europe and has a relatively high population density. Its main rivers include the Rhine, the Danube, the Weser, the Elbe and the Moselle. The Federal Republic of Germany comprises 16 Federal States or Länder, including Berlin. Though the seat of government is still Bonn, it is planned to move most of the federal ministries to Berlin.

Germany is a highly industrialized country with a strong service sector. Exports were the source of 29.2 per cent of gross national product in 1991, which made Germany the world's second largest exporter, following the USA but ahead of Japan. At the same time Germany is the world's largest import market. The most important manufacturing industries in Germany are motor vehicle construction, chemicals, electrical engineering and mechanical engineering. German products are renowned for their quality and reliability. Though German labour costs are high, so are levels of productivity.

Case Study—The Federal State of Thüringen

You work for a company which manufactures pharmaceuticals and chemicals. Your company wants to develop a more pan-European strategy and is considering the opening up of a factory at Thüringen, together with a number of other options. Briefly assess this option in terms of:

- demographics
- infrastructure

- physical location and accessibility
- the expertise of the workforce.

THÜRINGEN

Erfurt

Figure 2.9

Thüringen [Fig. 2.9] lies in the heart of Europe, in the centre of the Federal Republic of Germany. Being the smallest of the five new Länder with a surface of 16.251 skm it is home to 2.6 million people living in 1700 communities. This corresponds to 3.4% of Germany's total population and to 4.6% of its total surface. In the North Thüringen borders on to Saxony-Anhalt. Its neighbours to the West are Hesse and Lower Saxony. In the South it borders Bavaria, and Saxony in the East. Erfurt, the regional capital, is Thüringen's biggest city. At present, motorways, roads, railways and Erfurt airport secure good and dense connections which are currently being optimised.

Today's image of Thüringen has been coined in the age of industrialisation. Fertile soil as well as a well developed agriculture in an attractive low mountain range characterise the region. One third of Thüringen is covered with forest. The mild climate and pleasant setting soon brought Thüringen the name 'green heart of Germany'.

Thüringen consists of 5 cities and 35 districts. With 165 inhabitants per skm the population density is far below the federal average. The dense net of small towns and the high percentage of rural communities are typical of Thüringen's population. Approximately 40% of the inhabitants live in the towns along the Eisenach–Altenburg road. On this important axis, also known as the 'Thüringian pearl string' are located the five biggest cities of

Thüringen: Gotha, Erfurt, Weimar, Jena, Gera and the economically important districts.

Erfurt, the regional capital, is 1250 years old (1992) and thus the oldest city in central Germany. The former royal seat of Gera is the most important rail and road junction in Eastern Thüringen. The more than 1000 year old city of Weimar with its Goethe and Schiller memorial places is being looked at as being the region's 'secret cultural capital'. Weimar counted 4 million visitors in 1991 alone. Jena is commonly known for its university rich in tradition and for the performances of its old-established opto-electronical industry.

Due to its geographical location Thüringen has always had an important transit role strongly influencing the construction of new motorways and roads today.

The following old-established crafts have a long tradition in Thüringen:

- wood-processing and wood carving in Southern and Central Thüringen
- the toy industry in Southern Thüringen
- the production and refining of glass in and around Ilmenau and Lauscha where the first glass works took up production as early as 1594
- ceramics and porcelain mainly in Thüringen's South and East.

Thüringen is also known for the broad variety of its industries [Fig. 2.10] such as

- optics, precision engineering, electronics, mechanical engineering (in Erfurt, Sömmerda, Eisenach, Ruhla, Jena, Hermsdorf, Gera)
- mechanical engineering and the automobile industry (in Eisenach, Gotha, Erfurt, Weimar, Arnstadt, Nordhausen, Gera, Ronneburg, Saalfeld, Suhl)
- metal production and processing (in Saalfeld, Gotha, Bad Langensalza, Ohrdruf, Bad Salzungen)
- tools and ironmongery (in Schmalkalden and Zella-Mehlis)
- glass and ceramics (in Jena, Hermsdorf, Kahla, Saalfeld, Triptis, Blankenhain, Arnstadt, Ilmenau)
- wood-processing and furniture industry (in Eisenberg, Zeulenroda, Stadtroda, Nordhausen, Sangerhausen, Weissensee, Mühlhausen, Erfurt)
- textile, clothing and leather industry (in Altenburg, Gera, Greiz, Zeulenroda, Pössneck, Schleiz, Hirschberg, Leinefelde, Bad Langensalza, Erfurt, Apolda)
- chemical and pharmaceutical industry (in Rudolstadt, Schwarza, Greiz, Elsterburg, Eisenberg, Gotha, Waltershausen, Apolda, Jena).

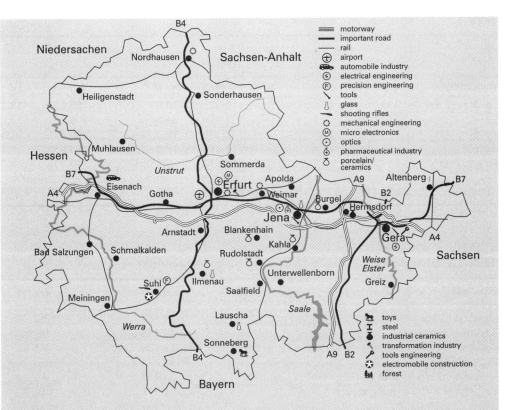

Figure 2.10   Thüringen an overview

Population

On 3rd October 1990 Thüringen counted 2 626 490 inhabitants, 52.2% of which are female. 19.5% of the under 15 year-olds will be entering the job market in the near future—this figure is particularly high in Thüringen. 66.8% or 1.754 million people in Thüringen are capable of gainful employment [Fig. 2.11] this is far above the federal average and also higher than in the other new Länder [see Tables 2.2 and 2.3].

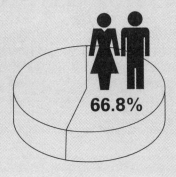

Figure 2.11

Table 2.2 Age structure: a young working population

Age	Total absolute	%	Male absolute	%	Female absolute	%
Under 15	512 723	19.5	262 795	20.9	249 926	18.2
15–25	338 782	12.9	173 228	13.8	165 554	12.1
25–40	615 620	23.4	311 470	24.8	304 150	22.2
40–50	313 622	11.9	157 286	12.5	156 336	11.4
50–65	487 573	18.6	231 618	18.5	255 955	18.7
65 and over	358 170	13.7	117 811	9.5	240 359	9.3
Total:	2 626 490	100.0	1 254 208	100.0	1 372 282	100.0

Source: Statistisches Landesamt Thüringen: 3 October 1990

Table 2.3 High percentage of skilled labour in industry and construction

Education/professional activity	No. of people	% of total
University	24 568	5.1
Technical college	44 153	9.1
Technician/master	21 728	4.5
Skilled worker	320 184	66.3
Skilled worker with part qualification	20 438	4.2
Employees with no qualifications	51 977	10.8
Total	483 048	100.0

Source: Statistisches Landesamt Thüringen: October 1989

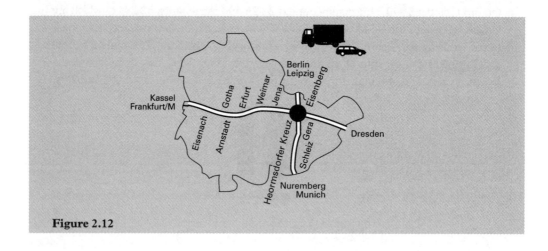

Figure 2.12

Road links

The strategic geographical location that has always been to Thüringen's advantage has gained even more importance since the reunification. Thüringen lies in the heart of Europe and right in the middle of Germany. This is crucial in view of the Single European market. Thüringen is at the cross roads of two motorways [Fig. 2.12].

In East–West direction the A5/E40/A4 Frankfurt on Main–Eisenach–Gotha–Erfurt–Weimar–Gera—Dresden–Görlitz.

In North—South direction the E49/E51/A9 Berlin—Leipzig—Hermsdorf junction—Nuremberg—Munich.

At present, improvements are being made to the A4 to accommodate six lanes of traffic between Eisenach and Dresden. At the same time the A9 is equally undergoing an expansion to six lanes from the Schkeuditz junction via the Hermsdorf junction to Hof. The construction of a new road is planned from the Bamberg/Schweinfurt region via Erfurt towards Magdeburg and Berlin. The 'Traffic Project German Unity' foresees the construction of another new road, the A82, running from Göttingen/Kassel towards Nordhausen/Halle. Throughout Thüringen the use of by-passes is being implemented.

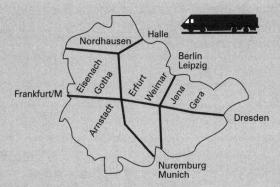

Figure 2.13

Rail links

In expanding existing rail links and constructing new lines Thüringen's connection with the rest of Germany is established [Fig. 2.13]. The modernisation measures apply to both the short distance and the long distance high speed lines. Selected lines are being electrified. The 'Traffic Project German Unity' foresees Thüringen's connection to the high speed track of the Bundesbahn. More precisely this implies the construction of a new line: Nuremberg–Erfurt–Leipzig–Dresden. The modernisation of the North–South axis Berlin–Halle–Jena–Nuremberg track also is to Thüringen's advantage. In East–West direction the expansion of the Erfurt–Bebra and Weimar–Jean–Gera–Göschwitz tracks brings about shorter journeys and better connections.

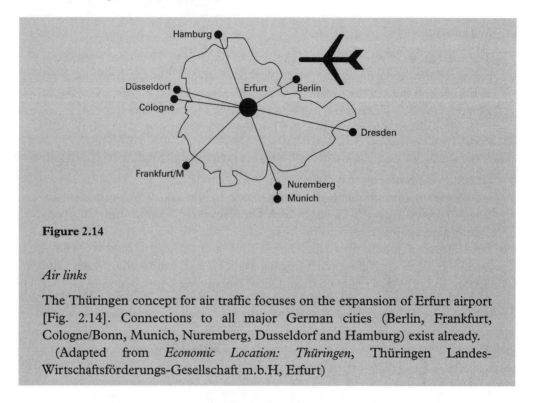

Figure 2.14

Air links

The Thüringen concept for air traffic focuses on the expansion of Erfurt airport
[Fig. 2.14]. Connections to all major German cities (Berlin, Frankfurt,
Cologne/Bonn, Munich, Nuremberg, Dusseldorf and Hamburg) exist already.

(Adapted from *Economic Location: Thüringen*, Thüringen Landes-
Wirtschaftsförderungs-Gesellschaft m.b.H, Erfurt)

Greece

Figure 2.15

Greece and its many islands stretch as far south as Crete and as far west as Corfu (Fig. 2.15). The north of Greece borders Albania, Macedonia, Bulgaria and Turkey. Greece is a mainly mountainous state, its tallest being Mount Olympus.

Though Greece joined the EC in 1981, it is a relatively poor country against the standards of other EU countries. The major industries of Greece include agriculture, particularly olives, fruit and tobacco, as well as merchant shipping and tourism. Exports include industrial products, wine, ores and minerals, textiles and chemicals. Though shipping has declined in recent years, tourism has developed.

 Task

Form small groups. In each group place at least one person who has been to either Greece or another Mediterranean country. List (a) the differences and (b) the similarities, between that country and the UK.

Iceland

Figure 2.16

Iceland (Fig. 2.16) is to the north of the UK and to the north-east of Norway. It has a small population with a low population density. Iceland's legislative assembly, the Althing, was established in 930 and is one of the oldest in the world.

Iceland's economy is heavily dependent upon fish, which provides about 70 per cent of visible exports. Almost one-third of the population is employed in service industries, 15 per cent in manufacturing and 9 per cent in construction. Unemployment in Iceland has always been low, and the country has a high standard of living and a large appetite for consumer goods. As only a few goods are manufactured in Iceland, it is heavily dependent upon imports.

Ireland

Figure 2.17

Ireland (Fig. 2.17) is an island on the western fringe of Europe. Its greatest length from Malin Head in the north to Mizen Head in the south is 486 km. Since 1921 the island has been divided politically into two parts: Northern Ireland is part of the UK and contains six of the nine counties of the ancient province of Ulster. The main rivers of Ireland are the Shannon, Lagan, Liffey, Blackwater, Suir, Lee and Slaney. The country has a mild and equable climate bathed by the relatively warm ocean waters of the North Atlantic Drift.

Ireland is an open economy which is highly dependent upon trade. Industry accounts for one-third of gross domestic product, about four-fifths of total exports and over one-quarter of total employment. Healthcare, pharmaceutical and electronics are key sectors of the Irish economy and Ireland has been the choice of approximately 50 per cent of new US electronics projects locating in Europe.

Italy

Italy (Fig. 2.18) is a Mediterranean country whose northern borders include France, Switzerland, Austria and Slovenia. It is identified by the familiar boot shape. To the east of Italy is the Adriatic Sea, while to the west lie the islands of Sardinia, Elba and Capri. Its main rivers include the Po, Tiber and Arno.

Though Italy has experienced problems of inflation, the economy has shown considerable growth throughout the 1980s. There is, however, still a considerable gap between the more industrialized north and the more agricultural south. In 1991 Italian exports were basic metal and mechanical products (34.3 per cent), textiles and leather clothing (17.6 per cent), wood, paper, rubber and other manufactured goods (12.2 per cent) as well as transport equipment (10.6 per cent). Italian products are frequently renowned for their design and style.

Figure 2.18

Liechtenstein

Figure 2.19

The Principality of Liechtenstein (Fig. 2.19) is a mini state lying on the Upper Rhine between Austria and Switzerland. It is less than half the size of the Isle of Wight and is closely linked with Switzerland. It lacks natural resources and is, therefore, dependent upon imports of energy and raw materials.

Since the Second World War, Liechtenstein has developed an industrial base in manufacturing machinery, precision instruments, textiles, ceramics for dental purposes and pharmaceutical products. It also has a formidable banking centre and is an important location for many trusts and investments. The country's workforce is considerably larger than the population. Nearly 60 per cent are foreigners and 31 per cent cross the border into Liechtenstein each day. There is virtually no unemployment and Liechtenstein's population enjoys a standard of living as high as that of Switzerland.

Luxembourg

BELGIUM

GERMANY

Luxembourg

FRANCE

Figure 2.20

The Grand Duchy of Luxembourg (Fig. 2.20) is an independent and indivisible state lying between France, Germany and Belgium and is one of the world's smallest countries. One-third of the country is covered with forest. In the north the uplands of the Ardennes are hilly, and, in the south there are rolling farmlands, bordered on the east by the grape-growing valley of the Moselle. The population is mainly bilingual and often trilingual. Luxembourg's position is very much at the heart of Europe and it has many close links with the Ruhr as well as with France and Belgium. Luxembourg City is the permanent host to the Secretariat of the European Parliament, the European Court of Justice, the Audit Office and some Commission services.

The Luxembourg economy usually outperforms the European Union average and GDP was at about 5 per cent per annum during the period from 1984 to 1990. Unemployment has been minimal at about 1.5 per cent. Luxembourg has a well-established steel industry, which is still the major employer. It is also a major manufacturer of heavy engineering products and machinery.

Case Study—Trading with Luxembourg

Table 2.4 Luxembourg's import/export with the UK for first quarter of 1991/2 (adapted from *Luxembourg*, with kind permission of the Luxembourg Embassy, London)

	Exports		Imports	
Section	1991	1992	1991	1992
Livestock and other animal products	0	1	62	29
Vegetable products	8	0	28	3
Oils and fats	0	0	1	0
Food, beverages, tobacco, etc	118	43	357	86

Table 2.4 (*continued*)

Section	Exports		Imports	
	1991	1992	1991	1992
Minerals (ore, slag, fuels)	14	6	19	8
Chemicals	242	125	305	119
Plastics (rubber products)	2284	1306	690	364
Leather, hides and skins	13	6	3	5
Wood and cork	4	1	7	4
Paper	159	139	403	312
Textiles and fabrics	1424	926	357	194
Footwear and headgear	0	0	11	7
Stone, glass and ceramics	1394	186	63	33
Jewellery	2	0	4	1
Base metals (iron and steel)	2138	1059	626	246
Electrical appliances	2026	1227	1524	598
Transportation equipment	95	43	226	114
Photographic and precision instruments	207	105	86	32
Arms and ammunition	0	0	1	0
Others (furniture, toys, sport requisites)	446	245	86	77
Works of art, antiques	411	25	13	14
Total	10967	6043	4872	2246

Table 2.4 itemizes the trading figures (in millions of francs) between Luxembourg and the UK for the first three months of 1991/2.

Questions

1. Look at the location of Luxembourg. Is this an accessible place for the UK to trade?
2. Comment upon the trading relationship between the UK and Luxembourg.
3. Examine the changes that have taken place over the two years.

Netherlands

The Netherlands (Fig. 2.21) lies between Belgium and Germany. More than a half of the country is below sea level, and there are many lakes, rivers and canals. The Netherlands is a constitutional monarchy and the reigning sovereign is Queen Beatrix.

Figure 2.21

The Netherlands is known as 'Europe's Distribution Centre' and the 'Gateway to Europe'. From the beginning the country expanded its inland waterway system and pioneered passenger and freight transportation. As a result Rotterdam is the world's largest and busiest port.

The Dutch economy has a broad base. More than one-half of the gross national product is exported, which compares with 29 per cent from Germany and 22 per cent from the UK. The main industries in the Netherlands are petroleum products, chemicals, agri-industrial products, transportation, medical instrumentation, electronics and bio-technology.

Norway

Figure 2.22

Norway (Fig. 2.22) lies to the west of Sweden. Much of the land is rugged and mountainous and there are considerable distances between major towns. Its major business centres are Oslo, Bergen, Trondheim and Stavanger.

Norway's main trading partners are Sweden, Germany and the UK. English is widely spoken and often used as a business language. Norway has a strong economy based on the natural resources of oil and gas, hydro-electric power, fish, forests and mineral oil. Its GNP per capita is the third highest in the OECD, almost twice as high as the UK's.

Portugal

Figure 2.23

Portugal (Fig. 2.23) is on the western edge of the Iberian Peninsula. It is bordered by Spain to its north and east and by the Atlantic Ocean to its south and west. It also includes the archipelagos of Madeira and the Azores, situated in the Atlantic to the south-west and west respectively of the mainland. The main rivers in Portugal are the Tagus and the Douro. Portugal became an independent state in 1140, making it one of the oldest countries in Europe. It has been a monarchy since its inception, and it became a parliamentary republic in 1910.

Portugal has been a member of the EC since 1986. Since then its economy has gone through a period of real growth at 4 per cent of GDP or more. Inflation has been a problem in recent years and though this is in decline, it is still the second highest in the EU. Portugal's main exports are manufactured goods, clothing, machinery, crude materials and food and beverages.

Case Study—Portugal's population in figures

Look at the population information published by the Portuguese National Statistical Institute (Tables 2.5–2.7; Figs 2.24 and 2.25). Comment upon the changes that have taken place since 1970. Use a charting device to display your analysis graphically.

Table 2.5 Resident population:estimages ('000's) at 31 Dec.

Year	Total	Males	Females
1970*	8663.3	4109.4	4553.9
1981*	9833.0	4737.7	5095.3
1982	9876.7	4761.1	5115.5
1983	9891.7	4770.1	5121.6
1984	9904.3	4777.3	5127.0
1985	9904.5	4778.0	5126.5
1986	9902.6	4777.8	5124.8
1987	9897.5	4775.9	5121.6
1988	9888.6	4771.8	5116.8
1989	9878.2	4766.8	5111.4
1990	9858.6	4757.6	5100.9
1991†	9853.0	4755.1	5098.0

* Population Census
† Resident population (Preliminary results Census 91)
Note: The Data from 1982 to 1990 were readjusted to the preliminary data 'Census 91'
Source: Portuguese National Statistical Institute

Table 2.6 Demographic indicators

Year	Birth rate (%)	Death rate (%)	Infant mortality rate (%)	Rate of natural increase (%)	Rate of population increase (%)	Expectation of life at birth (years)	
						M	F
1985	13.2	9.8	17.8	0.3	0.0	69.3	76.4
1986	12.8	9.6	15.8	0.3	0.0	69.8	76.8
1987	12.4	9.6	14.2	0.3	0.1	70.2	77.1
1988	12.3	9.9	13.0	0.2	0.1	70.1	77.3
1989	12.0	9.7	12.1	0.2	0.1	70.6	77.8
1990	11.8	10.4	10.9	0.1	0.2	70.2	77.3

* The indicators (excluding infant mortality rate) were adjusted in the preliminary data 'Census 91', so they are provisional.
Source: Portuguese National Statistical Institute

Table 2.7 Population (thousands) by district including Açores and Madeira

Regions	1970 Resident population (15–XII)	Density per km²	1981 Resident population (16–III)	Density per km²	1991* Resident population (15–IV)	Density per km²
PORTUGAL	8663.3	94.2	9833.0	106.9	9853.0	107.1
MAINLAND	8123.3	91.3	9336.8	105.0	9363.3	105.3
Aveiro	547.0	194.8	623.0	221.9	656.0	233.6
Beja	205.2	20.1	188.4	18.4	167.9	16.4
Braga	612.7	229.2	708.9	265.2	746.1	279.1
Bragança	181.2	27.4	184.2	27.9	158.3	23.9
Castelo Branco	255.8	38.3	234.2	35.1	214.7	32.2
Coimbra	403.0	102.1	436.3	110.5	427.6	108.3
Evora	179.7	24.3	180.3	24.4	173.5	23.5
Faro	269.0	54.2	323.5	65.2	340.1	68.6
Guarda	212.3	38.5	205.6	37.3	187.8	34.0
Leiria	379.0	107.8	420.2	119.6	427.8	121.7
Lisboa	1581.1	572.6	2069.7	749.5	2063.8	747.5
Portalegre	146.7	24.2	142.9	23.6	134.3	22.1
Porto	1318.8	550.6	1562.4	652.3	1622.3	677.4
Santarém	430.4	63.8	454.1	67.3	442.7	65.6
Setúbal	471.5	93.1	658.3	130.0	713.7	140.9
Viana do Castelo	251.6	111.6	256.8	113.9	248.7	110.3
Vila Real	266.4	61.5	264.4	61.1	237.1	54.8
Viseu	412.1	82.3	423.6	84.6	401.0	80.1
AÇORES	287.0	127.7	243.4	108.3	236.7	105.3
MADEIRA	253.0	318.6	252.8	318.4	253.0	318.7

* 'Census 91' Provisional data. (*Source*: Portuguese National Statistical Institute)

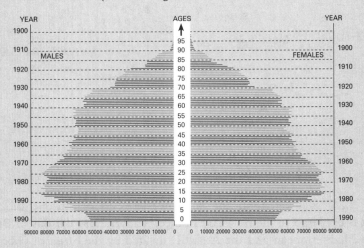

Figure 2.24 Distribution of resident population 31 December 1990 – estimate

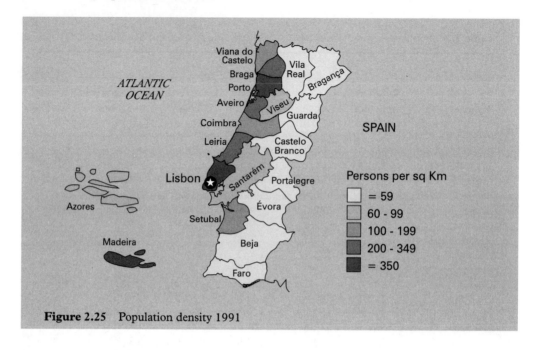

Figure 2.25   Population density 1991

Spain

Figure 2.26

Spain (Fig. 2.26) is located on the south-western tip of Europe on the Iberian Peninsula. It is bordered to the north by France, Andorra and the Bay of Biscay, to the south by the Mediterranean and the Atlantic, divided by the Strait of Gibraltar, to the east by the Mediterranean and to the west by Portugal and the Atlantic. In addition

Spain also includes the Balearic Islands in the Mediterranean, Ceuta and Melilla on the northern coast of Africa and the Canary Islands in the Atlantic Ocean. Spain is the second most mountainous country in Europe and the centre of Spain is a plateau.

The Spanish constitution was established in 1978 and Spain is a hereditary monarchy and a parliamentary democracy. Though many cultures influence Spain the predominant religion is Roman Catholic. Main Spanish exports include motor vehicles, machinery and equipment, edible fruit and nuts and iron and steel.

Sweden

Figure 2.27

Sweden (Fig. 2.27) lies to the east of Norway and to the west of Finland. Denmark lies to its south-west. The majority (85 per cent) of the population live in the south of the country around the principal commercial centres of Stockholm, Gothenburg and Malmö.

Sweden is ranked eighth in the world in GNP per capita. The economy is high-cost and high-quality and the Swedish market is highly sophisticated. To maintain this high standard of living Sweden depends upon international trade. The UK is Sweden's second most important trading partner after Germany.

Switzerland

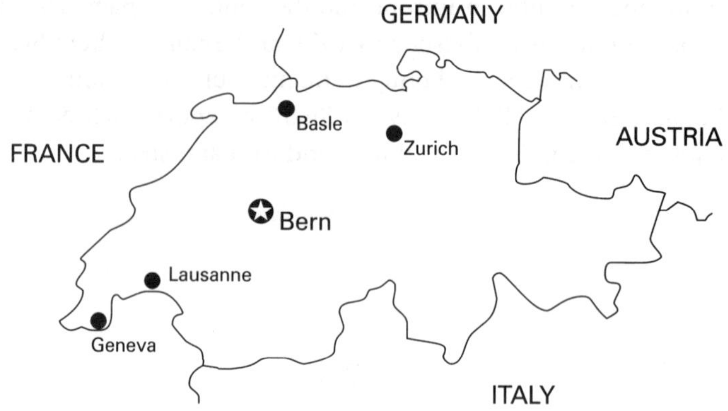

Figure 2.28

Switzerland (Fig. 2.28) is a relatively small country which lies at the centre of Europe between France, Germany, Liechtenstein, Austria and Italy. It is mountainous and its main cities are Bern, Zurich, Lausanne and Geneva.

Switzerland's per capita GDP is one of the highest in the world. Zurich is its financial and commercial centre and Nestlé is its largest company. Considering that Switzerland has negligible mineral reserves and no natural energy resources other than hydro-electricity, its success is outstanding. Main Swiss exports include pharmaceuticals, banking, finance and insurance services and food products.

United Kingdom

The UK (Fig. 2.29; Northern Ireland is shown with the map of Ireland (Fig. 2.17)) is on the west of Europe separated from the mainland by the English Channel. The Pennines run down the middle of the country separating east from west, from the Scottish borders to the Midlands. Main rivers include the Thames, the Severn and the Humber. The UK has four parts: England for which the capital is London, Scotland for which the capital is Edinburgh, Wales for which the capital is Cardiff and Northern Ireland for which the capital is Belfast.

The UK was the world's first industrialized country. However, its traditional industries such as coal, iron and steel and heavy engineering have since declined. Since 1979 Conservative governments have been in power and this has led to cuts in direct taxation, increases in indirect taxation, the movement of many organizations and industries to the private sector and laws to curb the powers of trade unions. Since this time the UK has also been through two significant recessions. The UK has been criticized for a lack of spending on research and development, on transport infrastructure and has a poor record in education and training. It has become a base for many overseas companies wishing to gain access to EU markets. During the early 1990s the UK had problems with budget deficits, unemployment and balance of payment deficits. However, by 1993 confidence started to improve and the UK emerged slowly from recession. Its main exports are manufactured goods, oil, gas and chemicals.

Figure 2.29

3

European identity

European culture

Europe is made up of many different groups of people with widely different *cultures*. In the same street of a large city you will find people who use different languages, have different styles of dress, varying tastes in music and have other cultural differences. However, perhaps more important than these differences will be the similarities and shared values of these groups of people.

There is no such thing as 'European culture'. Instead, Europe should be regarded as an area containing many cultural groupings that have interacted together for centuries. Most of the time different groupings get on well together and benefit from the knowledge gained by sharing ideas and customs with each other. At other times groups come into conflict, e.g. the ethnic tensions between Croats, Serbs and Muslims in the former Yugoslavia in the mid-1990s.

Europe is divided into many regions with particular *distinctive regional flavours*, e.g. Normandy in northern France, the highlands and islands of Scotland, Catalonia in Spain, etc. In 1992 *The Independent* newspaper produced a map of Europe which it called 'The Europe of the Regions'. The suggestion was that perhaps Europe should be looked at as being made up of many separate regions within countries, each region having its own distinctive culture and flavour as well as sharing many common features with other places.

> ## Case Study—The civilization of the European Union
>
> The following extract appeared in a publication *About Europe* produced by the Commission of the European Union to provide information to young people. Read the extract and then answer the questions that follow:
>
> > With its nine official—and numerous unofficial—languages and its hundreds of dialects, the Union often appears to be a Tower of Babel. What is frequently forgotten, however, is that this very diversity is an enriching factor and one that reflects the fundamental unity of the European culture

that has grown up over the last three thousand years on the soil of Europe's ancient civilisations.

The various migrations, invasions and wars have made havoc of frontiers, influenced the development of languages, changed customs and ways of life and have altered the face of the old continent, but for all this Europe has not lost its identity.

All the new arrivals have fitted into the European mould and have rapidly become some of the staunchest supporters of the new culture.

Questions

1. What are the nine official languages of the EU?
2. Why might the EU appear to be a Tower of Babel? Give examples of languages and dialects used in your own region.
3. Do you agree with the writer of the above extract that there is such a thing as a European Identity? Explain!
4. Do you agree that there is (or should be) a 'European mould'? Explain!

What is culture?

Different groups of people will have different ways of behaving. Culture consists of *behavioural patterns* which:

- have been acquired and are shared by a group of people in society
- are often historically derived and passed on from one generation to another
- may include ideas and values
- are a form of conditioning by society.

In learning about Europe, although it is impossible to find out about all elements of culture and the complexities of why different groups of people share such behaviour patterns, it is important to appreciate and be sensitive to all of the different things people do.

 Tasks—Portrait of a country

1. Working as a group produce a portrait of another country, e.g. Denmark, Spain, Portugal, France, Germany, the Netherlands. Work with three or four other students. Draw your information from what you already 'know':
    (a) about the country
    (b) about the people of the country.

At this stage do not use reference sources. Present your ideas on one large sheet of flip chart paper. Groups of students should present their ideas to the whole class. Now consider the extent to which your views of that country are based on poor information and stereotype. What aspects of culture do you focus on?

2. Carry out a survey to find out what views people in your area have of people from other countries. How stereotyped are their views?

The chances are quite high that your work on the previous task might show that we have only a limited view of the cultures of other countries. These views may be based on stereotypes—e.g. the Frenchman in a striped T shirt, beret and string of onions round his neck. Yet, when we visit other countries and meet people from these countries they rarely fit with the stereotype. Often our views of other countries are based on ignorance and poor information. Books and the media frequently paint a *stereotyped* view of other countries.

Real differences

There are, however, some real cultural differences between people which depend on their experiences, the environment in which they are brought up, and the society in which they live.

Children who are brought up in the same street in London—whatever their ethnic background, religion, or first language—may perhaps share more in common with each other than with a child who is brought up on a remote island off the north coast of Scotland. However, there will always be differences between children brought up in neighbouring houses. These differences can be celebrated. Life would be very boring if we were all exactly the same.

Culture and attitudes will vary according to *life experiences*. Examples of factors that might lead to differences would include:

(a) whether communities have developed in cities or rural areas
(b) whether communities have developed in areas where there has been a lot of contact with people and things from other parts of the world, or whether the community has been inward looking and/or isolated
(c) whether a community has a strong sense of history and tradition and whether this is passed on from one generation to the next.

   Task

What other factors can you think of which are likely to affect culture and attitudes?

Learning about culture

Learning about differences in cultures is important to all of us. We live in a *multicultural, multilingual society*. If we are going to work in and visit other parts of Europe we will also need to learn other languages and be sensitive to other people's beliefs and attitudes. Being sensitive to other cultures should start with cultures that are around us in our everyday life.

Learning about culture is also important for companies entering European markets. In order to understand why people might want certain products, they must find out how people behave. For example, the consumption of alcohol is an accepted part of life in some communities; it would, however, be forbidden in Muslim areas of Bosnia.

 Task

We all belong to groups in society which influence our behaviour patterns. Make a list of ways in which belonging to these groups influences the things that you do or don't do! (See Fig. 3.1.) For example, belonging to a particular religious group might prevent you from working on a Saturday or eating particular types of food!

Although culture passes on behaviour patterns from one generation to another, it can also change slowly over time. For example, our approach to doing things and our beliefs may be completely different from those of previous generations.

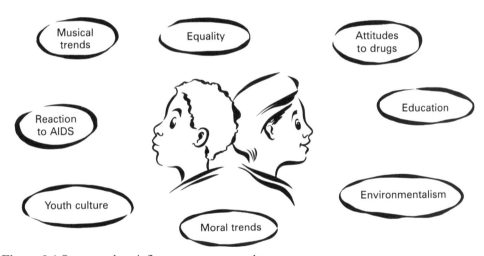

Figure 3.1 Some modern influences upon our culture

Social organization

In every society there are important *social institutions* that influence patterns of behaviour. For example, such institutions include: the family, the educational system, the strength of community, the influence of religion, and the legal framework (Fig. 3.2). The importance of these institutions changes over time and in different places.

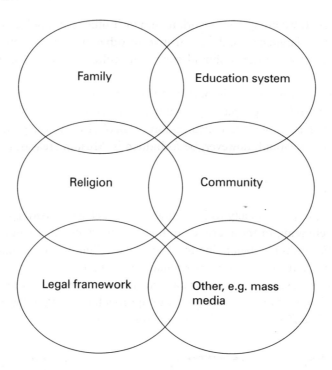

Figure 3.2   Institutions that influence culture

Attitudes and values change

This is illustrated in a survey that was conducted by *The Independent*/NOP in November 1993. This survey indicated a decisive slippage in belief in the *traditional family structure*. There had been a major change since opinions on one-parent families were previously surveyed: 48 per cent of people questioned in 1993 believed that a single mother could bring up her child as well as a married couple, against 31 per cent in 1989. However 58 per cent of people in 1993 still agreed that 'to grow up happily, children need a home with both their mother and father'; 33 per cent disagreed. This contrasted with a 1986 survey which gave 78 per cent and 12.5 per cent respectively.

The home is an important element in developing and influencing cultural values. Different societies place more emphasis on the traditional family made up of mother, father and children. In countries where the Church emphasizes the importance of the family—e.g. Spain, Ireland and Italy—the traditional family will have more influence. In contrast, where traditional family ties are less influential—e.g. parts of Denmark and the UK—the traditional family may have less influence.

A fascinating insight into the changing role of women in the European Union in the period 1983–93 was published by the EU's statistical office Eurostat in December 1993. This showed important changes in women's attitudes to marriage and divorce. Marriage is becoming less popular in the 1990s, and more women are choosing to marry later. The report stated that 'the institution of marriage is weakening in the European Union'. It went on to say, 'more and more women are living alone and bringing up children alone' and 'the marriage rate has fallen in every state'.

Between 1980 and 1992 the marriage rate in the EU dropped from 6.4 to 5.6 per thousand. French and Italian women have been the fastest to turn their backs on the institution of marriage and the Portuguese the slowest.

There is also a definite trend towards women having children later in life. In 1990 the average age for a woman to have her first child was over 27 in the Netherlands and the UK (compared with 25+ in 1980) but under 25 in Greece and Portugal (23+ in 1980). In most other EU states the age is around 26.

More and more women also feel able to bring up their children without assistance. Some 6.5 per cent of all women are single parents compared with only 0.4 per cent of men. The highest incidence is in the UK, where 10.1 per cent of women between 20 and 39 are single parents. The lowest incidences occur in Ireland (2.3 per cent) and Greece (2.4 per cent). (See Fig. 3.3.)

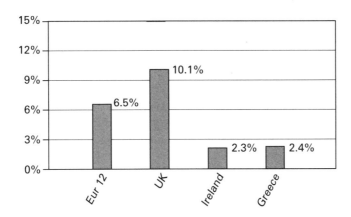

Figure 3.3 Incidence of women aged 20–39 bringing up children alone in the UK, Ireland and Greece

Another changing aspect of family life is that people in European countries are living longer (see Fig. 3.4). The chart shows a declining number of 15–44 year olds and an increasing number of those in the 65+ age range. Clearly this has an impact on family structures. Most EU countries (with the exception of Ireland) are faced with falling populations. At the same time there is an increasing burden of caring for the elderly. In recent years it has become apparent that it will be increasingly difficult for the working population to support those who have retired or are dependent in other ways.

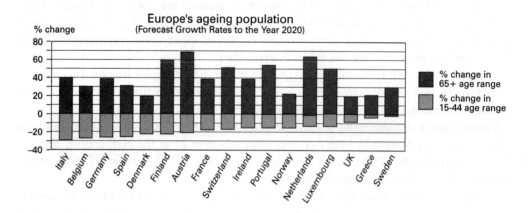

Figure 3.4

Task

Study Fig. 3.4. List six economic and six social consequences of this changing age structure? Is the ageing population a problem? Why?

The family as a social unit

In many European countries the family plays an important role in business, and businesses may be kept within family units for many generations—for example, in Italy, Spain, Greece and Portugal. There may also be strong links between businesses that are owned by relatives.

The ways in which families spend their money, the goods they buy and the leisure activities they enjoy provide us with important information about *lifestyles* in different European countries. For example, Fig 3.5 shows us that UK radio listening patterns vary significantly when compared with some other European countries.

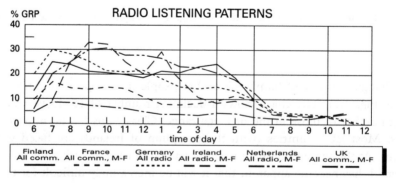

Figure 3.5

Task

How might you explain the differences in radio listening patterns between countries shown in the chart? When looking at differences between countries we need to be aware that there are:

- differences between regions in countries
- differences between individuals in these regions.

In the UK a high percentage of people own their own houses compared with France and Germany for example. However, this varies from region to region in the UK, and while some people strive to own bigger and better houses, others are content to rent property.

Case Study—Standard of living and patterns of life in Denmark

Surveys are sometimes used to give a picture of the average person in a particular country. However, be careful! There is no such thing as an average person. For example would you consider yourself to be representative of people of your country?

The following information comes from a Danish survey:

In Denmark, after the average family has paid taxes and put aside saving, disposable income is then spent as follows:

Food, drink and tobacco products	19.8 per cent
Clothing and footwear	5.1 per cent
Housing expenses	23.8 per cent
Fuel, electricity, gas and heating	7.6 per cent
Furnishings and household services	6.5 per cent
Medicines and medical expenses	2.1 per cent
Transport and communication	15.8 per cent
Leisure equipment, entertainment and education	8.6 per cent
Other goods and services	10.7 per cent

Of every 100 households in 1991 (figures for 1981 shown in parentheses: 54 (56) owned their own house or unit, 94 (89) had a telephone, 59 (57) had a car, 65 (59) had a washing machine, 95 (92) a TV, 91 (65) a colour TV, 42 (0) a video, 98 (96) a refrigerator, 90 (76) a freezer and 16 (0) a home computer. Of the 1.3 million households, 539 000 had satellite TV antennas—double the number five years ago.

Cigarette consumption has fallen from 7 billion in 1980 to 6.7 billion in 1990. At the same time consumption of smoking tobacco has grown by about 50 per cent.

Beer is a leading Danish export and Danes also drink the product themselves. More, however, have developed a taste for wine. In 1989 the average consumption of alcohol per person was 9.5 litres. Danish consumption (per thousand litres) has developed as follows:

	1980	1990
Beer	637 722	635 203
Wine	71 779	98 534
Spirits	18 244	17 638

Fitness is a key concern for more and more Danes. Jogging is often fitted in either before breakfast or after work. Danes eat rye bread and potatoes almost every day. It has been established that Danes spend an average of 45 minutes every day reading newspapers and books.

In 1991, 10 198 books were published, 48 papers had a daily circulation of 1.9 million, and 35 weekly magazines had a circulation of 3 million. Public libraries lent 117 million books. There were 9.2 million visits to cinemas.

Questions

1. Describe the major changes in family ownership of items between 1981 and 1991. Why might these changes have come about?
2. What are the major changing trends in alcohol consumption in Denmark? Why might such changes have taken place?
3. Do you think that the sorts of statistics provided in the article give a fair representation of aspects of patterns of consumption of Danish households?
4. To what extent do you consider the patterns of consumption for the 'average Danish household' to be (a) similar to and (b) different from your own?

Social classes

Most societies can be broken down into subgroupings based on *social class. Expenditure* and *consumption* patterns can then be viewed according to social class.

Each class may have its own patterns of behaviour and these will serve to reinforce their purchasing and consumption patterns. For example, it seems very probable that people who are better off will buy some items that are different from those bought by people who are less well off. People in supposedly higher class groupings may buy particular items because of the 'snob value' associated with a particular product (can you think of examples?).

In different states and regions differing levels of prestige will be given to varying occupations. For example, it is often said that in this country not enough *status* is given to engineers. We tend to give high status to professional people such as barristers and consultant surgeons but not to mechanical engineers. This contrasts clearly with Germany where engineers and people with technical backgrounds are given a lot of respect and command high incomes and status.

The *position of women* in society also varies considerably between states and regions. Though the right of men and women to equal treatment in the workplace is covered by a *Community Charter*, attitudes to women are very different in certain areas. All citizens in the EU are entitled to *equal pay for work of equal value*.

 Task

Which countries and regions do you associate with male chauvinist attitudes? Which countries and regions do you associate with a clearer emphasis on equal opportunities? How accurate are these pictures? Are they just stereotypes? Interview people who have visited these areas, or better still who come from these regions. What are their views? (Remember that one person's point of view only provides very limited evidence. Try to build up as broad a picture as possible.) Next, look at statistics that show the percentage of women in work in different states (see Fig. 3.6). Also try to find out for yourself information showing the relative pay of men and women in different EU countries.

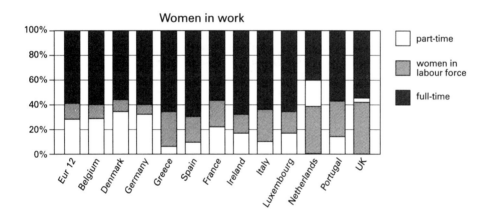

Figure 3.6 Women in work
Source: Eurostat

Women are slowly reaching equality with men in higher education, but this goal has not yet been achieved in all member states. In France, Greece, Spain and Portugal women outnumber men in higher education and in Ireland, Spain and Portugal the number of female students has increased by 30–40 per cent between 1988 and 1993. However, on a Union-wide basis there is still some catching up to do. In late 1993 there were 92 women for every 100 male students.

Women make up only 41 per cent of the workforce in the EU (and less in Ireland, Spain, Greece and Luxembourg). A report by Eurostat in December 1993 showed that 'women's jobs often reflect their traditional role in the home'. Women dominate textile, leather, footwear and clothing branches of industry, domestic services, health services and teaching. Significantly a high proportion of women—nearly 30 per cent—work part time. Women, especially young women, are more affected by unemployment. The unemployment rate for women is higher than for men in every EU state except the UK, and is particularly high in Greece, Italy and Portugal. Can you find information that shows the percentage of women carrying out managerial and professional jobs?

Case study - Varying household sizes in 1990

Table 3.1 contrasts household sizes in three EU states.

Table 3.1   Size of households, 1990

No of inhabitants per household	UK		IRELAND		DENMARK	
	Households (000)	%	Households (000)	%	Households (000)	%
1	5849	25.5	226	21.2	766	34.0
2	7662	33.5	236	22.1	743	33.0
3	3827	16.7	159	15.0	337	15.0
4	3779	16.5	175	16.4	295	13.1
5+	1785	7.8	270	25.3	110	4.9
Total	22 902	100.0	1066	100.0	2251	100.0

Task

Comment on the differences and the reasons for the differences shown in Table 3.1.

Religion

Religion shapes many aspects of culture in European society. However, European countries are characterized by many different religious groupings with different customs, beliefs and traditions. Even within the Christian tradition there are many churches, denominations and sects. You have only to look at the wide variety of ways of celebrating Christmas to appreciate the diversity in religious practice in the various communities and regions of Europe. Today, as always, there are also large Muslim, Hindu, Sikh, Jewish and many other religious communities to make up our European society.

Religious practice and belief affect the way society operates. For example, a Seventh Day Adventist and a Protestant will have different working weeks. Male and female roles will vary widely in Rastafarian, Jewish, Anglican and Muslim communities. Roman Catholic attitudes towards birth control may influence family size.

Some thinkers argue that there is a particularly strong relationship between religious values and attitudes and the shape of society. For example, Max Weber argued that the Protestant emphasis on thrift and hard work led to the development of capitalism in the Netherlands and in the United Kingdom. Religious differences also play a major part in creating conflict and tension, e.g. between Catholics and Protestants in Northern Ireland.

Case Study—Religion in the Netherlands

The Constitution of the Netherlands guarantees freedom of religion. The figures in Table 3.2 show the percentage changes that have taken place within religious denominations since 1900.

Table 3.2

Denominations	1900	1930	1960	1989
Roman Catholic Church	35	36	41	36
Dutch Reformed Church	49	35	28	20
'Gereformeerd'	7	8	7	8
Other denominations	7	7	6	4
None	2	14	18	32
Total population (in millions)	5.1	7.8	11.5	14.9

The most striking feature of these figures is the decling membership of the Dutch Reformed Church and the rise in the number of people who do not belong to any denomination. Denominations are regionally distributed. Roman Catholics tend to be found in the provinces of Limburg and North Brabant and Protestants are strongest in a broad band running from Zeeland (south-west) to Groningen (north-east).

Questions

1. What do the figures in Table 3.2 tell you about religious observance in the Netherlands?
2. Explain how religion could affect the things that people do.

Education

Education systems vary considerably across Europe. Some place more emphasis upon vocational training and preparing students for their role in work, while others concentrate upon a more academic approach which tries to develop learning and thinking patterns. Education systems help to develop the potential of young people and also in developing skills and understanding can help people of all ages to appreciate many more aspects of life.

The German system of education is frequently quoted as the best in Europe and is often considered to be a model for others to follow. For example, in Germany many school leavers enter a formal apprenticeship which is government approved and supervised and which still involves part-time education. Even though the costs are large, the benefits of developing a skilled and well-educated workforce outweigh the costs.

In France the education system is characterized by a two-tier classification. The Grandes Ecoles system creams off the top 6 per cent of students which then develops an élitist training and education system.

The UK has a poor record on education and training. For example, France and Germany produce two to three times as many craftspeople and ten times the number of individuals obtaining middle-ranking vocational qualifications. There have been many arguments concerning the causes of the problems in the UK education system and also many problems with some of the 'solutions' that have been introduced. The National Curriculum and allowing schools to opt out of local authority control have caused some controversy. Over recent years the National Council for Vocational Qualifications has developed NVQs and GNVQs, which endeavour to help young people to develop competences which facilitate entry into further employment, education and training.

The Italian education system has also been criticized for failing to provide young people with appropriate education and training. As many businesses in Italy are small, the cost of providing training, and the lack of help from the government, have made it very difficult for young people in Italy to develop the appropriate skills.

Poverty

It is very easy to take our standard of living for granted and then make assumptions that others have a similar lifestyle. But we cannot do this in the UK, let alone across the EU. There are distinct differences between the rich and poor of Europe (see Fig 3.7). Though these differences are unlikely to be eliminated, social policy decisions can eliminate many disadvantages in areas where low incomes and poverty predominate.

The Social Charter (see page 99) emphasizes that the social aspects of the EU must carry the same weight as economic aspects and covers many areas such as equitable pay, equal treatment and minimum incomes on retirement. The European Council has emphasized that social aspects of European unification must carry the same weight as economic considerations.

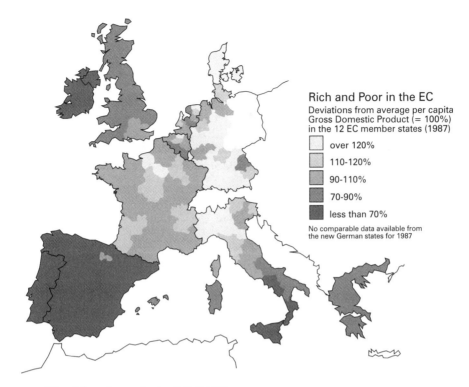

Figure 3.7   The rich and poor in the EC (1987)

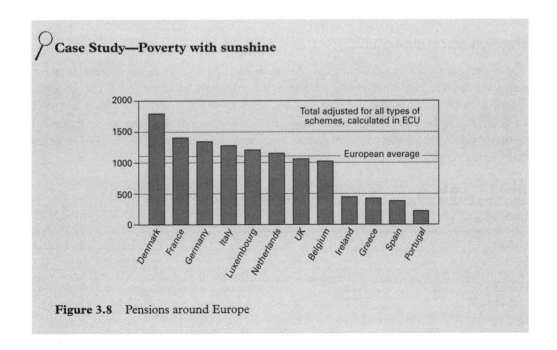

Figure 3.8   Pensions around Europe

Though 1993 was the European Year of Older People and Solidarity Between the Generations, research reveals a gulf in living standards between pensioners in different parts of the EU. For example, in Denmark, Germany, Luxembourg and the Netherlands, the large majority of pensioners regard their pensions as adequate. Elsewhere opinions on the adequacy of pensions is divided, except in certain countries such as Greece, Spain and Portugal where pensions are clearly not adequate (Fig. 3.8).

The main division between the living standards of the elderly is between the north and the south of the EU. Another aspect is that in the southern part of the EU few countries have the social services infrastructure to help pensioners with their problems. For many of these pensioners it is a case of poverty and sunshine in their twilight years!

Questions

1. After having read this short study and having looked at the chart in Fig. 3.8, which countries in Europe are (a) the most prosperous and (b) the least prosperous. Is there a north/south divide?
2. Why, if at all, should we help to overcome many of the problems of poverty in some of the least prosperous countries in the EU?
3. What sort of help should the EU provide?

Gross domestic product

There are many differences between the economic performance of various member states in the EU and these will influence the standard of living of each country's inhabitants. Gross domestic product (GDP) refers to the net output or value added of an economy by measuring the goods and services purchased. The figures in Table 3.3 compare GDP per person for 1991 in EU countries. At the top of the list are Denmark and Germany and, at the bottom, Greece and Portugal.

Table 3.3   Per capita GDP figures for EU countries (US$000s, constant 1985 prices)

Country	1991	Country	1991
Denmark	12.28	UK	9.06
Germany	11.53	Italy	8.65
Luxembourg	11.49	Ireland	6.84
France	10.72	Spain	5.35
Netherlands	9.72	Greece	3.63
Belgium	9.42	Portugal	2.67

Language

Language has been described as the 'mirror of culture'. It is a key ingredient in culture which provides a mechanism through which various aspects of culture can be transmitted. Language may also provide different patterns of thought process and also provide an understanding of the different motivations of others. One of the problems of language is that translations may be misinterpreted, fail to convey the meaning required or even offend others. There have been many arguments about the adoption of a common EU language, but such a language has not yet been chosen. English, however, is a commonly used business language, with widespread acceptability.

Case Study—'Du' or 'sie'

There is a close link between the use of parts of the German language and the type of relationship you might wish to have with another person. This relates particularly to the word 'you'. To 'siezen' someone indicates that you either do not know somebody particularly well or that you have respect for them because of age or professional position. In contrast, to 'duzen' someone indicates a certain element of intimacy, such as knowing a person well and being on first-name terms.

Imagine the confusion that this may lead to. An older colleague at work at a social function with a younger colleague might, after one or two drinks, start using the 'du' form. Having relaxed their relationship, they might then react indignantly if the younger colleague responds with 'du' as well. The following day discord might prevail and both sides move back to the 'sie'!

There is still a custom where many Germans who, having decided to scrap the business of calling each other 'sie', stand up and hug and kiss each other to celebrate their new-found closeness. There are also regional, social and political differences in using the 'du' form. It is a lot easier to get on 'du' terms with a southern German from Bavaria than with a northerner from Hamburg. In eastern Germany the 'du' form was widely used by communists as the 'sie' form was considered unegalitarian.

The duzen/siezen habit will probably never change. Unlike Germans, it is easy for English speakers who do not have to change their form of address because of a generation gap or because of different levels of status!

Questions

1. Make a list of words or parts of the English language that you feel it would be difficult for people from another country to understand.
2. To what extent do your answers to question 1 reflect the British culture?

Language skills

Though there is a growing awareness of the need to develop a second language in the UK, particularly in terms of work opportunities, roughly three-quarters of the population do not speak another language. This figure is roughly comparable with other poor second-language speakers such as Portugal, Italy and Ireland, but in stark contrast with the Netherlands where 80 per cent of the population speak at least one other language. There are many reasons why people in the UK seem to be poor at developing language skills. One point which is frequently made is that languages have not been given sufficient prominence in the school curriculum while another is that in the UK we tend to have rather nationalistic and often arrogant attitudes to languages and expect others to speak English.

Humour

Many people refer to the British sense of humour and it is often thought to be a strength in the workplace, particularly in building and developing relationships. For example, humour is often used at meetings to break down barriers and to keep the conversation flowing. However, it is possible for humour to be misinterpreted. Sometimes it can give the impression of a 'couldn't care less' attitude. Humour, therefore, needs to be handled with caution when dealing with other people, particularly in working relationships. When you meet people who are intent on getting on with a particular work task it would be sensible to approach the task with a sense of purpose. Humour can then be used to temper the relationship once both parties understand that there is a strong focus on agreeing objectives and work targets.

Case study—Oh no, not another stereotype!

Some of the biggest barriers to inter-cultural exchange are the stereotypes that confront us regularly. Some of the worst perpetrators of stereotypes are:

- The mass media: this is particularly true among the British tabloid press. For example, in 1990 *The Sun* newspaper ran a series of anti-French and particularly anti-Jacques Delors articles. The campaign used the expression 'Hop off you Frogs!' *The Sun* reader was invited to sit on the white cliffs of Dover with a Union Jack round his or her shoulders, with a pint of beer in hand and shout 'Hop off you Frogs!'
- Comedians: there is a brand of comedian who makes a living from peddling xenophobia and weak racist jokes.
- Politicians: in November 1993 Michael Heseltine criticized some of his colleagues for the pitiful nationalistic anti-European attitudes they were presenting.

The following description of Belgians provided in a tourist brochure exemplifies the stereotypical approach to national types:

> There are 320 Belgians to every square kilometre! Even if they speak different languages, they have similar characteristics. Their blood combines Nordic hardiness and vivacious Latin charm. If they are dogged at work, so they are with their friendship. But rarely do they open up on the first encounter. They are always tolerant and courteous, and have always been sincere hosts and allies. They love their comfort, look after their health, and enjoy living in the neat and cosy atmosphere they have created. They are individualists who enjoy company, and extroverts noted for their discretion. Belgians are realists with imagination. Serious and fun loving. Calm and active. Thoughtful and daring. Adaptable and determined. Reserved and warm. This is why, from continent to continent, they spread their ideas, roll up their sleeves and lend a hand.
>
> *Source*: The Belgian Embassy

Questions

1. Is it possible to generalize about national characteristics in this way?
2. What major criticisms would you make of the way the extract is written?
3. Could the extract be written in a more appropriate way? How would you go about it?
4. Do you think that this extract could be regarded as being offensive? To whom?
5. What problems are created by developing national stereotypes?

Etiquette

Etiquette refers to the *habits* and *customs* associated with the ways in which people interact with each other. It might include the clothes people wear, time-keeping, ways of addressing others, friendships, eating out, socializing and many other aspects of daily life.

Different groups of people become used to different codes of etiquette based on *existing practice*. You will notice this when dealing with people from different families, groups and organizations. It is hardly surprising, therefore, that patterns of etiquette can vary from region to region within the EU. *Lateness*, for example, may be seen to be particularly discourteous in some groupings whereas informality may be quite normal with others. When dealing with people from another community you should always try to find out something about their *codes* and *patterns* of etiquette. In this way you can prevent yourself from appearing rude and impolite in social and business situations.

Leadership

Groups and organizations have their own *distinctive* cultures. In business terms we refer to the culture of an organization as being '*the way we do things around here*'. Some organizations have a culture based on *strong leadership* from the top in with a clear *hierarchy of offices* (or positions). Other organizations are more *democratic*, being based on *shared decision making*. In the past many companies in European states worked on hierarchical lines. Today it is more common practice to *de-layer* organizations to give fewer layers of authority and to allow more democracy within the organization.

Adapting to different cultures

We are all shaped and influenced by our *cultural environment*. This cultural environment can limit the way we see the world around us and can lead us to build up stereotyped views and prejudices. This is a narrow vision.

It is important for us as individuals, for the organizations in which we work and for the communities and states to which we belong that we try to *understand* and *be ready to accept* the culture of others as well as to value our own culture. The world has always benefited from diversity as there is so much that we can learn from each other. We are tremendously fortunate to be part of a Europe of many regions, which is part of a world of many more regions. People with different backgrounds, ethnic groups, languages, religions, views and many other aspects can come together to share their lives and talents with each other in a shared space.

The most noticeable thing when people come together is how many similarities they share, and then how much they can benefit from and learn from differences, e.g. in foods, dances, games and music.

There will be occasions when we find it difficult to *communicate* or *understand* how colleagues from other EU countries think or work—in the same way that misunderstandings arise in our own communities. On these occasions failing to understand someone's culture may put us at a disadvantage. In the future, however, greater European understanding will help us to develop a much wider European perspective so that we shall not just be able to understand cultural differences but shall be able to celebrate and value them.

4

The Union at work

Today we live in an area called the *European Union* (EU). The EU was born on 1 November 1993. It includes the *European Community* and all its activities. The EU is a political organization of 12 democratic states. (As we shall see on page 119, this Union is likely to be enlarged by new members.)

The 12 states of the EU are *interdependent*. They have surrendered some national sovereignty so that they can co-operate on specific policies. (*NB*: The word 'sovereignty' means the power that an individual, group or nation has to run its own affairs. When a country gives up sovereignty, it hands over responsibility to another body, e.g. the EU, to make some decisions on its behalf—see Fig. 4.1).

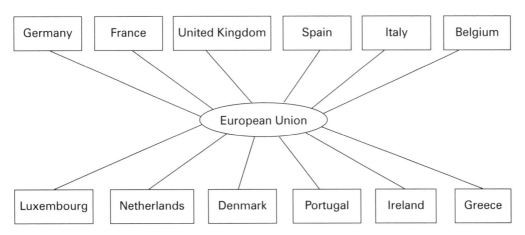

Figure 4.1   European Union laws are binding on member states.

The move towards 'federalism'

Important issues facing members of the EU are:

* How much power should individal countries have in running their own affairs?
* How much power should be given to *supranational* EU bodies?

To put it crudely: Should we, in the UK, be governed from Brussels and the European Commission, or from Westminster?

The EU is changing constantly—it is like a cyclist that has to keep moving to prevent falling off. As shown in Fig. 4.2, the European Community (EC) was originally a marriage of convenience between Adenauer's Germany and Fourth Republic France. This has proved to be one of the greatest success stories of the post-war world and has helped to give Europe nearly half a century of peace.

Throughout the 1950s and 1960s the EC increasingly involved co-operation between member states to manage resources such as coal and steel through co-operative ventures. New bodies were set up for particular purposes, e.g. the development of EURATOM, the European Atomic Energy Community, in 1957 to oversee the safe development of nuclear energy for peaceful purposes. These bodies were run by employees working for European rather than national institutions.

The 1970s and 1980s have been characterized as a period in which EC national governments met together to make joint decisions about common matters of concern. Real power in the EC was still very much in the hands of national governments.

The 1990s may come to be seen as a period in which the Union is given greater powers to make decisions from the centre. In recent years we have seen moves to strengthen the powers of community organizations.

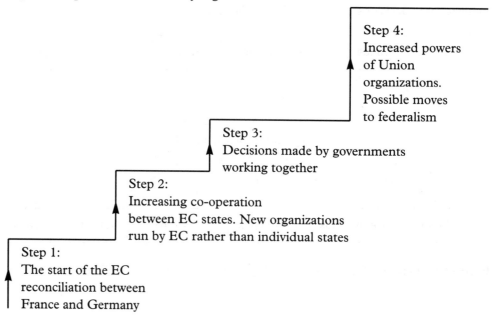

Figure 4.2   The steps of the European Community

What is federalism?

A *federal state* is likely to have the following features:

1. Shared institutions belonging to all member states (e.g. a common parliament, high court, etc). Decisions in these institutions will be made by majority voting (rather than a unanimous vote).
2. The transfer of some powers of internal government to the federal government. (Some powers would be kept by national governments.)
3. The federal government would take over the responsibility for external powers, e.g. dealings with countries outside the federation.

Case Study—How European do we feel?

A Eurobarometer poll carried out in 1993 showed that 80 per cent of people favour the efforts to 'unify Western Europe', but the majority of people in Western Europe still do not feel European. Almost half the population told a 1991 survey that they never feel European.

People were asked: 'As well as feeling your nationality, how European do you feel?' Some 49 per cent of respondents replied 'Never'; 33 per cent 'Sometimes'; and only 15 per cent 'Often'.

 Task

Construct a short questionnaire to find out how 'European' the people of your area feel. Begin by setting out some pilot questions to try on a small sample of people; then produce a final questionnaire that you can try on a larger sample. Try to interview people in different categories, e.g. young/old, male/female, those who have travelled in other parts of Europe/those who have not, etc. What factors seem to influence people's attitudes to feeling European?

Who makes the decisions in the European Union?

Some people think that the idea of 'Europe' involves groups of like-minded European states co-operating together to make decisions that serve their shared interests. Others think that we should go beyond this. They argue that co-operation is no longer sufficient to meet the needs of individual states. They argue that the best way of meeting the needs of all our peoples is through working together through shared institutions.

If we look at the working of the EU today we can see elements of both of these ideas. For example, we can see a contrast between the *European Council* and *Council of Ministers* on one hand, and the *European Commission* and *Parliament* on the other.

The European Council and Council of Ministers are directly accountable to national parliaments. These institutions continue to have a lot of power in EU affairs. They represent the idea of European co-operation based on the national interest. In contrast, EU institutions such as the Commission and the Parliament more genuinely represent the interests of member states as a united group (see Table 4.1).

Table 4.1 The role of the EU institutions

Decision-making bodies representing national groupings and interests	Decision-making bodies representing the whole community
The European Council The Council of Ministers	The European Commission The European Parliament The European Court of Justice The Court of Auditors etc.

We can now look at the structure of each of the major EU organizations in greater detail.

The European Council

Figure 4.3

The European Council brings together heads of state of the 12 member states. It provides the political leadership in the EU. It meets twice a year to give overall direction to the Union's work. *Heads of State* take it in turns to be *President* of this body for a term of six months. Each president will introduce new proposals for items to be discussed during their presidency. Today the presidency is involved in organizing close co-operation on foreign, security, immigration and judicial policies.

 Task

Who are the current 12 Heads of State of the EU countries? Find out this information using your existing knowledge, and by referring to recent articles in the national press (including *The European* newspaper, and *The Economist* magazine).

The Council of Ministers

This body decides on all the laws that set up Union policies. Councils are made up of Ministers from each of the 12 countries. For example, there is a Council of Ministers of Education, of Health, of Defence, Sport, etc. Each Minister represents his or her own government and parliament.

Decisions are made by *unanimous* agreement, *qualified majority voting* (where the number of votes depends on the population size of the countries), or a *simple majority* vote, depending on the subject.

On many important issues for national governments (e.g. tax) decisions must be unanimous. Each member state takes it in turn to hold the presidency of the Council, setting the agenda and chairing meetings for a six-month period.

Council meetings handle decision making on everything from agriculture to finance. The work is then coordinated by *ambassadors* of the 12 who meet at least once a week.

 Task

If the UK put forward a proposal to the Council of Ministers to increase safety at sports grounds:

1. How many votes would it need for a unanimous decision?
2. Which countries would it need support from to carry its decision by qualified majority voting?
3. How many votes would it need for a simple majority decision?

The European Commission

Figure 4.4

The Commission has three main tasks:

- to make proposals for Union laws
- to ensure that laws are carried out
- to manage EU policies such as the policy to ensure fair competition within the EU.

There are 17 Commissioners who are appointed by national governments. The Commission has real power in that it is the body that introduces actions or laws.

Those people who support the idea of 'Federalism' see the Commission as the basis for a future government of Europe. The Commission has a staff of 13 000 people and is based in Strasbourg. The Commission sets out to put Council decisions and Union laws into practice. The Commission is involved in negotiating international agreements (although these agreements have to be approved by the Council).

The European Parliament

Figure 4.5   The European Parliament

In 1994, there are 567 Members of the European Parliament (MEPS). The number from each country is shown below:

Germany	99	Spain	64	Belgium	25
France	87	Netherlands	31	Denmark	16
UK	87	Portugal	25	Ireland	15
Italy	87	Greece	25	Luxembourg	6

MEPs are elected every five years, the next election being in 1999. The Parliament is consulted on draft laws and may propose changes. Together with the Council, it is responsible for setting the EU budget.

In the past the European Parliament had a reputation for being a meaningless talking shop (for example, some sections of the press took photographs of MEPs sleeping during debates). However, the Parliament is designed to bring democracy to the EU, and is elected by citizens who choose the MEPs. However, MEPs are rarely household names.

 Task

Find out the name of your local MEP. To what party does he or she belong? What contributions has he or she made to recent European Parliament debates?

Perhaps you might be able to invite your MEP to talk to your class about the European Parliament.

Alternatively why not carry out a survey to find out how well known your local MEP is. If your MEP is, for example, J. Bloggs, set out a survey question, such as:
Who is J. Bloggs? Is he or she:

(a) a pop star?
(b) a Member of the European Parliament?
(c) the managing director of BP?
(d) the presenter of a TV chatshow?
(e) a trade union leader?

MEPs are paid the same as MPs in their home countries and they sit in cross-national political groups rather than by nationality. The main powers of the Parliament (at the moment) are to question the Commissioners and Council about decisions they are taking, to accept or reject the Budget, and in extreme cases to sack the entire European Commission. The European Parliament is based in *Strasbourg* (however, it has committee meetings in Brussels, and its officials are based in Luxembourg).

 Task

Figure 4.6 shows the main grouping of parties to which MEPs belonged at the end of 1993. In 1994 there was a new election of MEPs. Redraw the illustration to show the current breakdown of MEPs into different parties.

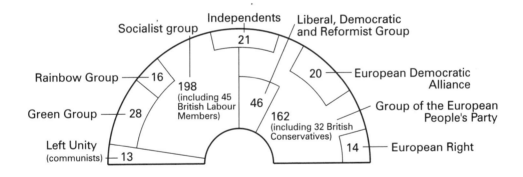

Figure 4.6   The political forces within the European Parliament

Case Study—Big nations and small nations

In Chapter 2 we saw that European countries are widely different in many ways. If we look at countries in the EU we can see that there are clear differences, for example:

- rich versus poor states
- big versus small states
- urban versus rural states
- northern versus southern states

- founding versus new member states
- pro-federalism versus anti-federalism states.

(Can you place France, the United Kingdom and Ireland in their appropriate category/categories, as listed above?)

Currently there is a lot of discussion in the EU about the influence that smaller states should have. This has become even more pressing with the possibility of the entry of new smaller states in January 1995 to bring the number up to 16. The big four—France, Germany, Italy and the UK—would like to see things change. They fear that the arrival of new, smaller members will make the European Commission unwieldy, weaken the presidency of the European Council and, under the complicated weighted voting procedure in the Council of Ministers, allow countries representing only 12 per cent of the EU population to block policies favoured by all other governments. Britain has argued that the number of Commissioners, the rotating Council presidency and the way votes are weighted towards small countries should all be reviewed before new members are accepted. This suggestion has been opposed by smaller countries and the applicants themselves: Finland, Austria, Norway and Sweden.

Questions

1. Why do you think that the larger countries may be opposed to (a) the current system of a rotating presidency and (b) the system of having 17 Commissioners?
2. What are the smaller countries of the EU?
3. How will the enlargement of the EU to 16 members increase the powers of smaller countries?

Implementing new laws and regulations

Once a new piece of community legislation has been passed it is up to individual countries to implement the new laws (failure to do so can lead to prosecution). However, the ways in which laws and directives are implemented varies from country to country, depending on politics, communication and how effectively laws are administered.

EU directives require member states to change their own laws to conform to EU law. In the UK this is either done through an Act of Parliament or by Regulations. Regulations are rarely debated in Parliament. Such Regulations do not get the same publicity as Acts of Parliament. As a result individuals and organizations are sometimes surprised to find that they are breaking new regulations, e.g. European Union VAT and insurance regulations. Some commentators argue that the increased number of regulations in recent years leads to a spreading of Brussels bureaucracy. The Conservative government in the UK has been trying to reduce the number of restrictions and regulations that hold business back, but it feels that it, in its turn, is being held back by Brussels.

An example of this is the number of regulations affecting small businesses. At the end of 1993 there were several thousand regulations concerning small business; an estimate that was given at the time was that 4 per cent of the turnover of a small business would need to be spent on meeting such regulations. For example, a retailer stocking cream would need to check the freezer compartment three times a day to make sure that the temperature was correct. Clearly such regulations cut into profit margins. In countries where regulations are carefully monitored, enterprise might find itself with a competitive disadvantage.

However, there are also times when the UK government feels hindered because the European Council has failed to make regulations in certain areas. For example, in November 1993 there was a horrific coach crash on the M2 in Kent in which ten passengers died. The UK government wanted the European Council to make regulations that all coaches should have passenger seat belts (every bus manufacturer in Europe is capable of providing coaches with this facility). However, the UK government has still not been able to persuade its partners to make this a Union-wide regulation. UK bus companies are therefore still able to operate without passenger seat belts.

The European Court of Justice

13 judges   6 advocates general

Figure 4.7   The European Court of Justice

The Court interprets and adjudicates on European Union Law. There are 13 judges, one from each member state and an extra judge to prevent deadlock. The Court is assisted by a Court of First Instance which handles certain cases brought by individuals and organizations.

The Court of Justice has responsibility in six main areas:

1. To rule in disputes between member states
2. To rule in disputes between the EU and member states
3. To rule in disputes between the institutions (e.g. a dispute between the European Parliament and the Commission)

4. To rule in disputes between individuals and the Union
5. To give opinions on international agreements
6. To give preliminary rulings, i.e. when disputes waiting to go before national courts are referred by the national court to the Court of Justice.

The *13 judges* are supported by *6 advocates general*. These advocates investigate cases and submit their findings to the court. The advocates are impartial, i.e. they do not take sides.

The Court of Auditors

The Court of Auditors is responsible for auditing the Union's budget. It helps to prevent and to detect waste and fraud.

Making Union Law

The procedure for making laws is complicated. Figure 4.8 presents a simplified version of what takes place.

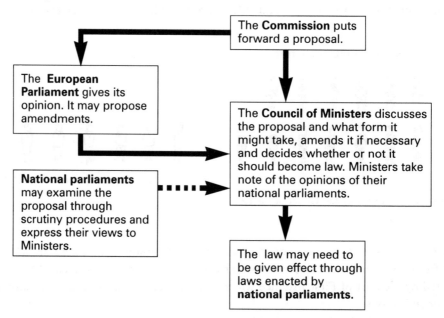

Figure 4.8   Making Union laws

Making Community laws is different from making national laws. Most national governments prepare their laws with some degree of secrecy and then present them when they are ready. This is not the case in the European Union where decisions are made after seemingly endless public discussion.

The Union Budget, for example (which outlines how the EU will raise its revenue to meet its spending), will be discussed, changed, and altered several times through open public debate before it is eventually agreed.

The Union Budget

The Union's activities have to be financed by contributions from its member countries (see Fig. 4.9).

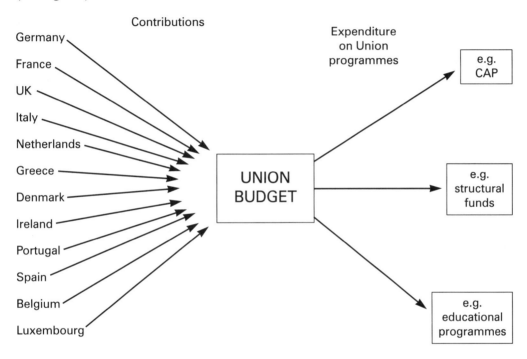

Figure 4.9 The Union Budget

In 1992 the EC spent over £50 billion (about 3.5 per cent of total central government spending in all EC member states).

About half of the total expenditure goes towards supporting the Common Agricultural Policy (mainly subsidies to farmers) and about one-quarter supports the poorer regions of the EU.

All countries receive money as well as paying into the budget. Countries with large farming communities and poorer regions benefit most from expenditure. Germany, France, the Netherlands and the UK are examples of countries who are net contributors to the budget (they pay in more than they take out).

What is involved in European citizenship?

Article 8 of the Maastricht Treaty sets out that:

1. Citizenship of the Union is hereby established. Every person holding the nationality of a member state shall be a citizen of the Union.
2. Citizens of the Union shall enjoy the rights conferred by this Treaty and shall be subject to the duties imposed thereby.

The idea of European citizenship involves creating a sense of identity among citizens of the Union, e.g. through youth exchanges and symbols, such as the flag. Today citizens of European Union countries can hold a Union passport as well as one for their own country.

European citizens are some of the most privileged on the planet (although we should not discount the plight of the 18 million members of the Union who are unemployed, and those others living in poor conditions). Some commentators argue that Europeans today have responsibilities that go well beyond the bounds of geographical Europe—e.g. responsibilities for world development and the conservation of scarce resources; responsibilities for human rights and the preservation of peace in other continents, etc.

The concept of citizenship is also linked to a person's ability to vote in European elections and in local elections if that individual is the national of one Union member state but resident in another.

Currently citizenship of the Union has only a limited effect on legal right; for example, it does not change a person's legal rights when arrested. These will continue to be determined nationally. Nor does it make a citizen eligible for military service if he or she happens to live in another country of the Union, such as France, whose nationals are obliged to enlist. Tax systems are still nationally determined and depend on where you live.

5

The development of the European Union as a trading area

In Chapter 4 we looked at how the European Union (EU) has increasingly developed into a closer political union with its own institutions. At the same time it has developed increasingly close economic ties (Fig. 5.1). In this chapter we set out to look at these *economic ties*, particularly focusing on the opening up of trading relations.

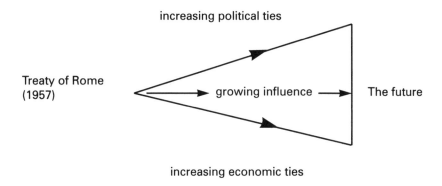

increasing political ties

Treaty of Rome
(1957)

growing influence

The future

increasing economic ties

Figure 5.1   The European Union economic ties

The benefits of trade

Before we move on to explore ways in which free trade has been created between the 12, it is helpful first to look at the benefits of trade. We can illustrate this by means of a simple example.

Once there were two islands separated by a sea that was too dangerous to cross. On the first island, which was very flat, wheat could be grown in plenty, but the waters around the island contained few fish. The second island was very hilly and only a little wheat could be grown. However, around this second island, fish were plentiful (Fig. 5.2).

Figure 5.2 Two islands—two economies

One day an explorer found a sea passage, to the south of the two islands, that was not dangerous to cross (Fig. 5.3).

Figure 5.3

Let us suppose that before the trade route was discovered, half of the people in each island spent their time farming, and the other half spent their time fishing. In a year, the amount of wheat and fish that could be produced is:

	Wheat	Fish
Hilly island	20 baskets	100 baskets
Flat island	100 baskets	20 baskets

 Tasks

1. Explain how the people of these two islands could benefit from the opening up of the sea passage.
2. Are there any problems that could be caused by the opening up of this sea passage?
3. Supposing that all the people of the flat island now just grow wheat and the people of the hilly island just fish. Can you show how the people on the two islands could be better off than before?
4. Why might this not always be true?

The advantages of specialization

Different areas are *endowed* with different resources. Some districts, for example, have a climate particularly suitable for certain products (e.g. the highlands of Kenya for coffee growing, the south of France for wine production, etc). Other districts possess minerals, gases and oils which are not found elsewhere, e.g. gas and oil in the North Sea. It is easy to understand why Italy exports citrus fruits and Scotland whisky.

Different kinds of labour are also *unevenly distributed* between countries. For example, trained chemists are relatively abundant in the United Kingdom and Germany and therefore these countries export chemical products. A *factor of production* (i.e. land, labour, capital and enterprise) which is relatively abundant in a given district will be relatively cheap there, so goods requiring a relatively large proportion of that factor can be produced more cheaply in that district than elsewhere.

In the two-island economy that we looked at above, we can see that with *specialization* the two islands will be better off. Without trade links, the two countries cannot specialize on what they do best. When trade links are opened, both islands benefit.

Without trade links, the combined annual production of wheat was 120 baskets and the combined production of fish was 120 baskets. After trading, the combined totals could be 200 baskets of each:

	Wheat	Fish
Hilly island	—	200 baskets
Flat island	200 baskets	—

Of course, this may be a simplification. For example, each island may want to produce some of its less plentiful products to avoid being dependent on the other island (or to maintain employment). A possible limitation is the rate at which the two islands are prepared to trade the two items. Another limitation is the time taken to transport the goods.

The reasons for trade

Countries trade with each other:

1. To gain products that they cannot produce in their own country
2. To gain products that are very expensive to produce in their own country
3. To increase the variety of goods available in their country
4. To build up good relationships with other countries so that there is give and take, i.e. importing and exporting
5. To create jobs by producing goods that are exported.

Barriers to trade

We do not live in a world in which goods and services are traded freely between countries. Often individual countries or groups of countries restrict imports from other countries, which they do for a number of reasons.

1. Countries *protect* their own industries. Industries develop over time and involve considerable investment. Specialist machinery needs to be bought and the labour force builds up the skills to run industries. Countries are therefore reluctant to see their domestic industries destroyed by cheaper foreign imports.
2. Countries *restrict* imports to protect firms and employment. They also protect industries to maintain a way of life. For example, some European countries have large farming communities. The farming community will live in rural areas in villages and small towns with a distinct lifestyle. If cheap food imports force farms to close down, we might see the destruction of the rural way of life, pushing unemployed agricultural workers into the already overcrowded cities.
3. Trade restrictions are used to protect new or '*infant*' industries. Once these new industries are established they may prove to be the lifeblood of an economy.
4. Countries may also want to restrict the import of *strategic goods*, e.g. basic sources of energy, fuel, materials and defence goods.

Types of barrier

There are a number of methods of restricting imports from other countries (or groups of countries).

Import duties (tariffs)

An import duty is a tax. The price of the taxed commodity will be higher inside the taxing country—by the full amount of the duty plus transport charges—than on the world market.

Subsidies

A subsidy is the reverse of an import tax. A government can subsidize domestic producers by giving them a sum of money according to how much they produce. This gives domestic products an advantage in competing with imports.

Quotas

An import quota lays down the maximum amount—not value—of the commodity that may be imported during a given period. For example, the EU imposes quotas on the import of Japanese cars.

The development of a trading community

The development of an economic community within the EU can be seen as involving a number of steps, with each step leading to closer co-operation (Fig 5.4).

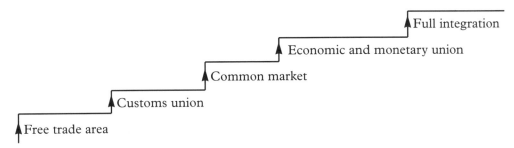

Figure 5.4   The development of a trading community

Free trade area

Developing a free trade area involved getting rid of some of the barriers to free trade. In particular it involved the removal of quotas and tariffs between members of the trading community.

Customs union

In 1986 the EC created a customs union with moves towards positive integration of economies. In addition to the free trade area member states operated a common external tariff. This meant that an import from a non-EC country, e.g. from Canada, would pay the same tariff whether it entered France, Germany, Belgium or any other member state. Within the customs union the member states developed common trading policies and moved towards equal conditions for individuals, firms and groupings operating within the customs union.

Common market

The creation of a common market took the integration process a step further. A common market involves the free movement of factors of production (land, labour, capital and enterprise) as well as the free movement of goods. Over the years we have seen a *harmonization of policies* designed to create freedom of movement. The *Single European Act* of 1986 highlighted what are known as the *four freedoms*, shown in Fig. 5.5.

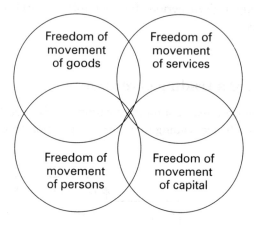

Figure 5.5   The four 'freedoms'

Economic and Monetary Union

It would appear that complete economic and monetary union is still a long way off. The aim of Economic and Monetary Union (EMU) is to provide a *fixed exchange rate* or *single currency* at some stage in the future.

A fixed exchange rate would exist if a given amount of pounds sterling could be changed into a set number of French francs today, next week, next year, and into the foreseeable future. A single currency would exist if an ECU could be used in Luxembourg, Athens, Lisbon or Dublin to pay for goods and services.

However, attempts to create exchange rate stability have not as yet been successful although an important new step has been the creation of a European Central Bank in Frankfurt in 1993. Germany, France, the Netherlands, Belgium and other countries have enjoyed some exchange rate stability and are working towards greater monetary union.

Full integration

Full integration of economies remains a future ideal. Integration would involve common economic policies decided upon by union institutions in conjunction with state governments through the creation of some sort of United States of Europe.

Case Study—The Single Market

The Single Market, which came into force on midnight 31 December 1992, affects every part of our lives. The simplest way of describing it is to say that people, goods, businesses and services can move anywhere within the EU without let or hindrance. That means that British workers can go to work in Copenhagen or Cagliari, restricted only by their personal ability or language capabilities. it also means that EU workers, from Corinth to La Coruna, can come to work in our factories, shops and offices—equally without restriction.

The Single Market means excellent export opportunities for British businesses. The EU already takes 53 per cent of our exports compared with 34 per cent in 1972. Equally, if most European countries are wide open to our exports then, of course, the UK is wide open to theirs.

Technical and tariff barriers, such as national product standards and quotas, are removed. So, other than transport problems, it is as easy to trade with Luxembourg as with Liverpool; with Athens as with Accrington. No longer, for instance, are individual EU nations able to restrict or block fellow members' goods on the basis of different testing requirements. The opportunities are even wider now that the seven European Free Trade Area nations have linked with the 12 of the EU to form the European Economic Area—adding EFTA's 32.5 million to the EU population of 345 million.

Questions

1. List five groups of people who stand to gain from the creation of the Single Market. What are the major benefits to each group?
2. List five groups of people who stand to lose from the creation of the Single Market. How can they lose?
3. How many people are now members of the European Economic Area?
4. Do large and small firms benefit from such an area?
5. Why is most of the UK's trade with the Single Market?
6. What is meant in the text by (a) 'technical' and (b) 'tariff' barriers? How can such barriers hinder trade?
7. Under Single Market regulations, European standards have been drawn up covering health, safety, food, consumer protection and the environment for everything from widgets to cutlets, toys to medicines, and cosmetics to animal semen. How do EU citizens benefit from such regulations?

Removing restrictions

It has not been easy to create economic integration. However, in a world that is increasingly dominated by huge trading blocs it has been essential. Since 1957 the EC

78   **European Business Studies**

has expanded internally from 6 to 9 in 1973, 9 to 10 in 1981, 10 to 12 in 1986 and 12 to 16 in 1995 (perhaps). Each step involves the need to *integrate new markets*.

During this period the EC had to cope with a changing external environment, e.g. sudden rises in oil prices during the 1970s and early 1980s and global recession in the early 1990s. Throughout this period the EC lost its competitive edge to the United States and Japan and, more recently, we have seen the emergence of the Pacific Rim countries.

Great importance has therefore been attached to the Single European Act and the creation of the Single Market.

Case Study

In the early 1990s the European Commission carried out a survey of business to find out what barriers within the Community particularly annoyed them. Business people were asked to answer the question: 'How important do you consider the removal of this barrier to be?' They then had to rank their answers from 1 (most important) to 8 (least important). Table 5.1 shows the ranking in the UK to the 12 countries as a whole.

Table 5.1   Ranking of market barriers by business

Total industry	UK	The 12
1. National standards and regulations	1	2
2. Government procurement	4	8
3. Administrative barriers	2	1
4. Physical frontier delays and costs	3	3
5. Differences in VAT	8	6/7
6. Regulations of freight transport	5	6/7
7. Restrictions in capital market	7	5
8. Community law	6	4

Clearly, if industry is going to be competitive it needs to cut costs. All of the barriers outlined above give UK and EU businesses a competitive disadvantage.

Questions

1. What are the three main barriers that UK business people saw as problems in the early 1990s?
2. Give an example of how a national standard in another EU country might put off a UK exporter.
3. Explain what is meant by an 'administrative barrier'. How can administration add to costs?
4. Explain what is meant by physical frontier delays. Why might this be a particular problem for food exports?

5. Government procurement means that a national government buys from its domestic producers rather than importing from other EU countries. Does this go against the spirit of free trade?

The costs of regulation

The main costs of having such barriers are:

- the high *administration costs* in dealing with different national standards and requirements
- higher *transport costs* because of border regulations
- the higher cost of *smaller production runs* to meet different national standards (e.g. the extra cost involved to European car companies in producing left-hand drive models for the UK)
- *duplication of costs* as a result of having separate research and development projects
- the high cost of *non-competitive government activities*, e.g. buying only from producers in your own country (rather than cheaper, higher quality goods and services from other EU countries)
- *higher prices* and *reduced choice* for national consumers.

Failure to coordinate economic policies must surely lead to a further decline in competitive ability. If the EU is to be competitive on a global scale it will need to create an internal market which is at least as competitive as those of other *huge global trading areas*, e.g. the North American Free Trade Area (NAFTA), the Pacific Rim countries, and the Commonwealth of Independent States.

Benefits of the Single Market

Benefits to EU citizens of the Single Market should include:

- a *wider choice* of goods and services as barriers to trade are removed, and greater assurance about the quality and safety of imported products as clear guidelines become legally binding on businesses
- *easier travel*, for example, hopefully cheaper air fares, as competition increases
- *more jobs* as business opportunities grow (although unemployment is a major problem facing all EU member states as we move into the twenty-first century)
- *wider recognition of qualifications*, making it easier for people to live and work where they choose in the Union
- an *end to routine customs controls* at ports and airports and the freedom to bring back any goods bought, duty- and VAT- paid in other EU countries for personal use.

A number of overseas countries—particularly Japan—have been attracted to invest in the UK in order to get inside the Single Market. The EU has also been extended by joining together with EFTA (the European Free Trade Association) made up of Austria, Finland, Iceland, Liechtenstein, Norway, Sweden and Switzerland to form the European Economic Area. This gives UK businesses a home market not of 55 million but of 377.5 million consumers. Less bureaucracy, e.g. by simplifying the paperwork required for trade, reduces business costs.

1992: The Cecchini Report

The Cecchini Report set out to measure some of the *benefits* that would be achieved as a result of cutting out red tape, and breaking down trade barriers. For the business sector it identified four main consequences of a well-organized Single Market (Fig. 5.6).

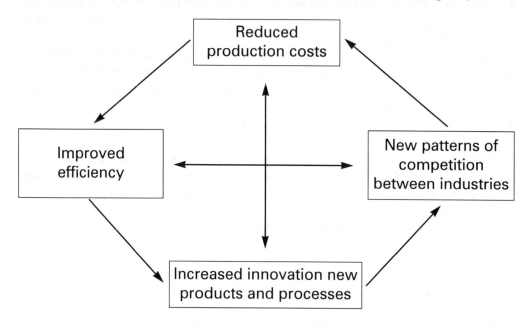

Figure 5.6 The benefits of a single market

- *Cost reductions*   Because companies would produce on a larger scale in a new mass market this would lead to falling costs for each unit of production.
- *Improved efficiency*   Industries would need to reorganize to serve mass markets. This reorganization, coupled with competition, should increase efficiency.
- *New patterns of competition*   Those industries and areas with the most effective resources would make the most gains.
- *New innovations, processes and products*   These would flow from the larger more competitive market.

The Cecchini Report also sets out to measure the potential gains in economic welfare for the EU resulting from the creation of the Single Market in a four-step approach, shown in Table 5.2.

Table 5.2   Potential gains in welfare for the EU

Step	ECU (billions)	% of national income
1. Gains from removal of barriers to trade	8–9	0.2–0.3
2. Gains from removal of barriers affecting overall production	57–71	2.0–2.4
Gains from removing barriers (subtotal)	65–80	2.2–2.7
3. Gains from exploiting economies of scale more fully	61	2.1
4. Gains from intensified competition reducing business inefficiencies and monopoly profits	46	1.6
Gains from market integration (subtotal)	62–107	2.1–3.7
Total: For 12 member states at 1988 prices	174–258	4.3–6.4

- Step 1 takes into account the removal of barriers to intra-EU trade, especially customs holdups.
- Step 2 takes into account the removal of barrier to production, e.g. different national standards and protective government procurement.
- Step 3 takes into account the benefits of being able to use economies of scale more effectively in a freer market.
- Step 4 takes into account gains in efficiency due to more intense competition.

 Task

Carry out a survey of 20 local businesses to find out what they consider to be the main advantages of the Single Market to them. Try to choose a sample of businesses that export at least some of their output to our partner countries.

Exchange rates

The Snake in the Tunnel

In 1978, EC member states agreed to establish an *Exchange Rate Mechanism* (ERM) that would limit fluctuations in the currencies of members who chose to join. Over time, all member states except Greece joined, but the tensions in the ERM became so acute that in September 1992 Italy and the UK decided to suspend their membership.

At Maastricht (see page 84), the European Community agreed a process and a timetable for moving towards Economic and Monetary Union (EMU) and negotiated the right for the British Parliament to decide whether or not to join the final stage in which a single currency could be established.

During 1993 a number of European currencies had rocky rides—for example, it looked at one stage as if the French franc would crash and tumble out of control. However, after a difficult spell (see headline, Fig. 5.7) it managed to pull through. The Germans in particular would like to see steady moves towards a single currency.

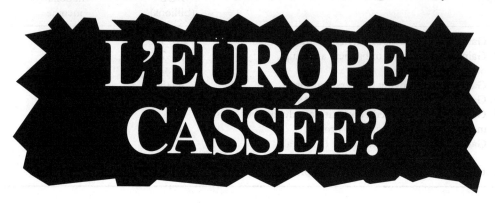

Figure 5.7

The idea behind the *Snake in the Tunnel* is to provide relatively fixed exchange rates between member states. The main advantage of fixed rates is that they provide stable trading conditions. If I export goods to Germany expecting payment in 3 months' time (a common period of credit in international trade) then I want to receive in payment the same value of money as I would receive if I was going to be paid today. If instead when I receive payment in Marks and convert them back into sterling I find that the value of the pound has fallen so that I receive fewer pounds, I will be disappointed (and perhaps stop trading with Germany).

The snake in the tunnel (Fig. 5.8) allows currencies to move up and down over time (the snake) within fairly narrow upper and lower limits (the tunnel). The Central Bank of a country must take action to stop its currency moving out of the tunnel.

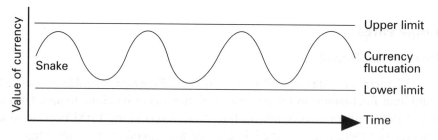

Figure 5.8

The Central Bank will sell its own currency when the value is rising too high, and buy back its currency when the value is too low. It buys currency with its reserves of gold and other currencies.

 Task

Keep a record over a two-month period of the rate of exchange between the pound and the franc, and the pound and the Mark. Keep a diary to explain the changes in the value of the currencies against each other. Use current newspaper and magazine articles to find out why the changes occur.

What causes the value of a currency to fall?

The value of a currency will fall when the quantity of that currency in international markets increases. This often happens when the country is selling fewer exports and increasing the quantity of imports. More of the domestic currency is going on to the international markets to pay for imports. Less of the domestic currency is wanted by foreigners because they are buying less of the country's exports.

Once a fall starts then *speculators* add to the problem by getting out of that currency (currency speculators make money from buying and selling currency).

A currency cannot be allowed to get into a state of free fall. The government needs to stop the value of its currency falling over a period of time. This may involve taking measures to discourage spending in the domestic economy, e.g. *raising taxes and interest rates* so that fewer imports are necessary.

Problems for the UK economy in the ERM

In the ERM currencies need to keep within the tunnel. Countries must maintain the value of their currency against an average value of other currencies (sometimes called a *basket of currencies*). Currencies that fall are forced into a position of using reserves to buy their own currency. In addition, they need to take measures such as raising interest rates to try to maintain the value of their currency. This can be deeply damaging for a country's economy. When the UK joined the ERM in the early 1990s, it soon became necessary to raise interest rates to keep within the tunnel. This had the effect of prolonging the recession in the UK, leading to increased unemployment. The UK economy abandoned the ERM. The stronger currencies in the ERM put pressure on the weaker currencies. In recent years there have been a number of references to a two-speed Europe. Stronger economies like Belgium, the Netherlands and Germany want to move towards greater monetary union, but weaker economies prefer to hold back.

6

Union and Community developments

In this chapter we examine some of the major features of the European Union and Community in addition to those covered in Chapters 3 and 4. In particular we focus on:

- The Maastricht Treaty and the European Union
- The Common Agricultural Policy
- Environmental policy
- Social policy
- Restructuring policy
- Committee of the Regions.

The Maastrict Treaty and the European Union

In 1991 the Maastricht Treaty set out to strengthen the European Community. However, it is important to remember that different countries have different views about the objectives of the Community. For example, the UK Conservative government want to create a more effective and efficient Community but to avoid *centralization* (government by a 'Brussels bureaucracy') or weakening of national political institutions.

> **Case Study—'Edmund Thatcher'**
>
> In November 1993, Edmund Stoiber, the Bavarian Prime Minister, was criticized for his comments to a German newspaper. In the article he renounced the idea of a federal Europe, which is a cornerstone of Germany's foreign policy.
>
> Mr Stoiber is the deputy leader of the CSU, the Bavarian sister party of the Christian Democrats, led by Chancellor Helmut Kohl. Mr Kohl's vision is of a united Europe.
>
> The German newspaper *Die Zeit* has condemned Mr Stoiber's words as being 'high treason' and referred to him as Edmund Thatcher. Mr Stoiber's words followed the week in which Germany had officially ratified the Maastricht Treaty. His words are clearly at odds with German foreign policy ever since the

Second World War. Mr Stoiber is critical of the centralizing power of Brussels. In particular he is worried about the state of Bavaria losing power in Germany, and in Europe.

Questions

1. What is the attitude of Germany's Chancellor Helmut Kohl to the idea of Europe?
2. Why do you think his party favour a Federal Europe?
3. Why has Mr Stoiber been called Edmund Thatcher?
4. Why do you think Mr Stoiber might be opposed to increased central powers in Europe?

What is involved in the Maastricht Treaty?

The Maastricht Treaty was finally ratified in November 1993, with the following main points:

- It helps to build closer co-operation on *foreign policy* and *justice/home affairs* on an *intergovernmental* basis without the Commission and European Court having the roles they enjoy under the Treaty of Rome, which initially created the European Community.

  Decision making on joint foreign policy and justice/home affairs under the Union is the responsibility of the European Council and the Council of Ministers. For example, in late 1993 European leaders agreed that under their common foreign and security policy they would tackle Yugoslavia, stability in Central and Eastern Europe, the Russian elections, democracy in South Africa and the Middle East peace process. These decisions were made by the Union, but not on behalf of the Community.

- It extends the responsibility of the *European Community* (EC) part of the Union— run by the Commission. The EC will deal mainly with *social* and *economic issues*. Its responsibilities include new areas such as economic and monetary policy, industry and trans-European networks. The EC also has increased powers on transport, social policy, economic and social affairs, research and development, and the environment.

- It increases the part played by the European Parliament, allowing it to *block laws* in some areas.

- It enshrines the principle of *subsidiarity*, limiting the EC's involvement in national affairs. In areas where both the EC and member states have power to act, the EC will only do so if the objectives of the proposed action cannot be sufficiently achieved by an individual member state. Any action by the EC in any field must not go beyond what is necessary to achieve the Treaty's objectives. If there is a dispute, the European Court of Justice can judge whether EC action is necessary. This principle should ensure that:

(a) the EC does not stray into areas where it is not needed;

(b) where EC action is needed, it should go no further than is required.

- It enables the European Court of Justice to take action on those who do not implement agreed EC rules.
- It defines the *scope* for EC activity in such areas as education and training and health by setting out the sort of action the EC should take.
- It enables EC action in other areas, such as the environment, which affect all countries.
- It makes the European Commission more *accountable* to the European Parliament.
- It establishes *new rights* for European Union citizens.
- It provides for movement towards *economic and monetary union*.

The Maastricht Treaty also set out a new framework: the European Union (EU). This is made up of *three pillars of co-operation* under the European Council (Fig. 6.1)

EUROPEAN COMMUNITY (Treaty of Rome, Single European Act, Maastricht Treaty)	COMMON FOREIGN AND SECURITY POLICE (Maastricht Treaty)	JUSTICE AND HOME AFFAIRS (Maastricht Treaty)
Full Community rules and procedures apply	Inter-governmental co-operation	Inter-governmental co-operation

Figure 6.1

National Parliaments will be encouraged to play a greater role in EC affairs through *Scrutiny of EC laws*. The European Parliament has been given new powers, including the approval of the appointment of the European Commission, and to carry out *inquiries into poor administration* of EC laws, as well as to have some say in EC law making.

- The European Court of Justice has new powers to *fine* countries that do not comply with judgements.

- The Court of Auditors is now required to provide a *statement of assurance* about the reliability of the EC's budget.
- A new *Committee of the Regions* (see page 101) now advises the Commission and Council of Ministers on Regional Policy.
- A *European Ombudsman* now has powers to investigate maladministration in the European institutions.
- Maastricht also contains a chapter on *social policy* (see page 99).

The Common Agricultural Policy

The Treaty of Rome set out that the central aim of the Common Agricultural Policy (CAP) was to: '*Ensure a fair standard of living for the agricultural community*' (Article 39). The main effect of this policy has been to *guarantee incomes* to farmers by setting *minimum prices* for agricultural products. These minimum prices set out to ensure that farmers earn enough to keep farming. The price that the CAP guarantees will normally be higher than the *free market* price (Fig. 6.2).

Figure 6.2

EC producers are also protected from cheaper imported foodstuffs from non-EC countries (e.g. American cereals). Imported non-EC foodstuffs can only be sold at a 'threshold price' (Fig. 6.3). Import taxes are placed on these imports to bring them up to this threshold price. The effect of this import policy is to make EC foodstuffs more competitive within the internal market.

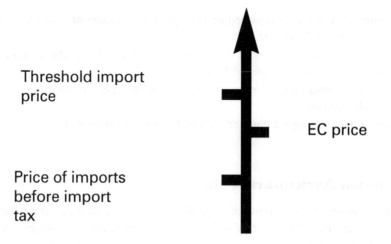

Threshold import price

EC price

Price of imports before import tax

Figure 6.3   Some EC foodstuffs can be given a competitive edge in the internal market.

We can illustrate the impact of this policy on imports by looking at the volume of Australian exports of selected foodstuffs to the EC during a period in which the CAP policy had a major influence (Table 6.1).

Table 6.1   Australian exports of selected foodstuffs to the EC (kilo tonnes)

	1966–8	1982–3
Beef and veal	26.7	8.9
Barley	7.0	0.0
Sugar	400.0	0.0
Butter	57.1	0.3

(*Source*: National Westminster Bank Review, February 1987)

The result of guaranteeing farmers minimum prices is that more goods are provided than can be sold (because consumers can't afford to pay the artificially high prices). The EC therefore has to buy *surplus produce* and *store* it. This has given rise to the notorious wine lakes, butter mountains and beef mountains (Fig. 6.4).

Butter mountains   Wine lakes   Beef mountains

Figure 6.4

This is a very costly policy to run because not only does the EC have to buy up all the surplus stocks. It also has to build huge *storage* areas for products that often need to be refrigerated. Periodically, surplus stocks are sold off at the lowest possible prices to, for example, Russia and other East European economies. In a widely acclaimed book *1992—The Struggle for Europe*, Tony Cutler and a team of writers argued that the CAP goes against the principles of a free market in Europe. Cutler contrasts the principles of the Internal Market and CAP in Table 6.2.

Table 6.2   Internal market vs CAP

Principles of the internal market	CAP
Removal of barriers to trade push down market prices	Prices administered by CAP
Open markets and competition leads to the survival of only the most efficient enterprises	Guaranteed prices allow inefficient farmers to survive
Removal of physical controls	Quotas used to restrict growth of output
Consumers will gain from price falls	Consumers will pay prices well above competitive world market prices

The original arguments for CAP

The numbers of people employed in agriculture vary widely within the EC. For example, in the late 1980s the figures were France 23 per cent, Italy 35 per cent, and Germany 15 per cent. In each of these countries there was thus a very strong agricultural pressure group. In addition, agriculture is always seen as a *strategic issue*— i.e. a country should provide much of its own foodstuff. The *principles* of the CAP that were set out in the Treaty of Rome were to:

- *increase agricultural output* and efficiency through better use of resources and technology
- ensure a *fair standard of living* for agricultural employees
- provide *stable markets*
- make sure that *supplies* of agricultural products are *readily available*
- make sure that *prices are reasonable*.

Preserving the agricultural community is often seen to be essential to the stability of society. In large countries like France there are many scattered towns and villages with their traditions and way of life. These are seen as havens of stability compared with the social problems associated with the suburbs of large cities like Lyons and Paris. If these communities were to collapse we would find the spread of empty villages and deserted communities, and the decline of traditional values.

However, agricultural subsidy leads to huge stockpiles of unused foodstuffs. Each country has its own *intervention agencies* for buying up these stocks. The purchase of stocks is funded by the *European Agricultural Guidance and Guarantee Fund* (EAGGF).

Criticisms of the CAP

There are a number of major criticisms that have been made of the CAP:

1. It is seen as a massive waste of resources. Currently, agriculture and fisheries account for over half of the total EC budget. (The percentage of the budget spent on agriculture has decreased over the years, e.g. in the 1970s it accounted for about 75 per cent of the budget, but this figure had fallen to 64 per cent in 1987 and 53 per cent in 1992. A major reason for this reduction is the growth of the size of the budget, thus enabling an increasing amount to be spent on regional policy.) Some people question whether subsidizing inefficient producers and building up huge stockpiles makes sense.
2. The agricultural policy is *divisive*. The UK government, for example, has in recent years complained about the contribution it has to make to support inefficient producers in other countries and the wastefulness of stockpiling.
3. The agricultural policy has created *international tension*, particularly between the EC and the United States. The EC has been accused of 'dumping' its products and causing loss of income for other countries. This heavily protected European market prevents other, perhaps more efficient, farming nations from selling their produce. In the 1990s international governments are hoping to reduce tariffs and quotas on a world scale. The CAP is one of the stumbling blocks in the way to international agreements (particularly under GATT—see below, page 93).
4. A review of the CAP in 1991 made a number of important points. Price guarantees had successfully ensured a supply of agricultural products, but the supply of many products was greater than the demand. The costs of buying surplus stock were too high. Price support tended to favour the larger, more efficient farms, which meant that nearly 80 per cent of EAGGF spending was going to only 20 per cent of farmers. As a result the policy was not ensuring a fair standard of living for all farmers, or ensuring reasonable prices to consumers, and was leading to unequal treatment to farmers in different regions.

Removing some of the problems of CAP

In recent years attempts have been made to make CAP more workable. However, there have been strong criticisms of some of these changes. In particular, you may have seen film of some of the protest actions taken by French farmers, e.g. blocking motorways and other roads. What has happened is that guaranteed prices for a number of products have been reduced, e.g. for butter; at the same time quotas limiting the amount of some agricultural products have been strengthened, e.g. for milk and beef production.

There has also been an increase in the use of machinery and equipment by large farms and the numbers of people employed in agriculture has fallen. However, many small farms are still operating.

Incomes in agriculture have fallen in recent years, particularly in cereals, oilseeds, milk, beef and veal, and pigmeat. Figures show that farm prices (in *real terms*) fell by 3–4 per cent a year in the EC, and that in certain member states (Belgium, Denmark, Germany, France, Italy and the UK) the *real income* of people engaged in agriculture was lower in 1990 than in 1973. It is important to to remember that some member states have an above-average dependency on agriculture and that cuts in the agricultural budget will have a harsh impact on farmers in these states (particularly Greece, Spain, Portugal and Ireland).

 Task

Do you think that recent falls in farm incomes mean that the 'EC ensures a fair standard of living for the farming community'? How important is it to ensure a fair income for all farmers?

Delors' strategies

In 1988 the so-called *Delors package* set out a five-year plan for reforming CAP (i.e. for the period 1988–92). In 1993 a new Delors II package (Fig. 6.5) was set out to continue these policies (for the period 1993–7).

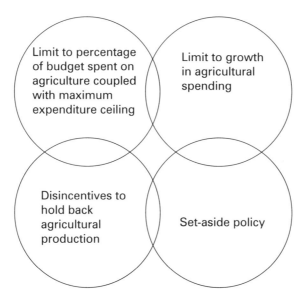

Figure 6.5 The ingredients of the Delors package

1. A *limit* was to be put on the amount of the EC budget that would be spent on CAP, i.e. 1.2 per cent of the national income of the 12 member states coupled with a maximum expenditure of 27 500 million ECUs.
2. *Growth in spending* in agriculture was to be limited to 74 per cent of the growth rate of income in the EC.
3. *Disincentives* were established to hold back production. For example, in cereal production if farmers produced more than a certain quantity then guaranteed prices would be cut.
4. The introduction of a *set-aside scheme* for land. Farmers were to be paid to take part of their land out of production for a five-year period. They received a sum of money for each hectare they set aside.

It is possible that the restrictions in support for overproduction in agriculture may lead to reduced food prices for consumers. On average, households in the 12 member states spend about 20 per cent of their household income on food, tobacco, alcohol and soft drinks. However, there is considerable variation, e.g. in countries where average incomes are lower, such as Greece and Portugal, households spend about 33 per cent of their income on foodstuffs compared with between 13 and 15 per cent in Germany, UK and the Netherlands.

Under the recent *MacSharry proposals*, however, it is suggested that 'savings' from lower price support should go into supporting rural activity—e.g. developing new forests, early retirement schemes for farmers, and measures to develop more environmentally friendly agriculture.

 Task

The following letter appeared recently in a national newspaper. Read the letter and then carry out the tasks that follow:

Dear Editor,

I am disgusted by the Common Agricultural Policy. Over 90 per cent of the European Union's budget is spent on this policy. It is of absolutely no use to hard working British farmers. It simply serves to put money into the pockets of the French and German farmers who go on to produce butter mountains, and wine lakes. Under this scheme these farmers are paid according to how much they can produce. They don't have to sell what they make. In fact they can leave their products to rot on the land. The UK never subsidized its own agriculture. British farms were simply the best in the world. Today our farmers are told not to grow produce on their acres. They have to set it aside. This is so that French farmers can compete. The whole policy is a huge con. The sooner we scrap the CAP the better it will be for our farmers.

Yours Angrily, A Disgusted Farmer.

1. Make a list of points that are inaccurate in this letter.
2. Is there *anything* with which you agree in the letter?
3. Set out a letter in reply to 'Disgusted Farmer'.

CAP and GATT

The General Agreement on Tariffs and Trade (GATT) involves trading countries throughout the world developing agreement to reduce restrictions to free trade. The *benefits of free trade* are enormous (see page 71). Free trade is restricted by subsidies, tariffs and quotas (see pages 74–5).

Over the years, successive rounds of talks between world trading countries have led to reductions in trade restrictions. However, the GATT Uruguay Round of talks broke down in 1990 and hopefully today is now stumbling towards an agreement. The successful completion of these talks is expected to lead to a boost to the world economy of $200 billion. Failure to reach such an agreement would be disastrous.

The biggest stumbling block has been CAP. Because EC agricultural products are subsidized, this gives them an advantage against such groups as American soya bean producers and low-cost food producing countries such as New Zealand and Australia. The Americans in particular have been determined to make sure that the EC cuts back on its farming subsidies. In 1992 the *Blair House agreement* between the EC and the USA a decision was reached to reduce subsidized farm exports (by 21 per cent in volume over six years). However, this agreement is still bitterly opposed by French and other European farmers.

Case Study—A Serpent in the Garden of Eden (Source: *The European*, 28 October 1993)

Italian farmer William Signani needs little reminding that the Emilia Romagna region has been Italy's land of milk and honey for the past 20 years. With 8.5 hectares of land, Signani has helped to make the region a major contributor to a national agricultural economy which accounts for 4.5 per cent of national product. Fruit and vegetables are among his main products, together with 18 000 litres of white wine each year.

Now, however, a serpent of anxiety has entered his Garden of Eden in the form of the EC's Common Agricultural Policy reforms and the Uruguay Round of the GATT talks. The new version of CAP is intent on reducing agricultural surpluses. The new CAP limits him to cultivating 17 000 kilos of grapes per hectare compared with 25 000 in 1992.

However, it is the GATT talks that are particularly worrying. At first, the trade and tariff negotiations excluded such Mediterranean produce as fruit and wine. The Blair House agreement then threw fruit, vegetables and wine on to the bargaining table and Italian farmers are calling for their government to adopt a hardline approach.

Concern followed when, in 1992, the US government threatened to block Italian imports of wine after soya producers—Italy is the biggest producer in Europe—lobbied Brussels to maintain trade barriers on US soya exports. 'Italy simply cannot be forced to fit in with what the US government wants,' said Signani. 'For us it's a good sign that any agreement seems a long way off. Let's hope that, when it comes, it doesn't leave us on our knees.'

Questions

1. What will be the likely effect of reductions in CAP support for William Signani (a) on his output of wine, (b) his cost of producing that wine and (c) the profitability of his farm?
2. How might he be encouraged to use some of his land for other purposes?
3. Why do you think that he is worried about the successful completion of GATT talks?
4. What arguments would American farmers put forward for free trade in agricultural products?
5. Why is the successful completion of GATT agreements so crucial for the world economy?
6. What are the possible disadvantages of successful GATT agreements? Who would be likely to suffer from such agreements taking place? How would they suffer?

NB: GATT negotiations to reduce trade barriers were successfully completed in the summer of 1994.)

Environmental policy

Our environment can be defined as that part of our planet and its surrounding space which contains all living things, and supplies all the requirements for survival and growth (with the major exception of energy from the sun). This is the 'living' environment.

This living environment, sometimes called the *biosphere*, is a comparatively thin layer of soil, rock, water and air. It extends downwards no more than a few thousand metres below the surface (sea creatures can exist at depths of up to 12 000 metres) and several thousand metres up into the atmosphere (people, animals and plants can live at heights of about 4000 metres—in the Alps for instance).

During the last quarter of the twentieth century we have become increasingly aware of our shared responsibility for the environment, and European states have now taken on increasing responsibilities for looking after our shared environment.

Agreement on the need to develop European laws on the environment dates back to 1972 when it was decided to put an environmental policy into practice. By 1990 there were nearly 130 separate laws on such things as the protection of wild birds and the control of discharges of harmful substances into the water supply. The Single European Act of 1987 introduced a *common environmental policy* as part of the Treaty. The environmental policy of the 12 member states sets out to meet the following objectives:

- to preserve, protect and to improve the quality of the environment
- to help to protect human health
- to make sure that natural resources are used carefully and sensibly.

EC policies are based on three principles:

1. The destruction of the environment should be prevented.
2. Environmental damage should be put right at source.
3. The polluters should be made to pay for the damage they cause.

In preparing environmental measures the EC is expected to consider the following:

1. *Available scientific and technical data.* The UK government in particular feel that this is important; for example, a number of 'experts' refuse to accept that there is enough evidence that emissions in the UK cause acid rain in Scandinavia.
2. *Environmental conditions in different regions.* Some people argue that some countries—e.g. those with more wind and rain—may not need such high controls as countries in which pollutants are less likely to be dispersed.
3. The *advantages* and *disadvantages* of taking environmental measures need to be weighed against each other.
4. Consideration needs to be given to the *balanced development* of different regions, e.g. some countries may find that the costs of introducing environmental protection may not be economically affordable (e.g. the poorer regions).

The Maastricht Treaty thus includes an *Environmental Chapter* which sets out to achieve a 'high level of protection' of the environment. Individual countries are, however, allowed to set higher national standards (as is already the case, for example, in the Netherlands, Germany and Denmark). Many states have a poor record of implementing environmental regulations. A good example of the way in which different interpretations were put on environmental regulations was that of public bathing. Countries were expected to take samples of water in public bathing places where there was 'a large number of bathers'. Amazingly in 1985 the UK had only identified 27 bathing waters at a time when Luxembourg with no coastal waters had identified 10. At the same time Denmark had identified 1374 and France 1796. (The UK government justified the lack of samples at Blackpool by stating that holidaymakers there rarely went for a swim. The UK press gave reports on Blackpool, claiming that its beaches were the dirtiest in Europe.)

Recent developments in Environmental Policy indicate that the European Union is seeking to establish the legal framework for environmental protection, leaving it to the member states to implement regulations.

Methods of ensuring environmental standards

Environmental standards can be grouped into emission standards, process standards, product standards, environmental quality standards, and biological quality standards.

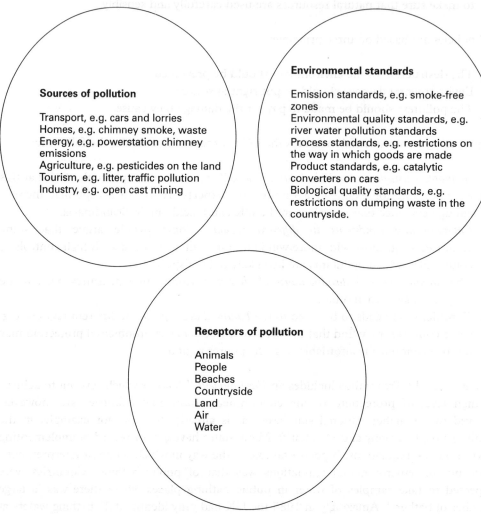

Sources of pollution

Transport, e.g. cars and lorries
Homes, e.g. chimney smoke, waste
Energy, e.g. powerstation chimney emissions
Agriculture, e.g. pesticides on the land
Tourism, e.g. litter, traffic pollution
Industry, e.g. open cast mining

Environmental standards

Emission standards, e.g. smoke-free zones
Environmental quality standards, e.g. river water pollution standards
Process standards, e.g. restrictions on the way in which goods are made
Product standards, e.g. catalytic converters on cars
Biological quality standards, e.g. restrictions on dumping waste in the countryside.

Receptors of pollution

Animals
People
Beaches
Countryside
Land
Air
Water

The various standards are detailed below and illustrated in Fig. 6.6.

Figure 6.6   Setting environmental standards to limit the effects of pollution sources

- *Emission standards* set limits on, for example, emissions from car exhausts, factory chimneys, etc. Emission limits are set according to the best available technology.

- *Process standards* are set to control production processes. They must be set at levels that protect workers' health and minimize discharges of pollution.
- *Product standards* concern what goes into a product, e.g. the substances it contains.
- *Environmental quality standards* establish the quantity of particular substances that is permissible in the air, water, soil, etc. Only when such substances reach a certain concentration is pollution said to exist. Clearly the level depends on when these concentrations become harmful, e.g. to the food chain.
- *Biological quality standards* relate to the limits of certain substances in living organisms. The costs resulting from pollution measures should be borne by the polluter.

The EC has recently introduced an *eco-label* to indicate environmentally sound products. Maastricht has gone some way towards tightening up responsibility for environmental policies with new regulations being made by qualified majority voting.

Case Study—Different methods in different states

It is not easy to come up with common solutions to common problems; however, shared responsibility for the environment in Europe is vital because of the *cross-frontier* nature of so many environmental problems. The single market requires a framework of the same standards in the field of the environment if barriers to trade are to be avoided. Member states are responsible for putting into practice a common approach. However, there are different views as to the best possible environmental approaches. For example, we can see this in Table 6.2, which shows the different methods employed to dispose of waste.

Table 6.2 What happens to waste?

Country	Combustion	Landfill	Composting	Recycling
Germany	36	46	2	16
France	42	45	10	3
Greece	0	100	0	0
UK	8	90	0	2

Germany has a target to recycle 64 per cent of all household plastics and paper and 72 per cent of all glass by 1995. This scheme has proved to be very popular. Most of the waste is thrown into special yellow bins of the Duales System Deutschland (DSD), a company set up to run Germany's recycling scheme. However, the system has been *too* successful. By November 1993 there was already 70 000 tonnes of plastic packaging piling up in warehouses, and although much of this waste was being exported to neighbouring European states for disposal (French wastepaper collectors held up traffic in Paris in October 1993 to protest that cheap imports had driven down the price of

French recycled paper), storage fees were almost crippling the Duales System Deutschland company.

In contrast, the French feel that burning rubbish with energy recovery would be a more practical way of reducing Europe's waste mountain. Burning household waste to produce energy is well-established practice in France. Some people argue that this form of waste disposal is often more economically and environmentally sensible because it is expensive to sort out small items of plastic and other waste, and it would be better to burn the lot and use the energy.

It is also very expensive to transport waste for recycling (with transport wasting energy and leading to further pollution). For recycling to be successful there needs to be a market for recycled products. It is not sufficient for goods to carry eco-friendly labels; they also need to be cheaper and less wasteful of resources.

However, in Germany incineration has a very poor public image—particularly the thought of rubbish being burned to create energy close to where you live. It seems likely that there will be no easy solution to the best way of dealing with European waste! The Germans argue that we should take responsibility for *substance cycles*. All those involved in the marketplace must take responsibility for their products, so that production, consumption, and final disposal form one single, closed system. The disposal of used products must in future have the same priority as supplying the consumer with goods.

Questions

1. Why do you think that different states emphasize different methods of dealing with waste products?
2. Would it be sensible for the EC to demand that all wastes are disposed of in the same way, e.g. by recycling? Or is it better to allow different approaches?
3. How does this case study illustrate the way in which one state's policies can have a cross-border impact?
4. What are the main arguments for and against:
   (a) a recycling approach?
   (b) a combustion approach?
5. Why do you think that landfill is so popular?
6. Which of the solutions outlined do you think would be better (a) in the short term and (b) in the long term?
7. Find out how waste is disposed of in your locality. To what extent is this waste disposal influenced by EC policy and regulations?

Social policy

The Treaty of Rome enshrines the principles that member countries will:

- ensure that every citizen enjoys the *freedom to take a job or set up in business* anywhere in the community
- establish *minimum standards for health and safety at work*
- ensure *equal treatment for men and women* in employment.

At Maastricht, many governments wanted to expand the range of areas of social policy covered by EC laws. The UK government would not agree to the acceptance of new laws that would increase regulation of the labour market. The UK therefore *opted out* of the Social Chapter.

The Treaty's Social Chapter gave legal force to the social charter signed by 11 EC leaders in December 1989. This gave the European Commission powers to develop social legislation *without* facing a national veto. For the first time, minister from the 11 countries are able to agree on the basis of *Qualified Majority Voting* directives on:

- health and safety
- working conditions
- information and consultation of workers
- sex equality in treatment at work and applying for jobs.

If they are *unanimous*, the 11 can agree to directives on:

- social security and social protection of workers
- protection of workers where the employment contract is terminated
- representation and collective defence of the interests of workers and employers
- conditions of employment for third country nationals living in the community.

Before Maastricht the only area of employment law enforceable by Qualified Majority Voting was health and safety. The reforms, therefore, involve a big increase in community powers.

Restructuring policy

The Delors proposals covering the periods 1987–1997 set out to provide an increasing emphasis in the European Union (EU) towards economic and social cohesion. This involved finding the money through the EU's budget to support this growing emphasis.

The *Delors proposals* recognized that the growth of free trade in the internal market would not lead to benefits for all regions. Therefore it was essential to provide assistance and support for *economically backward* and *declining* regions. Economic and social cohesion policies set out to make sure that the less favoured regions also benefit from the advantages of the Single Market. The Delors package therefore set out to double the money available for restructuring policies. Between 1987 and 1992 the proportion of the EC budget allocated to structural funds increased from 17 to 27 per cent.

The Maastricht Treaty set out that in formulating all EC policies the impact for social and economic cohesion should be taken into account. In addition, funds were to be channelled to the four poorer nations among the 12—Ireland, Portugal, Greece and Spain—particularly for developing infrastructure, e.g. transport and communication systems, and for training projects. In addition, moneys for training and retraining projects and other programmes were to be made available to poorer regions in richer countries. The Delors package set out that 33.5 per cent of the entire EC budget should be made available for economic and social cohesion policies by 1997.

The EU is made up of an advantaged *core* and a disadvantaged *periphery*. The 'depressed south' is the most serious regional problem facing the EU at present. The European Commission identifies a number of types of 'disadvantaged' regions. These are:

1. *Lagging regions*: These are regions that have never really started to develop. There are a number of such regions in the Mediterranean zone with poor communications, low output agriculture, and very low incomes for many people.
2. *Declining industrial regions*: These are areas in which industry was once important but has now gone into decline, e.g. areas such as the north-west of England, and parts of south Wales.
3. *Peripheral regions*: These are regions that are too far from the centre of large markets, e.g. The Highlands and Islands of Scotland, Ireland and Sicily.
4. *Border regions*: In the past a number of border regions were favoured because of the services they offered, e.g. warehousing for goods being traded between countries. With the lifting of border restrictions these areas now require assistance.
5. *Urban problem areas*: The big cities of Europe—e.g. Paris, Lyon, London—have particular social problems associated with crime, congestion, drugs, pollution, etc.
6. *Rural problem areas*: Some areas with poor climates for farming have particular problems. These areas have been adversely affected by reductions in subsidies to agriculture.

The EU has a number of *structural funds* which provide help and support to these areas—for example, for projects in declining coal and steel communities, helping with assistance and training schemes to deal with long-term unemployment, the promotion of development schemes in rural and lagging areas, increased employment help for young people, etc.

Committee of the Regions

One of the great failures of the EC has been lack of acknowledgement of the role of local and regional authorities as part of the European democratic system. Maastricht addressed this 'democratic deficit' by setting up an advisory Committee of the Regions. The Committee has aroused great interest in Germany, Spain and Belgium, each of which has powerful regional governments. The German *Länder* will be represented by their elected presidents and the UK by elected local councillors.

7

European Union economies

An economic system

The Europe of the 12, and in the near future the Europe of the European Economic Area, will increasingly come to operate as a single system. The beginning of 1993 saw the completion of the Single Market. We can represent the increasing interdependence of these economies in Fig. 7.1, which indicates how the move to economic union has progressively led to common economic policies.

	Removal of trade restrictions between members	Common external trade policy towards non-members	Free movement of factors of production between member states	Harmonization of economic policies under supra-national control
Free trade area	✓			
Customs union	✓	✓		
Common market	✓	✓	✓	
Economic union	✓	✓	✓	✓

Figure 7.1

Member states will increasingly be concerned with shared economic issues and policies. Concerns over issues such as unemployment, inflation, exchange rates and growth will increasingly come to be seen as European problems rather than national problems.

Economic management

Managing an economic system involves working to create a number of ideal economic conditions. The issues outlined below are increasingly being seen as European concerns requiring joint efforts and initiatives from European governments (see Fig. 7.2). These issues include:

1. Minimizing unemployment

Involuntary unemployment exists when people who want to work cannot find jobs. Unemployment occurs for a number of reasons, e.g.:

- A lack of demand for products on a wide scale. This occurs in a period of recession when there is a reduced demand for all goods, from building blocks to industrial machinery, from confectionery to cars, etc.
- A change in the structure of demand. As times move on the whole structure of demand for products changes—new products come in to replace outmoded products, e.g. CD players replace record players, synthetic fibres replace natural fibres, etc.
- Technology means that some products and processes can be carried out with a much smaller labour input, e.g. the use of machinery in farming, the use of automated production lines in car factories and breweries, etc.

Unemployment leads to a great waste of resources in an economy. It is also socially demoralizing. Combating unemployment therefore requires the generation of fresh demand in an economic system, the training and retraining of employees to take on new jobs, and other policies.

2. Minimizing inflation

Inflation occurs when there is a general rise in price levels. Inflation is a highly destabilizing force. A small increase in prices can rapidly escalate as people whose wages and other incomes fall behind try to catch up, leading to further increases in costs and prices.

Inflation is harmful to trade. Exporters generally sell goods on credit. When they seek repayment they find that the money they receive is less than they expected. They therefore become reluctant to trade.

Inflation can also lead to unemployment. Businesses faced by rising costs may be forced to cut back on production and in the numbers of employees.

Controlling inflation is therefore usually given a high priority in running an economic system. Ways of controlling inflation include limiting the amount that government spends, raising taxes so that consumers have less to spend, and raising interest rates to discourage borrowing (which leads to spending).

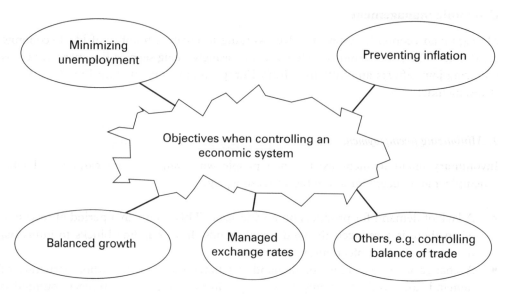

Figure 7.2

3. Controlling exchange rates

The exchange rate is the rate at which one currency will exchange against other currencies. When your currency rises in value against other currencies this makes your goods more expensive when you export them. It is important that your currency exchanges at a high enough rate to bring in good revenues from selling goods overseas. However, if the value rises too much, foreigners will become reluctant to buy your products. If the value of your currency falls too much it will be easy to sell products abroad—but it may not be worth doing so if each product does not yield much revenue.

It is important that exchange rates remain stable over a period of time so that traders know what to expect when they exchange goods. In recent years there has been a lot of emphasis on creating stable exchange rates within the EU. The ideal is that at some stage in the future there will be a common currency.

4. Maximizing growth

One way of measuring growth in an economic system is to compare the output or incomes generated by the system over a period of time. Growth occurs when output or incomes continue to rise. Growth leads to increasing standards of living. Citizens have bigger baskets of goods to consume. However, we need to be cautious about how we measure growth. Increasing output may be combined with increasing pollution, and environmental damage. We also need to consider the way in which income is distributed. Is the increase shared between many people or do just a few benefit?

Case Study—Unemployment in the European Union

At the start of 1994 the number of unemployed in the EU was officially measured at 18 million, i.e. 10.6 per cent of the workforce. The Commission's forecast for economic growth in 1994 was 1.3 per cent, which is hardly likely to reduce the unemployment figure by a great amount.

It was against this background that Jacques Delors set out a new agenda for the EU in his paper 'Growth, Competitiveness, Unemployment' at the end of 1993. 'Delors put unemployment at the top of the agenda. He argued that there was no miracle cure for unemployment. He proposed new rail, road and waterway links, improvements in airports, new telecommunications networks, more efficient energy and water distribution. These policies would bring permanent benefits to the EU economy. They would also be labour intensive and involve relatively low import costs. (Jacques Delors would like to see EU governments taking the initiative in paying for these projects).

Delors also raised the question of creating new, socially useful jobs. The elderly and handicapped need home helps, children in run-down areas need play areas, old houses need renovation, rural areas need transport services, polluted rivers need to be cleaned.

The White Paper also raised the possibility of work sharing at a time when some people work for more than 70 hours a week. At 47.3 hours, the average week for the full-time British employee is by far the highest in Europe. Portugal, at 41.9, is the next highest. (The UK government is currently opposed to work sharing, using the argument that job vacancies would be taken by less skilled and less productive people.)

The White Paper also called for low labour costs, deregulation and private sector investment in creating new jobs.

The target for the report was growth, which would hopefully create 15 million jobs by the year 2000, halving the rate of unemployment to about 5 per cent.

Questions

1. Why do you think that the Delors White Paper has put the emphasis on growth and reducing employment?
2. What are the main proposals for creating growth in the European economy?
3. Which of these proposals do you think the UK government is most likely to support? Why?
4. Which of these proposals do you think the UK government is most likely to oppose? Why?
5. Why is it important for these policies to be carried out on a Europe-wide level?

Variations in unemployment

Figure 7.3 shows that, at any one time, there are considerable differences in employment levels between EU countries. The figures show the percentages of the working populations that were unemployed in 1991 and 1992. You can see that at this time unemployment was rising in all countries. Contrast these figures with those available today.

Unemployment in the Community

	1991	1992
Luxembourg	1.7	2.1
Germany	4.2	4.9
Portugal	4.3	4.9
Netherlands	7	7.5
Belgium	7.8	8.6
Italy	9.9	9.8
The Twelve	9.0	9.9
Denmark	9.2	10
France	9.9	10.3
UK	10.1	11.6
Ireland	16.9	18.3
Spain	16.7	19.4

Figure 7.3

One effect of the creation of the Single Market and the reduction of subsidies to farmers through the Common Agricultural Policy has been to threaten the livelihoods of large numbers of people in poorer regions of the EU. In 1993, therefore, a new Cohesion Fund was set up to provide much-needed capital and bring down unemployment in the EU's four poorest countries: Ireland, Spain, Portugal and Greece.

Looking at the economies of member states

The state of the economy of an individual country or economic system is constantly changing. The economic indicators—such as the inflation rate, unemployment and the growth rate—change frequently. There is usually an underlying trend, e.g. unemployment increases for a period of time, but when this trend appears to be creating a problem the government takes measures to improve the situation by, for example, carrying out policies to create jobs. However, the measures that the government takes may lead to further problems, e.g. inflation may start to rise, or the exchange rate may deteriorate, etc. The section below looks at the economies of EU member states. It is important to remember that in the modern world the fortunes of these economies change quickly. You will therefore need to carry out some research by yourselves to investigate what is happening right now!

You may find the following statistics helpful. They are based on medium-term forecasts made by Barclays Bank in late 1993/early 1994. The indicators shown are:

- *Real GDP % change*: This can be used as a broad measure of growth in an economy.
- *Unemployment rate*: This gives the official figures indicating unemployment levels.
- *Prices (%) change*: This can be used as a broad measure of general inflation.
- *Current A/C ($bn)*: This shows the balance of current exports and imports in billions of US dollars.
- *Interest rates (%):* This is a rough indicator of the short-term cost of borrowing money.
- *Sterling ER*: This shows the rate of exchange of the relevant country's currency against the pound.

Country	Average 1984–91	1993	1994	1995	1996	1997
1. *Belgium*						
Real GDP % change	2.6	-0.8	0.3	1.0	1.4	2.0
Unemployment rate	9.7	8.8	9.0	9.2	9.3	9.0
Prices (%) change	3.1	3.0	2.5	3.0	3.5	3.7
Current A/C ($bn)	2.8	5.0	4.0	3.5	3.5	3.0
Interest rates (%)	8.9	8.1	4.0	4.0	4.2	4.5
Sterling ER	66.16	52.20	55.00	58.00	60.00	N/A
2. *Denmark*						
Real GDP % change	2.2	0.5	2.0	3.0	2.5	2.3
Unemployment rate	9.2	12.5	12.5	11.5	10.5	10.0
Prices (%) change	4.1	1.0	1.5	2.0	2.5	2.5
Current A/C ($bn)	-1.4	3.8	3.0	1.5	1.0	1.5
Interest rates (%)	9.9	9.0	5.5	6.0	6.0	6.5
Sterling ER	12.9	9.4	9.6	9.7	9.7	N/A
3. *France*						
Real GDP % change	2.5	-1.0	1.5	2.5	2.5	3.5
Unemployment rate	9.8	11.5	12.5	12.0	11.5	10.5
Prices (%) change	4.1	2.3	2.5	2.5	2.5	3.0
Current A/C ($bn)	-3.3	1.0	0.7	0.8	-0.5	-2.0
Interest rates (%)	9.2	8.2	4.0	4.0	5.0	6.0
Sterling ER	10.51	8.65	9.0	8.85	8.9	N/A

Country	Average 1984–91	1993	1994	1995	1996	1997
4. *Germany*						
Real GDP % change	3.1	−1.5	1.0	2.0	2.5	3.0
Unemployment rate	7.3	8.5	9.0	8.0	7.0	7.0
Prices (%) change	1.9	4.0	2.8	2.5	3.0	3.5
Current A/C ($bn)	31.0	−33.0	−32.0	−20.0	−15.0	−15.0
Interest rates (%)	6.1	7.1	4.0	4.0	5.0	5.5
Sterling ER	3.30	2.50	2.65	2.65	2.65	N/A
5. *Greece*						
Real GDP % change	3.5	1.0	1.5	2.0	3.0	3.0
Prices (%) change	13.7	14.5	10.0	8.0	6.5	6.0
Current A/C ($bn)	−2.1	−1.0	−1.5	−2.0	−2.5	−2.5
Interest rates (%)	20.5	22.3	17.5	15.0	12.0	10.0
Sterling ER	266	348	398	410	410	400
6. *Ireland*						
Real GNP % change	3.8	2.0	3.0	3.5	3.5	3.5
Unemployment rate	15.8	16.8	17.0	16.0	15.0	14.0
Prices (%) change	3.3	1.6	2.6	3.0	3.0	3.5
Current A/C ($bn)	0.2	3.0	2.9	3.0	3.4	3.7
Interest rates (%)	10.8	9.0	5.0	4.5	4.5	5.0
Sterling ER	1.11	1.01	1.06	1.05	1.03	N/A
7. *Italy*						
Real GDP % change	2.7	−0.2	2.3	2.7	3.0	3.5
Unemployment rate	11.3	11.5	11.8	11.5	11.0	11.0
Prices (%) change	6.7	4.5	3.8	3.5	3.5	3.5
Current A/C ($bn)	−7.3	1.0	6.0	11.0	15.0	15.0
Interest rates (%)	12.4	10.0	7.5	7.0	6.5	6.5
Sterling ER	2255	2345	2525	2520	2520	N/A
8. *Luxembourg*						
Real GDP % change	4.2	1.8	2.2	2.5	3.0	3.3
Unemployment rate	1.5	1.5	1.6	1.5	1.4	1.3
Prices (%) change	3.4	2.0	1.5	1.8	2.3	2.8
Current A/C ($bn)	2.2	3.8	3.5	3.3	3.5	3.8
Interest rates (%)	9.0	7.8	7.0	6.0	6.5	6.8
Sterling ER	68.35	51.60	54.50	54.50	N/A	N/A
9. *The Netherlands*						
Real GNP % change	2.7	1.0	2.0	3.5	3.0	2.5
Unemployment rate	9.2	7.5	7.0	6.5	6.0	6.0
Prices (%) change	1.6	2.5	2.8	3.0	3.0	3.0
Current A/C ($bn)	6.3	10.5	13.0	14.0	14.0	12.0
Interest rates (%)	6.7	7.3	5.5	5.5	6.0	6.0
Sterling ER	3.90	2.82	2.92	2.92	N/A	N/A

Country	Average 1984–91	1993	1994	1995	1996	1997

10. Portugal
See research task below

11. Spain

Country	Average 1984–91	1993	1994	1995	1996	1997
Real GDP % change	3.6	1.0	2.5	3.0	3.0	2.5
Unemployment rate	19.3	19.5	19.3	19.0	18.5	18.5
Prices (%) change	8.1	5.3	4.2	3.8	3.8	3.5
Current A/C ($bn)	−3.1	−22.0	−19.0	−16.0	−13.0	−10.0
Interest rates (%)	14.6	11.5	8.8	8.0	8.0	8.0
Sterling ER	204	175	200	200	0	0

12. United Kingdom
See research task below

NB: The information given in the tables above is based on forecasts made by economists working for Barclays Bank from 1994 onwards.

Tasks: Research and analysis of economic data

1. Can you supply the missing data for Portugal and the United Kingdom by using current publications? For example, you could use Barclays Economic Departments country reports, available free to Barclays Bank customers from The Librarian, Economics Department, Barclays Bank, PO Box 12, 1 Wimborne Road, Poole, Dorset, BH15 2BB. The DTI also produces country by country reports.
2. How accurate are the estimated figures from 1994 onwards? Check this against more recent figures for each of the 12 countries.
3. Analyse the figures in the following ways:
   (a) Which countries seem to be having the greatest problems with unemployment in the mid-1990s?
   (b) Which countries appear to be experiencing the fastest growth rates?
   (c) Which countries have deficits on their current account balances?
   (d) Which countries have the best/worst inflation records in the mid-1990s?
   (e) Which of the statistics appear to move together on a European Union wide level? Why do you think this is?
   (f) Which economies appear to have the greatest combination of problems? Which economies appear to have the fewest problems? Can you explain why?

Economic profiles of the 12

1. Belgium

There are nearly 10 million people in Belgium. It is a small country depending heavily on international trade because of the openness of its markets, the international role of its capital city Brussels and its geographical location. The Belgian economy is one of the stronger economies of the EU, with income per head about two and a half per cent above the average for the EU as a whole. It has a strong currency. Nearly twice as many women as men are unemployed in Belgium. Within Belgium there is considerable inequality; for example, unemployment in Flanders, the largest region of Belgium, is only 9.9 per cent (in 1992) compared with 18.4 per cent in Brussels and 20.6 per cent in the Walloon region. The Walloon region was based on heavy declining industries producing raw materials (e.g. coal, iron and steel) and semi-manufactured goods (including glass). In the mid-1990s only 20 per cent of people in Belgium are employed in manufacturing compared with 25 per cent at the beginning of the decade.

The Belgian economy is closely tied to that of Germany, which is its largest trading partner. Germany takes 25 per cent of Belgian exports. However, as Germany has tried to cope with the inflationary effects of reunification this has led to a reduction in demand for Belgian goods, leading to stagnation in Belgium. Three-quarters of all Belgian exports are sold in the EU. The fortunes of Belgium are therefore very much tied up with those of the EU.

2. Denmark

Denmark has shifted from being a rural to a predominantly urban society since the Second World War. Danes are on average relatively well off by EU standards. Denmark is one of the smaller member states with only 5.25 million people. Only about 15 per cent of Danes are involved in manufacturing. About 55 per cent of Danish exports are within the EU. In addition, over 20 per cent of exports are to former EFTA countries, i.e. mainly to neighbouring Scandinavian countries. Table 7.1 outlines Denmark's main trading partners in 1982.

Table 7.1   Trading partners (% of total) 1992

Exports to		Imports from	
Germany	23.6	Germany	23.1
Sweden	11.5	Sweden	10.5
UK	10.1	UK	8.2
Norway	5.8	USA	5.6
France	5.7	France	5.6
USA	4.9	Norway	5.4

During the 1980s the Danish economy had a number of problems associated with demand which seemed to be getting out of control, leading to price rises and an over-dependence on imports, and in that decade Denmark built up a large overseas debt. During the 1990s, however, this trend has been reversed—leading to increasing unemployment. It seems likely that there will be slow growth in Denmark over the next few years while neighbouring Germany comes to grips with reunification. Denmark has a relatively large public sector and welfare state system. Scandinavian countries also place an important emphasis on environmental concerns. The Danes, who produce much of their own gas and oil and make extensive use of wind power, plan to be self-sufficient in energy consumption by 1996.

3. France

France is the largest country in Europe by geographical area. Nearly 65 per cent of its exports are within the EU. Manufacturing industry is responsible for nearly 25 per cent of national output.

In recent years the French government has managed to hold back inflation and this has enabled it to achieve some slow growth although unemployment levels are relatively high and are likely to remain so.

In 1992 it looked as if the French franc might not be able to keep within the bands expected by the Exchange Rate Mechanism. However, the storm was weathered and the French economy now appears to be in a relatively strong position, enabling it to play an important role in Europe. Labour costs have been falling and, importantly, the level of inflation is lower than that in neighbouring Germany.

In the 1980s French businesses tended to concentrate on selling to a protected home market and to less-developed countries. In recent years there has been more emphasis on selling to industrialized markets. The French have been successful in this area, and that has been a major feature in improving external trade. The general economic policy of France is a balance between free enterprise and government intervention. In the past levels of protection were quite high; however, with the development of the EU more and more large French companies have looked outwards to international markets. Many companies have become international in stature, e.g. Chanel in cosmetics, and Peugeot and Renault in car manufacture. This has increased the strength of the French economy. In the 1990s the EU has reduced its subsidies to agriculture, forcing immense structural changes in the French economy.

4. Germany

East and West Germany were reunited as a Federal Republic of Germany on 3 October 1990. Since the Second World War West Germany has been one of the powerhouses of the world economy and a major force in the EU. During the late 1980s the German economy was starting to slow down. In the early 1990s the Germans have been faced with the tremendous costs of reunification as much of former East German industry became redundant overnight. The former West Germany was a free enterprise Western economy merging with a state socialist Eastern bloc country in which pollution had been a major external cost of industrial activity.

The process of unification led to a temporary boom as consumers in the East were able to purchase new consumer durables for the first time. The boom ended in the second half of 1992, leading the economy into a recession as sharp as any since 1945. Manufacturing took the brunt of the downturn.

Some commentators feel that German manufacture should have been reduced at an earlier stage. Today Germany typifies the high-cost Western economy with highly paid labour trying to compete with low-cost labour in the new Pacific Rim economies. It seems likely that manufacturing in Germany will need to be trimmed considerably, with smaller workforces, shorter working weeks and fewer producers. German growth is likely to be slow because of a loss of competitiveness within the EU.

A recent study by a German research institute has shown that, in 1992, West Germany had the highest hourly wage rates among developed economies. Major problems were caused by the strength of the German currency in international markets and by social security and welfare payments which amounted to almost 50 per cent of labour costs. Also, because Germany has excellent environmental standards, this adds to the cost of production.

5. Greece

In terms of output per head, Greece was the second-poorest country when it joined the European Community in 1981, and is now the poorest, having been overtaken by Portugal in 1991. Inflation is a major problem in Greece, running at a level consistently higher than that in other EU states. The Greek economy continues to run a deficit on current account which is higher than in any other European country. A major problem has been the deficit run by socialist governments. Conservative governments have tried to reduce state expenditure but this has been an unpopular measure. Greece benefits from the EU structural and cohesion funds which set out to put money into those regions which particularly lose out from growing competitiveness and free markets within the EU. EU structural funds are available to improve the infrastructure of weaker EU economies. The Greek government has been able to channel investment funds in recent years into major capital projects, such as those shown in Table 7.2.

A major emphasis in recent years has been on the deregulation of activities in Greece in order to reduce barriers to competition.

Greece is a relatively spread-out economy with many small islands in addition to its mainland. There are still many small farms in Greece and there is a dependence in the islands and coastal areas on tourism. Some 25 per cent of the population was engaged in agriculture in 1991 and 15 per cent in manufacturing. About 65 per cent of all exports are sold within the EU.

Table 7.2   Major infrastructure projects 1993–8

Project	Drachma (bn)
New roads and motorways	1292
Athens metro	500
Thessaloniki metro	40
Railway modernization	370
Diversion of River Acheloos	120
Athens airport	25
Evinos Dam	40
Others	183
Total	2570

6. Ireland

Since the end of the 1980s Ireland has made progress to improve its economic standing. The main thrust for growth has come in the manufacturing sector, largely as a result of expansion in the high-tech sector. One of Ireland's major assets is that it is a popular site for foreign investment.

Income per head in Ireland, however, continues to remain at under 70 per cent of the EU's average, and unemployment in Ireland tends to follow very closely that in the UK. Many of Ireland's problems arise because of its geographical location on the edge of the EU (its island status, poor access to (air)ports and inadequate roads and its high dependency rate).

Ireland's birth rate is one of the highest in the EU, and this has led to top-heavy youth unemployment and high emigration. In addition, the industrial sector until recently has been uncompetitive and small, depending on foreign investment. Overseas companies account for 50 per cent of industrial output and 75 per cent of industrial exports, with the largest presence in the chemicals and electronics sector.

Over the last 10 years the numbers of long-term unemployed have doubled. About one-third of the long-term unemployed are between the ages of 15 and 24.

The National Development Plan 1994–9 has been set up to combat some of the problems of the economy, particularly through new investment in industry, transport, training and energy. Along with Greece and Portugal, Ireland is the recipient of structural and cohesion funds which will enable it to invest in major capital projects— e.g. improving ports, airports and railways.

Over the last decade Irish trade has diversified away from the UK towards other EU countries and the United States. The UK's share of exports has fallen progressively from well over 70 per cent in 1960 to 37 per cent in the early 1980s to just over 31 per cent in 1992. Today over 40 per cent of exports are to other EU states.

7. Italy

Since 1989, Italy has replaced the United Kingdom as the third-largest economy in the EU. This has largely reflected the sharp upward revision made in 1985 to estimates of Italian national output. Previously, much of Italy's output had been hidden for reasons of tax evasion; some estimates put the 'black economy' in Italy as high as 25 per cent of all output. In addition, there have been other factors leading to real growth in Italy. An impressive productivity performance has stemmed from increased investment levels, particularly in machinery and equipment.

Italy's levels of investment exceeded the EU average in the 1970s, 1980s and 1990s (although recently this has dropped). Levels of productivity in services have, however, been lower than the EU average.

Italy has a much higher proportion of small- to medium-sized firms than most other major industrial countries, which can mean greater flexibility and drive. Other factors in Italy's growth may include superior design, more determined marketing and selling and the use of modern management and production methods.

In Italy the public sector has an above-average presence for the EU, but recently there have been moves towards increasing privatization.

A major characteristic of the Italian economy is regional inequality. The regions of the southern Mezzogiorno have much lower standards of living and higher unemployment rates than the more industrialized north. Consumption per head in the south was only 70 per cent of the north-centre level in the late 1980s. Productivity in the south is only 60% of that in the north-centre.

The south continues to be a drain on the resources of Italy and is a major reason why the government spends so much of Italy's national income in subsidies and welfare payments. Some pressure groups in the north-centre regions would like to see a split from the south.

Italy has a significantly less open economy than most other EU countries. Exports and imports of goods and services both amounted to only 20 per cent of national expenditure in 1992 compared with a 27 per cent average for the EU.

8. Luxembourg

Luxembourg is the smallest of the EU member states with only about one-third of a million people. It is a wealthy land-locked country which, during the 1980s and 1990s, has reduced its dependence on the steel industry, which at one time dominated the economy. In the 1970s Luxembourg produced more steel per head than any other country in the world; at that time 28 000 people were employed in steel production, but by 1992 the figure had fallen to 8000.

Luxembourg has now moved into other forms of production: for example, it has recently moved into financial services and other modern industries. The government, however, is concerned that an over-dependence on steel may have been replaced by an over-dependence on financial services. Luxembourg has a good competitive advantage for financial services in that it has a central location in the EU and a multilingual labour force. Services today account for 70 per cent of the national output of Luxembourg.

Restructuring of the Luxembourg economy has been based on tripartite agreement between industrialists, unions and the government. For example, the unions accepted a no-strike agreement as long as there were no forced redundancies in the steel industry.

Today, almost 20 000 people are engaged in financial services in Luxembourg and 190 banks are operating in the Grand Duchy. Luxembourg has benefited from free movement of capital, a strict bank secrecy code, an easy-going legal system and low taxes on investments. Luxembourg runs a deficit on visible trade and a surplus on invisibles, which is reflected in its trading figures (shown in $bn):

	1992	1993	1994	1995
Trade balance (visibles)	−2.0	−1.7	−1.3	−1.2
Current balance (visibles and invisibles)	4.0	3.8	3.5	3.3

9. The Netherlands

The Netherlands is a highly industrialized nation, with about a quarter of its workforce engaged in industry. Manufacturing, mining, quarrying (including public utilities) account for about one-third of the national income. The country has always been a centre of commerce and banking and about 70 per cent of people are employed in services. Under 5 per cent of people are employed in agriculture, forestry and fishing. Because of the scarcity of the land Dutch agriculture has tended to become highly intensive and specialized, producing mostly milk and milk products, meat, vegetables, flowers and similar products.

In the Netherlands there are marked differences in wealth between poorer peripheral areas in the rural north—which are characterized by industrial decline—and the more prosperous Randstad conurbation.

During the 1960s and 1970s some of the Netherlands' main industrial areas were hit by the reduction in size of traditional industries such as textiles, mining and shipbuilding. For example, in 1965 the closure of all 11 mines in the province of Limburg led to a slump in economic activity, leading to a loss of 75 000 jobs.

As a small open economy the Netherlands is strongly export oriented, with exports of goods and services accounting for nearly 60 per cent of national output. This is the highest ratio in Europe after Luxembourg and Belgium. The development of natural gas reserves and exports dominated the economy during the 1970s and early 1980s. Energy still accounts for 8.5 per cent of total exports. The services sector continued to grow during the 1980s and now accounts for over 40 per cent of GDP against 33 per cent for manufacturing. A major problem for the Netherlands has been the size of government spending and the national debt.

The main trading partners of the Netherlands have changed very little over the last 30 years, as can be seen in Table 7.3.

Table 7.3 Major trading partners (% of total) 1958 and 1991

Exports to	1991	1958	Imports from	1991	1958
Germany	29.3	19.0	Germany	23.5	19.5
Belgium	14.2	15.0	Belgium	13.0	17.8
France	10.6	4.9	USA	8.1	11.3
UK	9.3	11.9	UK	8.0	7.4
Italy	6.4	2.7	France	7.0	2.8
USA	3.8	5.6	Japan	5.4	0.8
Spain	2.5	0.8	Italy	3.4	1.8
			Spain	1.4	0.4
EU total	76.2	59.9	EU total	58.1	61.8

Although the United Kingdom and United States have become less important, Japan has risen in the import league. The top three export markets account for 54 per cent of total exports, and Germany's share of 30 per cent underlines the close relationship between the two states.

10. Portugal

Portugal, along with Greece and Ireland, is regarded to be one of the least developed states of Europe requiring the most support from structural funds. Substantial economic and technical assistance from the EU has helped to narrow the gap that existed between Portugal and other states when it joined the EU in 1986. Important infrastructure projects have included the completion and extensions of networks of roads and highways.

Progress has also been made in the development of export-oriented industries such as electronic component manufacture and assembly and textiles. Portugal benefits from some of the lowest labour costs in Europe, combined with good productivity levels. Foreign investors use the Portuguese base as a springboard into the European market. For example, multinational car companies use Portugal as a workshop to produce a variety of models.

Portugal benefited from relatively high growth rates in the 1980s. Between 1986 and 1990 growth rates averaged 4.5 per cent, which is well above the average for the EU. These slowed down to 2.2 per cent in 1992 and 2.3 per cent in 1993.

A rise in incomes in Portugal is expected to support growth through the home market. However, rises in wages may have a detrimental effect on international competitiveness.

Although Portugal is continuing to export more to other EU countries, rising living standards have helped to increase imports, thus giving the country larger balance of trade deficits.

EU funds have been crucial in helping to modernize the Portuguese economy. Between 1986 and 1992, for example, the annual rate of foreign investment in Portugal increased

37-fold. Direct EU aid and structural funds have provided a significant contribution in helping to modernize the economy; however, in terms of relative labour productivity, Portugal currently has only half the EU average. At current rates of progress it will take several decades for Portugal to catch up with the other countries in the EU.

11. Spain

After joining the EU, Spain, like Portugal, made rapid progress between 1986 and the early 1990s but this rate of progress has now slowed down. The boom in household spending in the years following EC membership accounted for almost 70 per cent of the 4.5 per cent annual growth in national income. Investment was important too, spurred on by deregulation and investment from abroad. Exports have been diverted to meet the high home demand.

Spain is the fifth largest economy in Europe, accounting for around 8 per cent of output. It is still relatively dependent on agricultural production, but tourism and services have become more important over the past 10 years. In terms of output or income per head it ranks alongside other 'less developed' EU countries, with an income level of only 73 per cent of the EU average. However, it is well ahead of Ireland, Portugal and Greece, and stands to gain further large regional and structural assistance from the EU over the next five years.

The Spanish economy has witnessed major structural changes over the past 10 years. The effects of these will still be important in shaping economic performance in the next five years. The most important of these changes are:

- Membership of the EC in 1986, which accelerated a major change in the pattern of external trade
- Deregulation in the shape of the Single Market, which opened up a previously closed economy
- Deregulation of financial services, which has prompted structural changes in the banking sector
- A shift to deflationary economic policies following entry to the Exchange Rate Mechanism and the acceptance of European Monetary Union.

Spain's membership of the EU signalled a fast-track policy to try to catch up with the rest of Europe.

12. The United Kingdom

The UK is the fourth largest economy in the EU behind Germany, France and Italy. The emphasis in the UK economy is very much on services and the City of London makes a substantial contribution to invisible earnings. However, the UK still has some important manufacturing industries including chemicals, whisky manufacture, pharmaceuticals and machine tools. Major British companies such as BP, Unilever and

ICI have a major international presence. Over the years there has been a recognition that competitive advantage has been lost in industries such as car manufacture, coal, iron and steel and textiles.

The 1970s and 1980s saw a considerable restructure of manufacturing companies. This was also a period of extensive privatization as telecommunications, gas, water, steel, electricity and other concerns were sold off to the private sector and substantially reduced in size. The emphasis is still on privatization but it has become increasingly difficult to place industries such as the railways and coal with private investors. The agricultural sector of the economy accounts for a very small proportion of the labour force, but it is highly productive. During the 1970s and 1980s the British economy benefited substantially from North Sea oil and gas. In the mid-1990s BP and Shell have again come up with intensive finds of oil off the Shetlands, but it is not clear how valuable these reserves will be with the current depressed price of oil.

The UK's trade is now predominantly with the EU and traditional ties with the United States and Commonwealth countries have reduced in importance.

Under a Conservative government the emphasis has been on creating a flexible labour market. Minimum wages have been abolished and workers in the UK work longer hours than anywhere else in the EU. The productivity of labour has increased, which has had the effect of increasing the competitive edge of UK industry. Japanese businesses have been welcomed into the UK and there has been substantial investment by foreign multinationals.

There is sometimes regarded to be regional variations in the UK. Depressed regions have included the south-west, Wales, Scotland, the north-east, the north-west and areas of industrial closure such as shipbuilding, mining, fishing, etc. There is a tendency to look upon the south-east, east Midlands and East Anglia as the more prosperous areas. However, during the recession in the early 1990s it was clear that the picture was much more complicated, with islands of prosperity in poorer regions and islands of decline in prosperous regions.

The UK government has opted out of the Social Chapter (see page 99) of the Maastricht Treaty and although it briefly entered the Exchange Rate Mechanism it has now left and shows no enthusiasm for European Monetary Union.

 Tasks

Use the information about EU countries contained in this chapter, together with your own research, to make some comparisons.

1. If you were going to rank EU countries into three bands:

   Band 1: the most prosperous
   Band 2: medium prosperous
   Band 3: poorer states
   how would you go about making this division? (Perhaps you would also want to make a comparison of poor and rich regions.)

2. Which countries tend to be involved most in trading with EU partner states?
3. Which states have the biggest problems with unemployment and inflation? Why?
4. Which states have been most affected by German reunification?
5. Which states still have large agricultural populations?
6. Which states are best placed to move towards a single currency?
7. How have all states become increasingly economically interdependent?
8. How have countries benefited from structural funds?

A wider Union

Negotiations are supposed to be completed by 1 January 1995 to extend the EU to include Norway, Sweden, Finland, Austria and Liechtenstein. Switzerland rejected the European Economic Area in December 1992 and is now having isolated talks with Brussels about an individual relationship. Figure 7.4 shows EU member states and potential member states.

Figure 7.4

Austria

Other than Germany and possibly Finland, Austria has been the Western nation most affected by the political and economic changes in central and Eastern Europe. At the same time economic relations with main trading partners in Western Europe are shifting with the establishment of the European Economic Area.

The theme of these developments is closer integration of markets to improve efficiency spurred on by competition. The opening of a market economy in central Europe has brought a net trade benefit for Austria, which shares a common border with the Czech Republic and Slovakia and Hungary. Pent up demand in these countries has led to a massive boom for Austria. Austria also benefits from the German market to which it sends 40 per cent of its exports.

Austria has a population of nearly 8 million people, about 25 per cent of whom are employed in manufacturing, and 65 per cent of its current trade is with the EU.

Finland

Finland is a relatively wealthy market economy. Output has expanded at a faster pace than other Western industrialized countries since the 1960s although the economy remains short of energy resources and raw materials. Finland traded extensively with former COMECON countries in exchange for energy supplies from the former Soviet Union. The virtual collapse of this trade with the spread of democracy in Eastern Europe led to a recession in Finland in the early 1990s. Finland is also heavily dependent on forestry and forest-related industries.

Finland is rapidly having to restructure its economy as it becomes heavily involved in Western markets. In the early 1990s unemployment has become a major problem, rising to 20 per cent from 3.5 per cent in 1990. Because of the peripheral position of Finland it is at a considerable competitive disadvantage. It will be interesting to see how Finland adapts to new circumstances. The population of Finland is just over 5 million.

Norway

The Norwegian economy in recent years has been heavily dependent on the massive exploitation of North Sea energy reserves. Oil and gas production has expanded to 2.7 million barrels (oil equivalent) per day, making it the second largest producer behind the USA of industrial countries, and 88 per cent of this production is exported. Petroleum output accounts for 20 per cent of total national output.

Oil revenues supported increasing living standards and employment in Norway, but there is always a danger of being too reliant on one product and this was realized by periodic collapses in world oil prices. Norway also has massive supplies of natural gas. Other exports include fish, timber and ferrous metals. The growth of the Norwegian economy has been at about 2–3 per cent per annum with a positive trade balance and stable prices. The Norwegian economy is tied up with its Scandinavian partners. It is possible that the Norwegians may vote not to join the EU in a referendum in 1994.

Sweden

Sweden is a small open economy with strong trading links with other members of the European Economic Area. The Swedish economy is a blend of capitalism and socialism with a strong emphasis on social welfare. The emphasis has been on full employment, relative wage equality and a high level of state welfare benefits. However, a problem of this policy has been to lower the competitive edge of Swedish industry. In recent times there has been an emphasis on the reduction of welfare benefits and state subsidies in preparation for Sweden's entry to the EU. In addition, Denmark and Sweden are looking towards extensive road and bridge-building projects to place Scandinavia in a more central communications position in Europe.

Although rich in timber and metal ores, there is an almost total absence of fossil fuels and 40–50 per cent of energy consumed is imported. Engineering is Sweden's most productive sector accounting for over a third of manufacturing output compared with a fifth for timber products.

Sweden has a population of nearly 9 million people. An opinion poll carried out in 1993 showed that 26 per cent of the Swedish people were in favour of joining the EU, while 41 per cent were against.

8

Doing business in Europe

In this chapter we have set out to show the importance to UK business of trading in Western Europe and in particular in the European Union (EU). We have set this against a background of the importance of trading to the EU as a whole. It is important to stress that the Single Market is now the *home market* for UK businesses. There are now 12 states providing goods and services to a combined home market. We then explore how and why UK businesses are developing trade links with Europe. We look at the importance of trade to domestic businesses and explore the impact of the removal of trade barriers in helping business to forge trading links and the procedures that need to be followed in trading. Finally we look at the processes and procedures involved in trading in the Single Market.

United Kingdom exports and imports

Today there can be no doubt that UK trade is closely tied to the EU; for example, over half of our exports by value go to EU countries. We can see the importance of Western Europe, and particularly the EU, to the UK in Table 8.1.

Table 8.1   The value of UK exports to selected European countries (£m)

	1982	1986	1990	1991	1992
Total trade	55 557.8	72 987.7	103 692.4	104 877.0	108 507.5
European Union: total	24 423.6	34 996.4	55 024.7	59 280.2	60 702.3
France	4491.8	6210.5	10 894.5	11 596.7	11 484.7
Belgium and Luxembourg	2309.6	3832.9	5649.4	5873.3	5715.1
Netherlands	4642.8	5441.7	7561.3	8257.7	8503.2
Germany	5412.5	8549.1	13 169.4	14 676.2	15 212.6
Italy	2024.3	3463.4	5553.0	6140.2	6146.9
Ireland	2889.4	3553.5	5313.0	5295.3	5738.9
Denmark	1098.2	1211.6	1419.3	1408.6	1560.6
Greece	255.1	356.0	682.9	667.9	770.9
Spain	871.4	1905.5	3620.9	4279.2	4405.3

Table 8.1 *continued*

	1982	1986	1990	1991	1992
Portugal	428.5	472.1	1031.8	9085.1	1164.1
Other W. Europe: total	6680.9	6961.1	9299.5	9085.1	8548.1
Norway	933.9	1147.6	1292.0	1357.7	1419.9
Sweden	1935.6	2307.8	2712.3	2471.2	2439.0
Finland	513.3	664.1	1041.1	845.8	997.0
Switzerland	1195.7	1575.2	2358.9	2104.7	1844.6
Austria	250.8	403.0	705.8	766.8	795.1
Turkey	218.1	433.0	614.0	730.1	692.0
Other countries	174.8	241.7	584.0	361.7	360.5

 Task

Enter the information provided in Table 8.1 into a spreadsheet and convert the information into charts using a graphics package. What are the main changes in exporting patterns highlighted by your charts?

We can now look at Table 8.2 to see the value of United Kingdom imports from Western Europe.

Table 8.2 The value of UK imports from selected European countries (£m)

	1982	1986	1990	1991	1992
Total trade	56 978.2	86 175.5	126 086.1	118 786.0	125 866.8
European Union: total	25 269.0	44 576.8	65 855.5	61 328.0	65 609.3
France	4266.9	7387.1	11 872.3	11 075.4	12 223.4
Belgium and Luxembourg	2857.5	4084.3	5732.0	5472.5	5741.1
Netherlands	4512.0	6623.0	10 483.2	9969.0	9907.8
Germany	7405.9	14 137.8	19 907.1	17 740.5	19 034.3
Italy	1415.8	4666.1	6732.8	6378.7	6765.7
Ireland	2003.4	3054.0	4497.4	4416.3	5070.0
Denmark	1335.3	1756.8	2278.5	2226.7	2385.0
Greece	151.3	309.1	400.5	377.8	372.2
Spain	941.0	1790.2	2870.7	2627.7	1170.8
Portugal	379.9	768.4	1176.2	1043.3	2939.0
Other W. Europe: total	8390.0	11 886.8	15 905.9	14 214.6	14 509.0
Norway	2019.2	3253.7	4132.8	4162.5	3885.7
Sweden	1672.9	2760.4	3594.5	3141.6	3282.7

Table 8.2 *continued*

	1982	1986	1990	1991	1992
Finland	921.8	1346.0	1775.7	1522.3	1676.6
Switzerland	1664.5	3020.1	4247.9	3754.2	3928.9
Austria	402.4	705.3	957.8	916.1	948.9
Turkey	207.8	406.6	550.8	401.9	457.0
Other countries	128.8	249.5	538.9	316.0	339.2

 Task

Enter the information provided by Table 8.2 into a spreadsheet package. Produce the information in the form of tables and charts. What changes in importing patterns are highlighted by your tables and charts?

 Follow-up task

Use a spreadsheet package to illustrate the net balance of exporting and importing between the UK and each of the following during the years covered by Tables 8.1 and 8.2:

- Germany
- France
- Spain
- Ireland.

Produce the information in the form of a chart. What does the chart tell us about UK trading with these countries over the years shown?

The European Union's place in world trade

In the early 1990s the EU had 20 per cent of the world market in goods and services, both for imports and exports. The United States import figure was slightly below this and its exports amounted to 15 per cent of the world total. Japan's share was just under 10 per cent. Three-quarters of the EU's trade was in goods and a quarter in services, as shown in Fig. 8.1.

The bulk of the EU's trade with other countries is with the Western industrialized countries (about 60 per cent), being made up mainly of manufactured products (64 per cent of imports and 83 per cent of exports). Machinery and transport equipment made up the biggest proportion of trade in manufactured products (40 per cent of exports) followed by miscellaneous manufactures and chemicals.

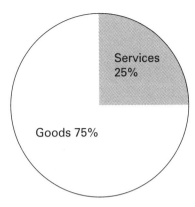

Figure 8.1 Relative market share of goods and services

The EU has to import considerable quantities of energy products (over 15 per cent of all imports) and raw materials (over 8 per cent). The EU runs a deficit on its trade in goods with other countries. However, the EU is a net exporter of services to other countries.

Why should businesses develop trade links?

When UK firms sell their goods in the UK they are selling to a market which, at most, contains 60 million people. When the same firm extends its horizon to the Single Market then immediately the opportunities are far greater, e.g. 80 million people in Germany, 56 million in France, etc. The arrival of the Single European Market on 1 January 1993 opened up golden opportunities for capitalizing on a huge 'domestic' market of 340 million customers. If a company can produce goods for a mass market, there are various benefits to be gained. On the *demand* side it is faced with a much bigger *target market*; on the *supply* side it has the opportunity of reducing the costs of production through producing to scale (Fig. 8.2).

Figure 8.2

Case Study—A Single Market for confectionery

Figure 8.3 shows the consumption of confectionery per head in 1992. Each year the size of the total market for confectionery is increasing. In the UK there are three main producers of chocolate, each with over 20 per cent of the market. These are Cadbury, Mars and Nestlé (which in 1989 took over Rowntree). Nestlé is a Swiss multinational.

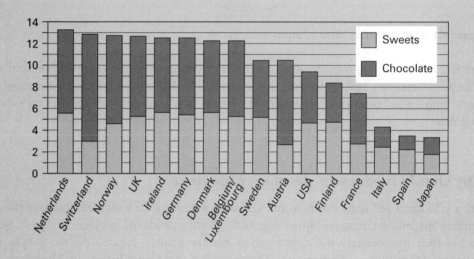

Figure 8.3   Consumption of confectionery kg/head/year

Source: Review of UK sweets market 1992

Questions

1. What are the current strengths of a British confectionery manufacturer e.g. Cadbury?
2. What opportunities are presented to Cadbury by the creation of the Single Market?
3. What are the possible weaknesses of Cadbury?
4. In what ways is the development of the Single Market a threat to Cadbury?

Market knowledge

Whenever firms export goods, they must get the following right:
- Price
- Quality

- Delivery.

These are areas in which, in the past, some UK businesses have not been too successful. Exporters must know their market. Information about overseas markets can be obtained from two main sources:

1. The government
2. Banks

The government and banks play a major role in overseas trade because of their experience. They will help to organize finance, give advice, help with insurance and assist with foreign currency. However, it is not altogether surprising that some businesses are reluctant to engage in international trade, as problems include:

- uncertainty in exchange rates
- language differences
- differences in tastes
- paperwork
- customs duties
- extra transport and insurance costs.

The Single Market and the development of new opportunities

Buying and selling within the Single Market takes place between member states. This is in many ways different from the idea of exporting and importing. Firms that buy and sell goods in the Single Market are dealing with their *home market*.

The significance of '1992' (more accurately 31 December 1992) was that it finally created the free movement of goods, services and people in the 12 countries of the EU. Until this time the movement of goods without restriction had been prevented by a range of national restrictions, such as:

- technical barriers (e.g. different national product standards)
- public purchasing policies which distorted competition
- red tape
- differences in food law (e.g. additives and labelling)
- barriers to the sale of financial products
- controls over capital movements
- limitations on the establishment of professions
- differences in company law
- competition policies and state subsidies
- differences in external trade policy and consumer protection
- language barriers.

By removing such barriers it is hoped that new opportunities will arise for businesses within the EU. The creation of the Single Market for goods and services should cut down business costs, encourage more efficient organization and, hopefully, stimulate wealth and job creation.

Today businesses can take heart from the opportunities presented by the Single Market. It has been designed to remove barriers to trade and to ensure the free movement of goods, services, people and capital throughout the EU. It cuts across all sectors and affects most aspects of trading, changes that affect firms which trade solely in the UK as well as those already selling elsewhere in the EU.

Case Study—Is exporting for me?

This case study has been adapted from a DTI publication *Trading with Europe*.

With the whole of Europe as your home market, commitment to customers and consistency in meeting their requirements are no longer a luxury but a necessity.

. . . You will need to give your product and your sales effort as much support as you would in the UK. Look, for example, at the number of sales representatives you employ to cover the UK, and then consider how many you would need to cover other parts of Europe properly. France, for example, is geographically two and a half times the size of the UK. Quite often a company expects big results from a small sales force. If you have limited resources, it may be better to choose one key market (or even one key customer) and to concentrate your attention there.

. . . Remember that you may also face increased competition in the British market as other European companies compete to seize their new opportunities.

. . . To sell to other European countries involves four basic challenges:

1. Adequate management resources
. . . Successful export marketing requires the near-constant involvement of senior management not just in making decisions, but in making contacts with representatives and customers.

2. Adequate staff resources
Exporting means more paperwork and more correspondence, much of it in foreign languages. Some of this can be contacted out but even these activities will need careful supervision.

3. Adequate production capacity and flexibility
The object of export marketing is to obtain extra orders. Have you the capacity to fulfil them and the flexibility to incorporate the modifications that may well be required in order to meet the needs of different markets?

4. Access to adequate finance

Laying in extra raw materials, extra packaging, insurance and freight charges, and the longer periods often required to realize payment for overseas orders will put extra strains on your cash flow. Can you obtain the necessary bridging finance? And can you support other extra activities such as research?

Questions

1. What are the main costs outlined in the above article of extending a business's home market?
2. What are the costs of not extending your home market?
3. What are the main priorities that a business needs to consider in expanding into new European markets?
4. What types of business will be best placed to take up the opportunity of expanding into new areas of the Single Market?
5. What types of business will be least well placed?

Getting help with selling in Western Europe

There are many organizations that provide help to businesses wishing to sell in Western Europe.

- *Business in Europe Branch*: In particular, the DTI's Business in Europe Branch runs a hotline giving plentiful advice to businesses as well as numerous detailed publications. The address is:

    Business in Europe Branch
    Department of Trade and Industry
    9th Floor
    Kingsgate House
    66–74 Victoria St
    London SW1E 6SW

The BEB exists to help firms of all sizes to sell into other European markets by providing general market information.

- *Overseas Trade Services*: The DTI's Overseas Trade Services helps UK firms to make a success of selling abroad by providing information about exporting and helping with promotions overseas.

- *Chambers of commerce*: Many chambers of commerce have international links and some of the larger ones provide an extensive range of services and information for exporters.

- *Trade associations*: Many trade associations help their members by providing information about prospects for their products in overseas markets.

- *Export clubs*: These are associations set up by groups of local exporters who meet to discuss export matters and can often give useful advice to new exporters.

- *Banks*: All the main banks have export and international departments and give useful advice to customers about different markets.

- *Language centres*: There are a number of language centres in large towns and cities which help with the training of staff in European languages.

Selling in Europe

There are a number of key stages involved in selling goods and services in a wider European market. These are detailed below in their various stages and summarized in Fig. 8.4.

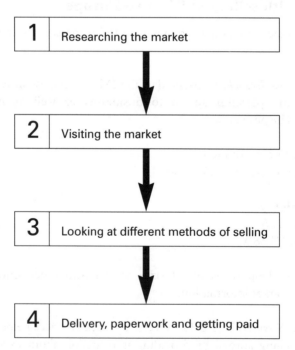

Figure 8.4

Stage 1: Researching the market

In their advice to exporters in Europe, the DTI makes the following recommendation:

> Clearly you can't take on every country in Western Europe at one time: it's essential to limit the number of markets. Choose one, or, at the most, two countries to begin with and concentrate your efforts on them. Which market you choose obviously depends on your product or service and your circumstances.

You therefore need a check-list like this to help you make comparisons between markets:

Size of market: ....

Growth of market: ....

Present state of market: ....

Potential competitors (the sales methods, prices, etc): ....

Distribution methods: ....

Legal requirements, e.g. standards: ....

Transportation: ....

The starting point for any market research is to look at your product and to have a clear idea of the sort of person you want to sell to. For example, are you aiming for bulk sales in a volume market or one-off specialist sales (Fig. 8.5)?

One-off specialist sales   or   Bulk sales

Figure 8.5

Published statistics can be a useful pointer to possible markets. The *Overseas Trade Statistics* of the United Kingdom, published monthly by HMSO, gives a detailed breakdown of the UK's imports and exports by product and principal countries of origin and destination. Statistics of intra-EU trade are now calculated from VAT returns (because customs documents have been abolished). These figures are collected by a system known as INTRASTAT. (Note that these are now collected differently from the way they were collected before the completion of the Single Market, so a comparison of today's figures with pre-January 1993 will be very difficult.)

Specialist information on overseas markets is provided by specialist agencies. For example, the Market Information Enquiry Service employs experts who can answer questions on opportunities in overseas markets. Export Intelligence gather information on new opportunities overseas, but exporters have to pay to use these services.

 Task

Identify EU countries that might provide a large market for UK:

- confectionery
- beer
- chemicals
- pharmaceuticals.

What problems might UK companies have in penetrating these markets? To meet customer requirements you may want to go beyond published sources: for example, an exporter of consumer goods might well discover more about customers' tastes by making a careful study of the shelves of a few supermarkets or other outlets in other countries.

Stage 2: Visiting the market

Figure 8.6

Research has shown that the best way of gaining export orders is by visiting the market place and making direct contact with customers and clients. When visiting another country you need to have clear objectives about what you want to achieve, e.g. market research, making contacts, etc.

When you visit a new market you will want to meet the right people. You should plan to call on the *commercial Department of the British Embassy*, the local *chamber of commerce*, or someone with contacts with your local *UK bank*. These sources of information will be able to tell you how best to conduct your business and how to make useful contacts. You should also find out about the strength of the competition and the nature of the target market.

The *translation* of literature about your goods or service is crucial. You will need to engage a good agency in the UK and check this with a native speaker of the country with which you are dealing. If you are giving out material with hideous language clangers, you can hardly expect to be taken seriously.

Stage 3: Choosing the appropriate selling method

There are a number of possible ways of selling abroad, e.g. by appointing an *agent*, by *dealing direct* with the customer, through an *export house*, or by setting up your own *local company* in the overseas market.

Figure 8.7

Employing an agent

Many businesses operating in new markets will employ an agent to do their selling for them. The agent may receive a *commission* for each sale made. The agent will have local knowledge and be able to take orders for the product. You may want to give the agent considerable responsibility, e.g. for sales promotion, advertising and after-sales service.

Dealing direct with the overseas customers

Selling direct to overseas customers gives you a lot of control over commercial aspects of your business. However, it also involves a lot of hard work and takes up time. You need to make and *maintain* reliable contacts. Also, once you have built up some business you may have to visit your market regularly to deal with problems that arise, say, in dealing with after-sales service.

Large businesses selling high quantities of consumer goods may find that it pays to sell direct because they can afford to employ specialists to deal directly with overseas markets. Firms selling expensive capital items may also benefit from selling direct.

Using an export house

Export houses (or merchants) operate in three main ways:

1. As *export merchants*. They will buy goods in the UK to meet the requirements of their overseas customers.
2. By acting as an *export department* for a business. The export house promotes sales abroad, deals with all the documentation and risk of selling overseas and may even manage the after-sales service.
3. By acting for an overseas buyer on a *commission basis*.

When an exporter uses the services of an export house the export house in effect really acts as just another UK customer. The export house takes the risk of selling overseas, handles the paperwork and settles the account in the UK.

Setting up your own local company

A fourth option is to set up your own local company. Clearly, this may prove to be the most expensive method in the short period; however it enables you to operate directly in a new market and to keep control over all aspects of quality. You can recruit local people to work for you who are well versed in the language and routine of that particular market. You can transfer your existing standards and procedures to the new company. Of course you will need to adapt some of your practices to local conditions. A disadvantage might be the difficulty of managing business units that may be hundreds or even thousands of miles apart. You may have to develop an entirely new organizational structure to organize the new company.

You may want to set up a *joint venture* with an overseas business. One way of doing this is to allow an overseas company to make and sell a product (using UK techniques and methods) and the partners in the venture then share the returns. An alternative is for the joint-venture partners to jointly own a business unit which makes and sells products. Many businesses also *license* a patented manufacturing process so that it can be made and sold by an overseas firm. A popular alternative is the *franchise* arrangement; for example, the Italian concern Benetton franchises out many small shops. The franchisee (the person buying the franchise from Benetton) operates and sells products using the Benetton label and shares profits with Benetton.

Stage 4: Delivery, paperwork and getting paid

When delivering goods overseas it is usually best to use the services of a *freight forwarding agency.* The freight forwarder will take responsibility for arranging the paperwork and transport of your goods. It is essential to work with a reliable freight forwarder. The choice of transport used depends on *speed, cost, reliability* and *product requirements.*

 Task

What method of transport would you use for sending the following consignments? Explain each choice.

1. A consignment of clothes for a fashion show between London and Paris.
2. Urgent medical supplies from Manchester to Denmark.
3. Crude oil from Rotterdam to Shellhaven.
4. Beer from Northampton to northern France.
5. Cut flowers from the Netherlands to Hull.

Transport options

Developments in the *express freight market* have made it possible for goods to be delivered overnight to destinations in Europe. This enables UK firms to be more competitive. The customer does not need to hold so much stock because supplies can be delivered very quickly.

A slower, but less expensive, method offered by transport companies involves *containers.* Containers/trailers are filled with goods from a number of exporters for delivery to given destinations.

Paperwork

With the arrival of the Single Market paperwork in the EU has been considerably reduced. The *Single Administrative Document* (SAD) was introduced in January 1988 to replace over 100 documents previously used.

Payment

Before selling goods overseas it is important to check that they can be paid for. Major banks and other specialist *status reference agencies* can provide reports on the creditworthiness of potential customers. Insurance, called *credit insurance,* can be taken out against non-payment. Insurance can be obtained from banks, insurance companies, and the government's *Export Credit Guarantee Department.*

When you sell exports abroad you will not be paid immediately. There are two main ways of financing exports:

1. *A bank finance scheme.* Most large banks offer export finance (Fig. 8.8), including credit insurance.

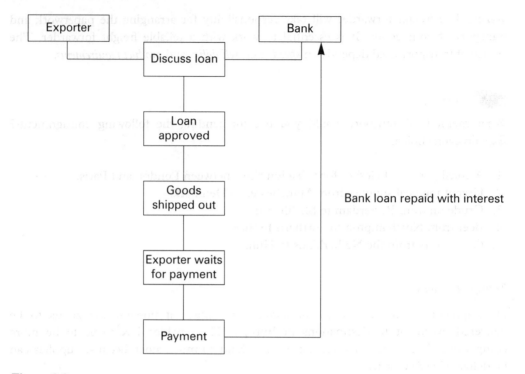

Figure 8.8

2. *Factoring*. Factoring involves selling to a factoring company (often owned by a major bank) your invoices for money you are owed. The factoring company immediately pays you about 80 per cent of the debt. The factor will then collect the money owed to you when it is due. You will then receive the balance of the money owed to you *minus* the factor's commission.

Selling through an export house can also give rapid payment, as the export house buys from you on its own account.

Thirty days' credit is a common credit period in the EU. Businesses need to negotiate a credit period when making deals. About 70 per cent of UK exports are sold on an open account basis, i.e. payment is made by settling up within a given credit period through bank payment. About 20 per cent of UK exports are sold using *bankers' letters of credit* whereby a reputable bank guarantees to make the payment at the end of the credit period. Letters of credit guarantee that customers get the goods they want and that the exporter is paid promptly. Exporters must give *proof of delivery* by submitting documents listed in the credit to the bank. If these documents are accurate showing that the goods are correct, then payment will be made within a few days.

Pricing

When quoting prices to overseas buyers there are several terms you can offer.

1. Many overseas firms will want the price quoted to be '*delivered*'. This means that the exporter is responsible for covering all charges involved in getting the goods to the premises of the buyer.
2. Sometimes prices are quoted '*ex works*'. This is the price of the goods at the premises of the exporter. The importer will then be responsible for organizing the transport of the goods.

Competition policy in the EU

It is important that '*fair competition*' takes place between organizations in the EU. Over the years the Commission has set out to create a climate of competition.

Organizations are forbidden to make agreements that set out to prevent, restrict or distort competition within the common market: in particular, agreements *fixing prices, sharing markets, discriminating against third parties* or *imposing territorial restrictions* that split up the common market. Of course, today this competition policy must now also cover the whole of the European Economic Area (EEA).

The European Commission, supported by the European Court of Justice, is responsible for safeguarding competition rules in the EU. In addition, a new body, the *EFTA Surveillance Authority* (ESA), has been set up to maintain these rules in the EFTA area supported by the EFTA court. The two bodies will work closely together. It seems inevitable that these bodies will merge at some stage in the near future.

Restrictive agreements and monopoly abuse

The Commission will handle cases which *affect trade or a dominant position* in the EU. The Commission will handle cases where trade between EU member states is affected and cases where more than 67 per cent of the EEA turnover of the undertakings concerned is within the EU. However, responsibility will pass to the ESA if the effect on trade within the EU is not great.

Mergers and takeovers

The Commission handles all cases where the combined worldwide turnover of the organizations concerned is greater than *5 becu* (5 billion ECU) and where the EU turnover of at least two of them is in excess of *250 mecu* (250 million ECU).

Pricing and exclusive distribution

As a general rule, firms are free under EU competition law to charge different prices for the supply of their goods in different parts of the EU or to different categories of consumer. The exception to this rule is where prices are fixed by agreement with other firms.

Consumer protection in the EU

In addition to measures covering competition between organizations, the EU has introduced directives aimed at protecting consumers. Examples of these are:

- *The Misleading Advertising Directive*: This was adopted in 1984 and aims to protect businesses and the general public against the effects of misleading advertisements.
- *The Product Liability Directive*: Introduced in 1985, this makes manufacturers and importers strictly liable for injuries caused by defective products.
- *The Doorstep Selling Directive*: Introduced in 1985 this brought in a seven-day cooling-off period for certain sales contracts concluded at the consumer's home or place of work.
- *The Consumer Credit Directive*: Introduced in 1987, this protects consumers entering into credit agreements.
- *The Toy Safety Directive*: Introduced in 1988 this harmonizes toy safety standards.
- *The Price Indication Directive*: Introduced in 1988, this requires the selling prices, and in some cases unit prices, of food and non-food products to be displayed.
- *The Package Travel Directive*: Introduced in 1990, this establishes minimum standards of consumer protection for package travel and package holidays and tours.

Developing a strategy for Europe

Paul Cecchini, in his 1988 study for the European Commission, *The Cost of non-Europe*, estimated that market integration will, in the medium term, trigger a major relaunch of economic activity, adding an average 4.5 per cent to the Community's National Income, and boost employment by creating 1.8 million new jobs. He said:

> If EC market integration is to succeed, so must business. The degree of its success depends on the *strategic response* of Europe's companies to the market challenge, and on their ability to seize the new opportunities on offer.

The DTI have responded to this by providing a very useful document entitled *Business in Europe: An Action Check-list*.

Tasks

1. Obtain a copy of *Business in Europe: An Action Check-list*. This publication suggests that the key questions that a business should be asking include:
   - How is the market, including the UK market, changing for our business?
   - Should we become a European business, looking upon Europe as our primary market rather than just the UK?
   - Would becoming a European business alter the scale of the targets in our plans?
   - In what ways will we be vulnerable to more competition in our present markets, whether solely in the UK or elsewhere in Europe?
   - Should we form links, merge or acquire business to strengthen our market presence, broaden our range of products and services and spread our financial risk?
   - Is our management and structure appropriate to exploit new opportunities or defend our position?
   - What training in languages and other skills do we need to be ready for trading in Europe?
   - Who in our firm is going to be responsible for deciding how to make the most of the new opportunities?

2. You work for a small confectionery business and realize that the changes that are taking place could affect your business. Working with a partner, consider the strategy you would take to improve your position in the new competitive business environment of the EU. Outline your strategy under the following headings:

   - Marketing
   - Sales
   - Distribution
   - Production
   - Product development
   - Purchasing
   - Finance
   - Training, languages and recruitment
   - Information Technology

NB: You will need to use the DTI publication *Business in Europe: An Action Check-list* to carry out this assignment.

9

Marketing goods and services in Europe

Imagine what it would be like to live in a country that did not trade with its neighbours. The goods and services that we take for granted would not be available. Domestic companies would be small because they would not be able to specialize and export their wares overseas. If we measured our standard of living in terms of variety of goods and services, it would be extremely poor. International trade is an economic necessity for the UK. Imports of raw materials and other products improve the quality of our lives and provide us with the opportunity to export our products across the globe. In the past, marketing in Europe and further overseas was frequently seen as the domain of the large company. We have all heard of the term 'multinational' and it immediately conjures in our minds an image of an organization with a household name such as BP, IBM or Ford. Today, however, since the advent of the Single Market of 1992, almost every business, no matter what its size, has to look beyond national and geographical boundaries and adapt strategies to develop a more European approach to running its operations.

The events of 1992 have effectively changed market structures. Organizations today cannot sit behind geographical barriers complacent in their belief that their product and market share are invincible. Such strategies make them sitting ducks! Marketing successfully in the new Europe involves adopting a different approach to running a business. Though this means developing defensive strategies to counter increased competition from their traditional markets, the reward is the opportunity to take advantage of all that is offered across Europe.

Case Study—AirBoss

The Oxfordshire-based company AirBoss Ground Engagement have recently developed long-lasting tyres for the construction industry. At its factory in Didcot, AirBoss is manufacturing a puncture-proof alternative to pneumatic tyres which are made from hollow chevron-shaped segments bolted on to a steel rim. The tyres simply cannot deflate and segments of tyre can be replaced where necessary. Andrew Helby, the MD of AirBoss, feels that the wheel would not have been so successful if it had not been for the Single Market. He says that 'The tyre might not have been granted a licence were it not for access to the whole EU market. ... The single market means that we have access to hundreds of millions of end users.'

Since having launched AirBoss in 1991, Andrew Helby and his team have tested their tyres in the UK market and developed connections with Germany, France and Italy. During this time their ideas have won awards at exhibitions, including the largest construction exhibition, BAUMA, in Germany, where the tyres attracted so much attention that the AirBoss exhibitors ran out of brochures.

Having developed and tested their product, the first step AirBoss took to enter the European market was to undertake market research. Market intelligence was supplied by the London-based Corporate Intelligence Group, who were able to provide information on sales of tyres by country and types of vehicle. This led to an immediate assault on the German market. At the same time discussions took place with potential agents in France and Italy.

In each case AirBoss decided to work with established distribution outlets. Overseas sales and marketing teams were set up to work with their chosen distributors. German, French and Italian speakers were recruited for the teams and promotional materials were translated into relevant languages. A quality engineer was also employed to keep a watching brief on common product specifications, testing procedures and European Directives that apply to the company's products.

Over the next three years some 90 per cent of AirBoss sales will be made to Europe, 30 per cent of which will go to Germany, 20 per cent each to Italy and France and, at the same time, markets will be developed in other European countries. With such an approach the AirBoss business plan forecasts that the company will become a multi-million pound operation by the mid-1990s.

Questions

1. Make a list of the advantages that AirBoss gains from trading in Europe.
2. Explain why AirBoss undertook extensive market research before entering the European market.
3. In what ways will the marketing of products in Europe be different from marketing products within the UK?

Identifying opportunities

In the AirBoss study we could see that, in order to sell overseas, AirBoss had to undertake key strategic decisions that were all part of a carefully constructed business plan in which corporate objectives such as profitability were matched with marketing objectives.

The Chartered Institute of Marketing defines marketing as:

> *'The anticipation, identification and fulfilment of a consumer need—at a profit.'*

The implication of this definition is that for an organization to pursue its marketing *goals* and *objectives*, it needs to discover what its customers are likely to buy and then set out to meet their needs. Effective marketing provides organizations with a framework for *planning* their activities. Marketing *strategy* involves establishing their major aims and objectives. Having established strategy, an organization will then use *tactics* to meet their strategic goals (Fig. 9.1).

Figure 9.1   Marketing goals, strategies and tactics

Though strategic planning will differ from market to market, the overall marketing process and the tools used by marketeers will remain roughly the same. Marketing in Europe, however, does involve recognizing that customers in different countries have different needs. For example:

- Customer behaviour, culture and customs will vary from country to country. Patterns of demand will be determined by lifestyles, incomes, religions, etc. By understanding such influences organizations can develop products to cater for specific needs.
- Communication systems will vary widely and promotional materials will have to be translated to take into account levels of literacy, types of media, etc.
- Protocols may differ when dealing with European customers, such as channels of negotiations between different levels of managers.

Catering for such differences can involve *greater risk* and will therefore require more detailed planning and research. Other differences and difficulties may also arise when trading in Europe: for example, marketing and distribution structures may be different and will have to be catered for, and exchange rates may present a problem. Since the UK left the Exchange Rate Mechanism (ERM) the pound could be subject to wide fluctuations against other currencies. If the pound falls in value, British goods become cheaper and this will affect the profitability of an overseas transaction. (NB: This is one of the main arguments for a single currency.)

The Single Market has had a marked effect on the activities of organizations throughout Europe. In the past an organization required detailed knowledge of different legal, financial and other bureaucratic regulations. The removal of such obstacles and the harmonization of requirements has served to erode barriers between states and create a freedom of movement that provides more opportunities to compete.

Identifying market opportunities within Europe will start with the process of *market research*, so that an organization can find out as much as possible about product requirements, customer needs and markets. This will help the organization to identify

- what a customer wants to buy
- when a customer will wish to make a purchase
- the alternative products available
- how the marketplace functions
- the nature of the competition.

The organization will then have to decide whether it has the capability to meet customer needs and also how to develop a competitive advantage over other organizations in that marketplace.

If an organization has already traded within the European marketplace a lot of useful *internal information* about the marketplace may already be held. For example, feedback from European sales representatives may be held on databases so that it can be regularly processed and accessed. Such information may help to identify types of customers, patterns of consumption, methods of payment, credit periods, profitability per customer, areas of expansion/contraction, etc.

Internal information simply provides a snapshot of an organization and its customers. It does not relate the organization to competition and other market activities. *External information* is more often called 'secondary data' because it is in the form of published materials collected by someone else. It will provide a broader dimension to data previously collected.

External information will help to identify and label characteristics of customers so that an organization wishing to enter a market can develop products to meet that specific need. It may also help to identify market potential, provide information upon competitors and put their performance within the context of external influences, such as economic and political factors.

The *Department for Enterprise* provides a range of services that are specifically designed to help organizations make the most of business opportunities within Europe and further afield. These include:

- The DTI's *Export Market Information Centre* (EMIC), which is a self-help information facility for organizations wishing to research a market. It provides statistics such as patterns of trade, production, employment, market reports etc. A search service may be used to select commercial on-line databases.
- The *Export Marketing Research Scheme* (EMRS) provides professional advice and offers financial support for marketing research studies overseas.
- *Export Intelligence* receives information from Diplomatic Service Posts about sources of new opportunities for businesses within Europe. This may include sales leads and published tenders.
- *Specialist market knowledge.* The DTI will put an organization in touch with a specialist who will tailor information to the company's requirements.
- Representation through *DTI representatives* will draw upon local contracts and expertise.
- Other services include *overseas trade missions, trade fairs, seminar support* and published information and help (see, for example, Fig. 9.2).

The **Business in Europe Hotline** is open 24 hours a day, 7 days a week. It can put you in touch with a wealth of information and advice about trading in Europe. It can provide you with:

- **Government contacts for specific sectors or areas of EU legislation**
- **Signposting to private sector sources of advice**
- **Free publications**

Remember the number

0272 444 888

Phone today

Figure 9.2   The DTI Business in Europe Hotline

The EU itself publishes a wide range of information. This includes periodicals, studies, reports, documents and booklets on almost every aspect of doing business. The Office for Official Publications of the European Union publishes the bulk of the material.

Other organizations which can offer advice and provide secondary material include:

- local chambers of commerce
- business clubs
- development agencies
- training and enterprise councils
- some educational establishments.

Specialist information may be provided by research and technology organizations such as the Furniture Industry Research Association and also by professional bodies such as the British Institute of Management.

Commercial agencies and publishers may also provide a wealth of general and highly specified information. For example: Romeike & Curtice provide an overseas press clipping service; Kompass publish details of companies and services that could be used to identify sales leads and new suppliers; and British Rate and Data (BRAD) provide comprehensive coverage of virtually all media advertising opportunities across Europe.

Case Study—Going into the electronics business

You have recently invested into a consortium of business people who are in the process of negotiating the purchase of a chain of electronic wholesalers. Considerable research has been undertaken into this proposition and the statistics researched include those shown in Table 9.1.

Table 9.1   EU spending on consumer electronics 1988–95

(million current US$)

	1988	1989	1990	1991	1992	1995
Belgium	625	635	644	654	662	690
Denmark	744	769	794	819	841	915
France	6323	6769	7217	7688	8227	9615
Germany	9665	10 271	10 872	11 447	11 942	13 679
Greece	393	376	359	341	322	268
Ireland	112	112	112	109	98	98
Italy	13 687	14 307	14 927	15 511	15 250	15 850
Luxembourg	11	11	11	11	11	12
Netherlands	212	221	230	238	245	271
Portugal	953	1089	1228	1358	1454	1888
Spain	1535	1617	1700	1780	1851	2106
United Kingdom	8236	8917	9598	10 275	10 941	12 978
EC total	42 496	45 094	47 692	50 231	51 844	58 370

Questions

1. In what parts of the EU are sales of consumer electronic products (a) expanding and (b) contracting?
2. Where would you prefer your electronic wholesalers to be situated?
3. What other information would you require before making your investment?

Internal and external data may not answer all the questions an organization may wish to ask before marketing its products and services in Europe. To meet its specific needs, a company may undertake *primary research*—which is the term used for information that a company compiles for its own requirements.

Surveys are usually the most common way of conducting primary research. For an organization wishing to export, face-to-face contact with potential European buyers and agents to discover the standing of a product or service is probably the most useful form of research. By doing this it is possible to obtain feedback about design, price, delivery dates, packaging, branding and many other areas. Mobilizing market research teams overseas can be expensive, and trade fairs and exhibitions can be used not only as a useful method of obtaining information but also as a means of evaluating the products of competitors.

Market research gives organizations the opportunity to develop an understanding of the behaviour of their customers, whether it be the UK market or the European market. Such knowledge can be used to target more appropriate goods and services. Customers can be divided into two distinct types:

*   consumers
*   organizations.

Consumer markets are composed of individuals who purchase items for domestic consumption, mainly from retailers. Domestic items vary considerably throughout Europe and research may help to clarify:

*   factors that affect their behaviour, such as tastes, fashions, incomes, etc.
*   social factors that motivate people to buy goods
*   cultural differences across Europe
*   socio-economic factors.

Organizational markets buy goods and services that are used either directly or indirectly in the production of other goods and services. Research may help to provide information on:

*   distribution channels
*   discounts/payment methods
*   variations in demand due to business cycles.

Developing policies and strategies

It is estimated that only 50 per cent of European businesses will survive the increased competition created by the completion of the Single Market. The remainder will disappear over the next five to seven years because of mergers, acquisitions or bankruptcies. There will be more competition in domestic markets and more opportunities in European markets. Given the nature of these changes, and in order to survive, they must look beyond the UK.

Competition takes place where two or more organizations act independently to sell their products to the same group of consumers. Direct competition occurs where organizations produce similar products—for example, the Renault Clio and the Vauxhall Corsa. Indirect competition occurs where suppliers provide slightly different ways of meeting the same need—for example, the Renault Clio and the VW Passat. It is argued that increased competition in the Single Market will

- increase choice
- lead to better products
- encourage organizations to become more efficient
- benefit consumers.

Market research, and the ways in which it improves the understanding of consumer behaviour and market operations, will help organizations wishing to trade within Europe to understand the different sectors of the marketplace. Within the total market it may be possible to group consumers with similar characteristics into *market segments*. By doing this an organization may use different strategies with different groups of consumers in different countries. This will help the organization to target specific groups of consumers more accurately. Within segments, organizations may then wish to position brands (e.g. up-market, mid-market, down-market) and then develop strategies for each position in each segment.

Figure 9.3   The marketing mix

By splitting the European marketplace into segments and developing strategies to position products, an organization can choose an appropriate *marketing mix* for each different group of customers. The marketing mix comprises a complex set of variables which an organization combines in order to achieve its objectives. This concept is usually analysed on the basis of the four Ps (Fig. 9.3). To meet customer needs an organization must develop *products* to satisfy them, charge them the right *price*, get the goods to the right *place* and make the existence of the product known through its *promotion*.

'Mix' is an appropriate word to describe the marketing process. Different mixes can be designed to suit the precise requirements of different parts of the marketplace. Given the vast difference between the various groups of European consumers, it is vital that organizations use the mix to develop policies and strategies to meet the needs of these consumers.

The product

The product is the central point upon which all marketing strategies depend. The main decision to be made by organizations trading in Europe is whether to standardize their products for the pan-European market (Fig. 9.4) or whether to differentiate them according to the specific requirements of each market (Fig. 9.5).

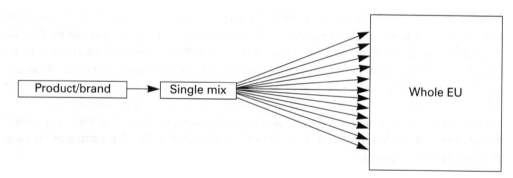

Figure 9.4   Undifferentiated marketing—standardizing for a pan-European market

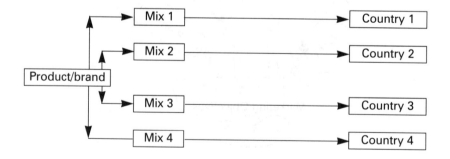

Figure 9.5   Differentiated marketing—developing different strategies for each country

Case Study—Creating a pan-European identity

Today it is no longer possible to buy a Marathon chocolate bar. The UK's fourth favourite chocolate bar was replaced by Snickers. The reason for this was to fall in line with Mars' global branding strategy as Snickers was known in every market except the UK.

Many other companies are harmonizing brands across Europe. Reckitt and Colman, the UK's multiproduct giant, has reorganized its brands and standardized packs throughout the EU. Lucas has unified its multibranded automotive components under its own name. Girling, CAV, Rotodiesel and Condiesel have all been replaced by the single brand name of Lucas.

The major benefits of harmonizing brands are economies of scale, standardizing of production procedures and processes and savings on promotional costs. It is also felt that unified brand names help to create a pan-European identity.

There is, however, a word of warning. It is important to understand how different names might be interpreted. Denmark's Plopp chocolate might not be too well received in the UK and Irish Mist liqueur in Germany translates to manure!

Questions

1. List the advantages of creating a pan-European identity.
2. Provide *two* examples of products which you feel have a strong pan-European identity. In each case explain why you feel the product has such an identity.
3. Explain how different consumer needs are catered for by pan-European products.

Though goods can be standardized so that they are viewed as pan-European, it is possible to make minor adjustments to products to cater for specific needs in certain parts of the Single Market. For example, recipes for tobacco brands vary slightly from country to country, even though they may be sold under a familiar name. There is, however, no doubt that though organizations that develop different products for different markets will not be viewed as pan-European and will lose certain cost and efficiency advantages, their products will be able to serve local needs more specifically.

One of the difficulties that has previously taken place between countries in the EU wishing to trade across Europe has been the massive range of technical standards. Such standards were often viewed as the biggest trade barrier! These barriers were frequently due to differences in:

- industry standards
- legislation in member countries
- the testing of products.

Since 1987 the harmonization of standards has made it easier for organizations wishing to trade their products throughout Europe.

The *DTI Standards Policy Unit* coordinates standards policy and its responsibilities include 'Community policy on testing and certification'. *Technical Help to Exporters* (THE) is operated by the British Standards Institution (BSI) and provides advice on European requirements including national laws in relation to safety, environmental protection, technical standards and certification processes in relation to customer needs.

Pricing

Of all of the parts of the marketing mix, price is the one that creates sales revenue. The importance of price within the mix varies from one market to another and between different segments in the same market. In low-cost, non-fashion markets, price may be critical—for example, in the sale of washing-up liquid. In fashion markets, such as fashion clothes, price may not be such an important factor.

There are a number of different pricing techniques (see Fig. 9.6).

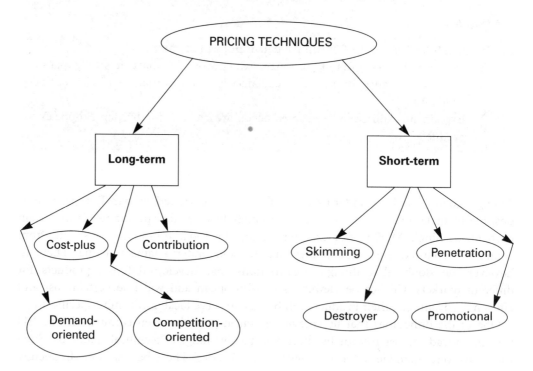

Figure 9.6   Pricing techniques

- *Cost-plus* pricing simply involves adding a mark-up on the cost of providing a good or service. This method of pricing is often used by small businesses.
- *Contribution* pricing separates costs into *direct* and *indirect*. Contribution is the sum remaining after direct costs are deducted from revenues. If the total contributions more than cover indirect costs, profits are made, and if they do not, losses are made.
- *Demand-oriented* pricing involves reacting to the intensity of demand for a product and then pricing accordingly. Before the Single Market, organizations frequently divided up the European market and sold goods and services at different prices in different countries according to demand. For example, cars varied in price throughout the community, with Britain being one of the most expensive countries in which to buy. Some distributors in the UK were buying UK-manufactured cars on the European continent and bringing them back to the UK for sale!
- *Competition-oriented* pricing simply involves pricing according to the nature of competition in the market. Where there are few competitors, prices will be higher and where there are many, prices will be lower. The impact of the Single Market will substantially increase the levels of competition in most markets. This expansion will lead to a wider variety of products and a tendency for prices in many markets to fall.
- *Skimming* involves setting a high initial price with new products which yields high unit returns. Consumers who wish to be seen to buy new products—known as 'adopters'—will be willing to pay this premium. Once this first group of consumers have had their needs satisfied, prices fall to skim new groups of customers. Products with a high technical input are often priced in this way. Increased competition should make it difficult for organizations to skim or should reduce the period over which they skim.
- *Penetration* pricing is frequently used to attract customers to a product—for example, a breakfast cereal. Once market share is established prices slowly increase. Many organizations will use this technique to gain access to European markets.
- *Destroyer* pricing may be used to undermine the sales of rivals or to warn potential rivals not to enter a new market.
- *Promotional* pricing may be used to inject fresh life into a product by lowering prices from time to time.

The overall trend in the Single Market will be for prices to move downward. In markets where price discrimination has previously taken place, *parallel importing* will occur as marketing intermediaries buy up goods in one market where prices are low and sell below current market rate in another where prices are higher. Increased competition and lower prices will inevitably reduce profit margins and organizations will have to become more efficient to maintain profitability. The real threat, however, is that, in the new market, organizations may become embroiled in price wars that will lead to the loss of key competitors.

Distribution

Distribution is the process of moving goods and services to the places in which they are required. This process may involve a single step or a number of steps. Export strategies for distribution will inevitably become more complex. Factors influencing choice of distribution systems might include speed, time and type of transit, effects of different climatic conditions and extra freight, packing and insurance charges.

It is important for any organization to identify the most appropriate route to reach customers. Identifying a channel may involve a long-term commitment which cannot easily be altered. The traditional channel of distribution within the UK is shown in Fig. 9.7. Though the nature of such channels may include various stages when exporting, the first decision organizations have to make is whether to export *indirectly* or *directly*.

Manufacturer

Wholesaler

Retailer

Customer

Figure 9.7   Traditional pattern of distribution

Indirect exporting involves the use of an export house or agent to act as intermediary. An export house or agent will link across many markets and countries and will be able to play a prominent role in promoting exports and providing valuable advice and experience for suppliers. By using intermediaries organizations can enter overseas markets without having to invest in the costly financial and administrative procedures required to cater for consumers abroad.

For example, export houses or agents may act as *merchants* by buying in the home market and reselling in the export market. They may act as the *manufacturer's or supplier's agents* and hold sole rights for the promotion and sale of products overseas on an agency basis. Broadly speaking, they will provide the functions of an *export department*, carrying out many specialist functions such as shipping, insurance, finance and credit and bearing much of the risk.

Case Study—In time for tea

Karen and Chris Adams decided that there was a gap in the market for medium-priced, good-quality teapots. Today their company, Pristine Pottery of Stoke-on-Trent, employs 35 people and exports 80 per cent of its production outside the UK.

Pristine Pottery began with the help of a Small Firms Loan Guarantee from the DTI. After establishing business in the UK, they began to pick up other business from European countries, based upon attendance at trade shows at the NEC and Frankfurt. Here, agents for Scandinavian and other markets approached them, and Karen's French and Chris's German came in very useful. They feel that their sales have been well served by agents. Agents know the markets, they know customers and also provide valuable advice on pricing levels. They say, 'If you have the right products, and you market yourself at trade shows and in the international trade press, good agents will find you.' (NB: The DTI keeps a list of reputable agents for European and other markets.)

Figure 9.8 Pristine Pottery products

Development of sales across Europe has been along the lines of targeting and then consolidating one country after another. Success has brought rewards and recognition. The company has gained awards from the local chamber of commerce and the British Overseas Trade Board.

Questions

1. What distribution difficulties might an organization encounter when entering export markets for the first time?
2. Make a list of the benefits of indirect exporting.

Direct exporting involves manufacturers or suppliers setting up their own export department, shipping their products overseas and selling their wares directly to their customers, using their own personnel. This might involve establishing offices and warehousing facilities overseas and employing staff to monitor and control operations. This may require considerable investment in time, money and staffing as well as knowledge of specialized administrative procedures.

As small firms, in particular, expand their operations beyond their domestic market for the first time, many will turn to the services provided by exporting intermediaries such as agents. Exporting indirectly will mean that they will not have to invest heavily in overseas distribution facilities and will reduce the risks associated with the venture.

The place is a very important part of the overall marketing mix for a product. Organizations in the Single Market will constantly seek new ways of supplying goods and services in their customers. For example, direct marketing has become an important marketing tool in the Single Market and is rapidly increasing in popularity. Direct marketing to customers avoids the necessity for other distribution channels and reduces competitive pressures upon margins.

Promotion

Exchanging information help organizations not only to communicate with customers but also to develop an image with the world at large. Promotion is simply a communication process in which organizations are the senders of information and consumers are the receivers.

The main problem with promotional strategies across Europe lies in being able to communicate across environments which include different cultures and languages. Given the range of differences, standardization of promotional materials is rarely possible.

To plan a promotional campaign an advertiser will consult an advertising agency. Such agencies act as a vital link between the advertiser and the consumer. Larger agencies will have widespread European experience which will enable them to:

- develop a broadly-based European-wide strategy
- utilize different media opportunities across Europe—for example, the use of satellite and cable television
- develop creative materials which cater for both cultural and language differences.

Specific restrictions on advertising do, however, appear in some European countries. These include:

- restrictions on alcohol and tobacco advertising
- curbs on the time when certain adverts can be broadcast
- upper limits on advertising expenditure
- limits on the radio and TV time that can be utilized by advertisers.

Marketing planning

The main implication of the Single Market for organizational strategy is that of change. Organizations have to take into account changes within the wider European context and adjust their strategies accordingly. Strategies are long-term decisions that can be translated into a series of short- and medium-term plans. Marketing planning involves planning today what is to be done tomorrow. Forward planning

- brings objectives into the open
- provides all parts of an organization with clear guidelines on what they are expected to achieve
- coordinates the activities of different parts of the organization
- provides a mechanism against which performance can be checked, modified and controlled.

In the Europe of the 1990s organizations will have to modify strategies to consider threats from new European competitors, adapt to European standards and requirements and improve their overseas competitiveness. In doing this the following three broad strategic options are open to them:

1. Improve efficiency and productivity.
2. Penetrate new markets.
3. Search for European link-ups.

Marketing planning should be viewed as the route to achieving such goals and objectives.

10

The European Union, Europe and the rest of the world

In this chapter we look at some of the important relationships between the European Union and the rest of the world. In this last decade of the twentieth century world politics and alliances between countries are changing rapidly. Today world trading patterns are increasingly dominated by huge internal markets such as:

- The Single European Market (SEM)
- The North American Free Trade Area (NAFTA)
- The Association of South East Asian Nations (ASEAN).

New 'huge' markets consisting of millions of consumers (e.g. China and India), are developing.

Competitive industry today is characterized by advanced technology and low-cost production. If the 12 EU member states are to capitalize on new opportunities and resist competition within their internal market, they will need to be increasingly competitive. This chapter, therefore, focuses on changes and challenges facing the EU; in particular:

- The development of new trade groupings
- Competition in international markets
- The opportunities presented by new huge markets
- Changes in the economies of Eastern Europe
- The challenge of German reunification.

A European crisis?

After the Second World War the European economy was able to rebuild itself. This rebuilding process was helped by the creation of the European Community and the development of a single market. However, a number of commentators today argue that the '12' have lost much of their early momentum. Today we have an ageing population, in an economy with relatively high costs of production, high taxes, high welfare, relatively old-fashioned technology in a number of sectors, high unemployment and low investment. A gap has developed between the growth rates of parts of Asia and Europe.

Generally speaking, the main European industries are still those that were established in the first half of the twentieth century. The '12' taken as a whole are neither high-technology, nor low-cost, they are mainly middle-technology with high costs. The so-called Pacific Rim economies are investing in advanced technologies which can be worked at lower cost.

The countries of the EU have a declining population. Only in Ireland is the birth-rate at the replacement level of 2.1 per woman. West Germany in the late 1980s had the lowest percentage of population under 15 of any state in the United Nations. Italy and Spain had a reproductive rate of 1.3. At the same time Europe has some of the highest welfare expenditure in the world. As the population ages, the cost of health and pensions increases, which is likely to lead to an overload on welfare and pension schemes in the twenty-first century. European economies will therefore have to carry a considerable burden of non-productive people.

The benefits of free trade

Those who believe in free trade argue that dismantling international barriers to trade encourages an international specialization of production that maximizes the economic welfare of the whole world. Countries can then specialize in what they do best. For example (see Fig. 10.1), China is a leading manufacturer of soft toys, the US and Japan world leaders in computers, and Germany probably the largest manufacturer of hi-tech machine tools.

Figure 10.1   Examples of international specialization

The EU stands to gain enormously from the freeing of world trade. A 1993 study by the Organization for Economic Co-operation and Development and the World Bank showed that the EU would make a gain of 1.4 per cent of its national income in the year 2000 if the *Uruguay Round* (see page 159) succeeds, whereas Japan would gain 0.9 per cent and the US only 0.2 per cent. These benefits would be gained because without tariffs and subsidies the countries and regions of the world could concentrate on making those things that they do best (see page 71).

Of course, a disadvantage would be that, in the short term, unemployment would occur as inefficient firms and industries closed down. Without a GATT deal the world might slip back into 'beggar-my-neighbour' policies (Fig. 10.2) with each country protecting its own industries (similar to creating an uncrossable sea in our example on page 72).

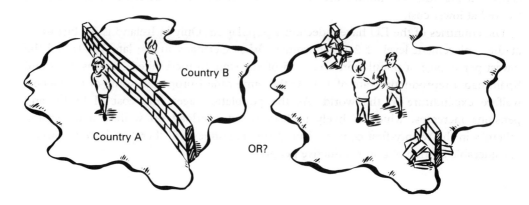

Figure 10.2   'Beggar my neighbour' or 'trade with my neighbour'?

Figure 10.3 presents a graph of what could happen if countries increased tariffs. It is drawn up by the London Business school and shows the effects of an increase in European and American tariffs worth 10 per cent of all imports. The graph shows the effect on prices (a) if things stay as they are now (dark) and (b) after an increase in tariffs (light). The immediate knock-on effect is to reduce output and incomes in countries.

% change

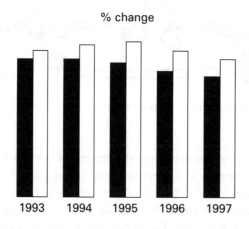

Figure 10.3   Effect of trade war on world consumer prices

The creation of the Multilateral Trade Organization

The General Agreement on Tariffs and Trade (GATT) was created in 1947 and operates on three levels as

- a set of trading rules (the 'rules of the road for trade')
- an international agency for helping to resolve trade disputes between countries and groups of countries
- a means for countries to get together to create freer trade and to cut down existing barriers.

For expansion, the period of growth during the 1980s was supported by a period of freeing of trading conditions in the world. At the end of 1993 there were 112 members of GATT, accounting for 90 per cent of world trade. With China and Russia joining the new Multilateral Trade Organization (see below) this was extended to nearly all of world trade.

With the completion of the Uruguay Round (a round of talks which started in 1986, the eighth such round of reductions in barriers to trade since 1947) the Multilateral Trade Organization (MTO) was created to replace GATT. The MTO is a powerful umbrella organization (Fig. 10.4). Underneath is an agreement on trade in goods, services and intellectual property. If there is a consensus among most member states the MTO is able to force terms even on members that do not want to make the changes. The MTO is in effect an international trade organization.

Figure 10.4   An umbrella organization

World trading patterns

World trade is dominated by huge trading blocs of countries. In 1991 there were three huge exporting blocs, accounting for a large proportion of world trade. These blocs were *East Asia and the Pacific*, the *European Community* and *NAFTA* (see Fig. 10.5).

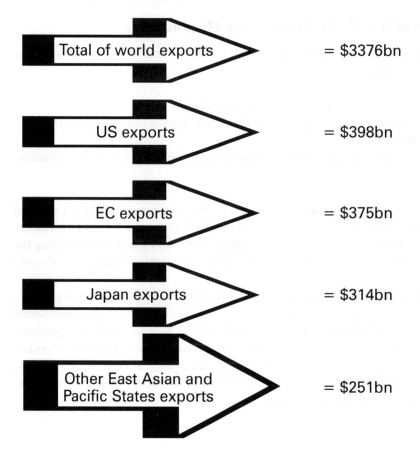

Figure 10.5

 Tasks

1. Use a desktop publishing package to produce a chart which illustrates the pattern of world trade highlighted by the figures in Fig. 10.5.
2. Use an atlas to draw a map showing (a)NAFTA countries, (b)European Union counties (c)Japan and other East Asian and Pacific States that are major trading nations (e.g. South Korea, Malaysia, Singapore, Taiwan, Australia).

Export growth

If we look at the growth of exports in recent years we can immediately see the importance of the East Asian and Pacific countries in contributing to this growth. The percentage increase in the volume of exports in the period 1980–91 was:

East Asia and Pacific	10.2
US	4
Japan	4
European Community	4.4
World	4.1

 Task

Present the information above in the form of a bar chart or pictograph.

Extending free trade areas

Countries in the EU will benefit from the expansion of the size of the internal market in which they operate and from the reduction in barriers to trade with other groupings and individual countries.

Case Study—Creation of an 18-country Single Market

An agreement creating an 18-country Single Market stretching from the Arctic to the Mediterranean came into effect on 1 January 1994. Billed as Europe's answer to NAFTA (the North American Free Trade Agreement that links Canada, the United States and Mexico), the European Economic Area (EEA) has finally arrived.

The agreement, linking 372 million consumers, was the product of an offer made by Commission President Jacques Delors to include the EFTA countries in the EU's Single Market programme. The deal was, however, held back by Swizerland's 'No' vote in a referendum in December 1992. Negotiators quickly set out to remove Switzerland from the deal and replace it with Liechtenstein, which had votes 'Yes' to the EEA.

Liechtenstein is expected to join in July 1994. EFTA's other EEA members, Austria, Finland, Sweden, Norway and Iceland, have offered to make up Liechtenstein's contribution to the new EEA Cohesion Fund—the special investment plan to compensate the EU's poorest members for incorporating the richer EFTA states, on condition that it pays back half if it joins in July.

Questions

1. Why is it important to increase the size of the EU and EFTA areas into a single European Economic Area?
2. What benefits might a British manufacturer gain from the development of the EEA?

3. How might some British manufacturers be at a disadvantage through the creation of the EEA?
4. How can consumers benefit from the creation of the EEA?
5. What is the purpose of the EEA Cohesion Fund? Who stands to benefit from this fund?
6. Why do you think people in Switzerland voted against joining the EEA?

 Tasks

1. Find Liechtenstein and other European Economic Area countries on a map. Draw your own map to show the European Economic Area.
2. Set out a database of European Economic Area countries showing: size of population, currency, whether they are a member of the EU, the capital of the country, the name of the central bank, and language spoken in the country.

Opportunities in new market economies

Until recently the world economy did not really exist. The Soviet Union and its East European satellites opted out because of communism. So did China. India closed its doors to international trade on a large scale. The same was true of many other smaller countries. Altogether, more than half the world's population was outside the market economy.

Today many of these countries, totalling 3 billion people, are trying to return. They are doing so at different speeds, faced by differing problems and with differing chances of success.

The potential gains from this process are enormous. Trade and investment have the ability to revitalize the world economy in a new period of growth. Already the Asian-Pacific area is the world's most dynamic economic area. It has become so without the huge markets of China and India. Japan and the Asian *tigers* of South Korea, Hong Kong, Singapore and Taiwan became prosperous through trading with America and Europe, not within Asia.

Links with Asian-Pacific countries

In 1989 Australia was instrumental in encouraging the development of a new trading organization and alliance, i.e. Asian-Pacific Economic Co-operation. This organization is made up of Asian and Pacific Rim countries. It includes the world's two largest economies, the US and Japan, and the fastest-growing, China. Also among APEC's 15 members are East Asia's up-and-coming economic powers: South Korea, Taiwan, Malaysia, Thailand and Singapore. APEC accounts for more than half the world's economic output and two-fifths of its trade, but is only a relatively loose organization of trading nations when compared with the EU. However, its significance is that it presents new alliances in trade.

Today, for example, United States trade across the Pacific is already 60 per cent higher than that across the Atlantic. The United States is increasingly trading with the Asian-Pacific region rather than with the EU. The United States also intends to expand NAFTA to include all of North and South America.

Challenge and opportunity

In the 1990s there has been a flood of capital and investment to China, South-East Asia and parts of Latin America, fuelled by the possibilities of growth in these regions. Many Asian countries enjoy annual growth rates in excess of 10 per cent. Attracted by the prospects of rapidly expanding markets it is understandable that companies increasingly want to locate production facilities in or near these countries.

The development of Asian economies presents both a threat and a challenge. Clearly, there are many areas of manufacture—e.g. computers, electronics, televisions and cars—which Asian economies can produce in large quantities and at low costs using automated technology. However, there are also considerable benefits to be gained from the expansion of these huge markets.

Case Study—Exports soar as Asia buys British

The following report has been adapted from the *Daily Mail*, Saturday 20 November 1993:

The economic recovery moved up a gear yesterday when John Major was treated to a taste of Eastern promise. Britain's trade deficit with countries outside Europe was cut to its lowest for nearly six years, thanks mainly to a boost in Far East business.

The cash value of sales to China has doubled this year, with a 38 per cent rise in Hong Kong, a 29 per cent jump in South Korea and a 20 per cent increase in Japan, whose trade barriers are notoriously tough.

It appeared to be a remarkable vindication of a deliberate switch of emphasis by the Major government. The Premier's autumn trip to Japan and Malaysia drummed up an estimated £2 billion in orders.

The growing taste for Western-style living in Asia made best sellers of British electronics, pharmaceuticals, cars and trucks, and clothing. In China, UK firms are selling aircraft, aero-engines, power stations and industrial machinery. Unilever has set up joint ventures in Shanghai to produce Lux soap and Timotei shampoo, and has struck a deal to produce both its Signal and Pepsodent toothpaste brands. In Thailand, British firms have won orders for top-quality sandpaper (£2 million) and are negotiating deals worth more than

£200 million. In Vietnam, construction giant John Laing has won a £33 million contract to build a new airport, based on the design of Birmingham's Eurohub terminal.

And in India, National Power and Rolls Royce have teamed up with local companies for £800 million worth of work in two power station projects. In Japan, Rover is linking with Honda to break into a ferociously tight car market and sell its four-wheel-drive Discovery.

Questions

1. Why is it important for businesses in the EU to look outwards to the rest of the world for export orders?
2. How does the existence of a huge internal market support firms who are competing overseas?
3. Why are markets such as China and India particularly attractive to EU businesses?
4. How can EU businesses benefit from developing joint products with manufacturers in East Asia?
5. Why is the development of East Asian and Pacific Rim countries both an opportunity and a threat for EU producers?

Changes in Eastern Europe

In the 1990s we have seen massive changes in the economies of Eastern Europe. Eastern Europe is made up of numerous countries, many of which are quite different from the others. The former Soviet Union was a massive area made up of many different types of peoples. The Czech Republic, Slovakia, Croatia, Hungary and Poland have a long tradition of economic and cultural ties with Western Europe, particularly with Germany and Austria. Romania, Serbia, Slovakia, Bulgaria and Albania have fewer economic and cultural ties to Western Europe and closer ties with Russia.

It seems likely that Poland, Hungary and the Czech Republic will be able to develop strong relationships quite quickly with the EU. These countries in particular have taken on *reforms* to their economic systems. In particular, they have moved towards privatization of industry, the development of private property, and allowed prices to find their own levels rather than being fixed by the government.

Western countries have been able to develop *joint ventures* with companies and to invest capital in Poland, the Czech Republic, Hungary and, to a lesser extent, other Eastern bloc countries.

Prior to the 1990s, much of the trade that took place in Eastern bloc countries was controlled by an organization called COMECON, which arranged exchanges between Eastern bloc countries—for example, oil from the Soviet Union for manufactures from other Eastern bloc countries. Today these countries need to exchange goods on the free market with other countries.

Until 1988 relations between Western countries and COMECON were very poor. The process of reform, however, changed this. By September 1989 the EC had signed trade agreements with Czechoslovakia, Hungary and Poland. Agreements were made with the Soviet Union in December 1989 and with Bulgaria in May 1990. Today a major problem is developing free trade with the former Eastern bloc countries is that the sorts of exports they generate—mainly low value added manufactures—are most likely to compete with products made in the poorer regions of the EU. This, therefore, adds to the problems for the poorer regions of the EU.

At the end of 1991 the EC, as it was then known, formed an arrangement for a free trade area with Czechoslovakia, Hungary and Poland. Quotas and tariffs on goods from these countries were to be removed up to 1996. After this date these countries were to remove their own tariffs and quotas so that EU goods could enter freely into their markets. These states should therefore be able to benefit from selling more textiles, steel, chemicals, and other goods in the EU.

The problem for the former Eastern bloc countries is that the transition to a Western style economy can be very harmful in the short period, leading to widespread unemployment. This is particularly the case where these countries try a 'short sharp shock' treatment of rapid reform. This was the case in Poland, which led to the return of the Communist Party in free elections in 1993. Other Eastern bloc countries have taken more gradual steps towards market reform.

 Task

Draw a map showing the countries of the European Union and their geographical proximity to Poland, Hungary and the Czech Republic. Are there any physical barriers, e.g. mountain ranges, that may limit trade?

The redevelopment of Eastern Europe

The EU stands to make tremendous gains from the reconstruction of Eastern economies. Eastern economies should, after a period of time, be able to grow rapidly. They will therefore demand increasing quantities of goods, services and 'know-how' from the EU. Consumers in these countries will increasingly want to purchase cars, and other modern household equipment.

Many Eastern enterprises welcome joint ventures with Western companies. The EU has developed a four-point programme to help Eastern Europe:

1. Developing free trade with Eastern Europe
2. Industrial, scientific and technical co-operation

3. Financial backing and assistance
4. The creation of political discussion and shared proposals for change.

The Baltic Republics of Latvia, Lithuania and Estonia have shown a keen interest in developing close ties with the EU. The Ukraine and Russia, because of their size, are also likely to become important trading partners for the EU. However, links with more remote areas of the former Soviet Union may be more limited.

The reunification of Germany

Figure 10.6

The reunification of Germany has taken place at great speed. The first step in the integration of East Germany into the European Community was the introduction on 1 July 1990 of monetary, economic and social union with West Germany. This introduced East Germany to the rules of the market economy, the abolition of price controls, and free trade between the two Germanies.

Community law has applied to the united Germany since 3 October 1990. Goods produced in the former East Germany must now meet EU standards and structural funds have been made available to help to rebuild and restructure East Germany.

The immediate impact of the reunification of Germany has been the creation of wide-scale unemployment in East Germany. East German business units have long been protected from market conditions by a state planning system.

Case Study—End of the line for the Trabant

In 1990 the new Germany was created. What had previously been East Germany had been a centrally planned economy. West Germany had been a mixed economy in which prices had been free from government interference.

Before the two parts of Germany reunited, a car known as the Trabant had been virtually the only type of car available in East Germany. More than three million Trabants had been sold since production began in the late 1950s. The same model of car was sold from 1964 to 1991. There was no other car available and because people could only buy the one model there was no competition. The planners saw no need to change the design because they could sell every car they produced. The car was functional (i.e. it served the purpose of getting a driver from place A to place B), it was cheap to run and it was more or less repairable with a hammer, a ball of string and chewing gum. However, it was an environmental disaster. It was made largely from a cheap fibre-glass material called Duroplast, which is everlasting. The car was noisy, gave off a lot of fumes, and the only way to destroy it was to burn it, which gave off poisonous fumes.

Before the two Germanies were reunited there had been a long waiting list for the Trabant (some people had waited 20 years). After reunification nobody wanted to buy a Trabant. The customers deserted to buy Western cars. The Trabant was obsolete in a modern market. It was no longer possible to continue producing an obsolete car at a cost of 11 000 Deutschmarks (£3,700) and to sell it for 9000 Deutschmarks. In May 1991 the company was forced to close down and lay off 9000 employees.

Questions

1. Why do you think that so little change was made to the Trabant over the years?
2. What would be the benefit to (a) producers and (b) consumers of sticking to the standard model?
3. Why would a free market force change?
4. How could the Trabant survive in a free market?
5. What problems do you think would have been caused by the disappearance of the Trabant?
6. Explain in detail why you think that the disappearance of the Trabant has been a good or a bad thing for (a) people living in what was East Germany and (b) the world economy.

East Germany, like many of the Eastern bloc countries, had been characterized by chronic states of soil, air and water pollution coupled with uncontrolled waste disposal and poorly maintained nuclear installations. One of the stipulations for integration of the former East Germany into the European economy was a rapid development programme to ensure acceptable environmental standards and safety of nuclear sites.

The costs of introducing the former East Germany into the Western European economy have been high. There have been widespread closures of industries and, because of CAP regulations, quotas have been imposed on agriculture. This has led to widespread unemployment and rapidly increasing programmes of social security. Germany as a whole in the mid-1990s has been characterized by falling production and output and huge structural changes in industry.

Case Study—Reducing Germany's payments to the EC

In November 1993 the Bundesbank called for a reduction in Germany's payments to the EC. It argued that the current high net level of contributions was no longer justified since unification.

Germany has slipped to sixth in the EU prosperity table as a result of incorporating the much poorer East Germany, but the country is still by far the largest payer into EU coffers, ahead of France and Britain. 'This position was justified up to German unification when West Germany lay in second place behind Luxembourg in terms of living standards in EC countries,' the Bundesbank said in its November 1993 monthly review.

Germany's net contributions to the EC rose from DM10.5bn (£4.2bn) in 1987 to DM22bn in 1992. The European subsidies to East Germany since unification have had little compensating impact on this increase. By 1997 it is estimated that Germany's net contribution to the EU will amount to DM30bn. The German Bundesbank is now worried that if the EU continues to spend money this could undermine financial stability in Europe.

Questions

1. Why is Germany the highest net contributor to the EU budget?
2. Is this fair given the costs of reunification?
3. Who should pay for the reunification of Germany?
4. Would it be possible to compensate Germany for the high costs of reunification? Explain.
5. Why might the Bundesbank be worried about the size of the EU's expenditure?

The EU and the developing world

The economic relationship between the EU and the developing world has been heavily influenced by the *colonial* history of many EU countries—for example: France's former colonies included Algeria, Morocco and Tunisia; Italy's included Libya; Portugal's included Mozambique; and the UK's included West Indian islands such as Barbados, African countries such as Kenya, India and, of course, Australia and New Zealand.

Before the development of the European Community countries had given preferential trading arrangements to their colonies. These arrangements were then built into the new Community. When the UK joined, a new agreement was made, known as the first Lomé Convention of 1975. This arrangement made sure that many of the favourable trading relationships enjoyed by the Commonwealth and other former colonies were an established part of the new Community. Today there are nearly 70 states benefiting from the Lomé Convention (Fig. 10.7), and every five years a new convention is signed giving preferential treatment in trade as well as a component of aid to these countries.

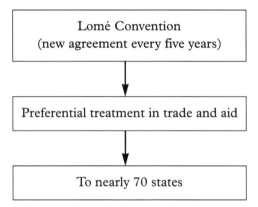

Figure 10.7

Each convention offers *duty-free access* for exports of manufactures and most non-CAP agricultural products (e.g. pineapples, bananas, etc.) from African, Caribbean and Pacific former colonies. The 'seven outside'—the bigger or more industrially advanced Commonwealth countries in South and South-East Asia (e.g. Singapore, Hong Kong, India)—were not offered membership of the exclusive Lomé club. In recent years, however, the EU has imposed some measures (e.g. on textiles) to protect businesses in the EU.

It is important to remember that many of the products and foodstuffs produced by African, Caribbean and Pacific colonies would enter the EU without trade restrictions regardless of the Lomé Convention because these products do not compete with those produced by the EU).

The *European Development Fund* exists to provide aid mainly to African, Caribbean and Pacific countries either in the form of direct grants or loans at low rates of interest. Four major sectors get most of the EU aid:

1. Rural development projects (by far the largest amount)
2. Industrialization
3. Economic infrastructure
4. Social development.

The Fourth Lomé Convention, which is the most recent, covers a 10-year period from 1990 to 1999. It is important to note that some of the safeguards given to African, Caribbean and Pacific countries have been reduced, exposing them to increased competition as we move towards the next century. In recent years, commentators have noted a reduction in the ties to former colonies; these ties have been replaced by a wider emphasis on a responsibility to the developing world as a whole.

The Western European Union

At the time of the Iraqi invasion of Kuwait it was felt that EU countries were moving towards common strategies on defence combined with the development of a world role in international affairs. This led to a growing confidence in the ability of the EU states to work together to share responsibility for global security.

This confidence was rapidly destroyed by the inability of EU states to develop a coordinated policy for the former Yugoslavia. Europe was suddenly faced with a massive inter-ethnic conflict on its own doorstep. No European state took any decisive action to do anything. European foreign policy crumbled so that the EU was made to look powerless to deal with matters close to home. The Western European Union (WEU) is the defence arm of 9 of the 12 member states. Some countries, notably France, are more excited about it than others. Britain fears that it could undercut NATO, to which it has more of a commitment; and Germany sees the WEU as strengthening NATO's European leg and underpinning Europe's own security. A *Eurocorps* of 10 000, combining German, French and Belgian forces, has already been established as the foundation for a European defence identity and the core of European armed forces.

The Venn diagram in Fig. 10.8 shows the relationship between the EU, NATO, and the WEU.

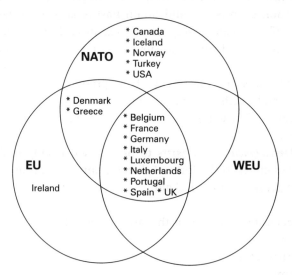

Figure 10.8

11

Transport in Europe

The transport system of any area is a key part of its infrastructure. The transport system serves to move goods and people and bring them into contact with wider areas. We are all familiar with the problems of a poor transport system—i.e. delays, accidents, high costs and, of course, frustration!

Transport accounts for about 5 per cent of the national income of the EU, as well as 5 per cent of employment, and is responsible for over a quarter of all energy consumption and 40 per cent of government investment. Transport has a tremendous impact on the environment; transport links pass directly through greenfield and urban areas, as well as generating pollution as fuel is burnt. The transport system provides the channels through which trade takes place.

Main forms of transport

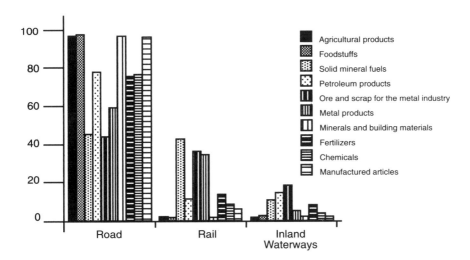

Figure 11.1   Goods transported by road, rail and inland waterways 1990

The EU has one of the densest transport networks in the world. This is particularly true in areas where a number of cities are close together. However, in *peripheral* regions, where populations are more spread out, transport networks are much less dense. The rail network is particularly dense in Germany, Belgium and Luxembourg. Germany, the Netherlands and Belgium have the densest motorway networks.

Road transport is easily the most common method of transporting passengers and goods, followed by rail and inland waterways. Figure 11.1 shows the percentage of various products that were transported using different methods in 1990.

 Task

Explain the advantages and disadvantages of carrying the following types of goods by (a) road, (b) rail and (c) inland waterways:

- agricultural products
- solid mineral fuels
- ore and scrap for the metal industry.

Integrated system

An integrated transport system is a key goal of the EU. Indeed this objective was established as part of the Treaty of Rome in 1957. However, only in recent years has there been a need for an integrated transport system linking air, sea, road, rail, canal and river routes.

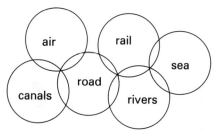

Figure 11.2

Countries on the periphery of the EU, such as Ireland, Denmark, Portugal and southern Italy are worried that they will be unable to compete economically unless transport links are improved.

 Tasks

Study Fig. 11.3, which shows the main motorway routes in the EU.
1. Which areas are best served by motorways?
2. Which areas have the poorest motorway connections?

3. How might the current pattern of motorway links support existing patterns of regional inequality in the EU?

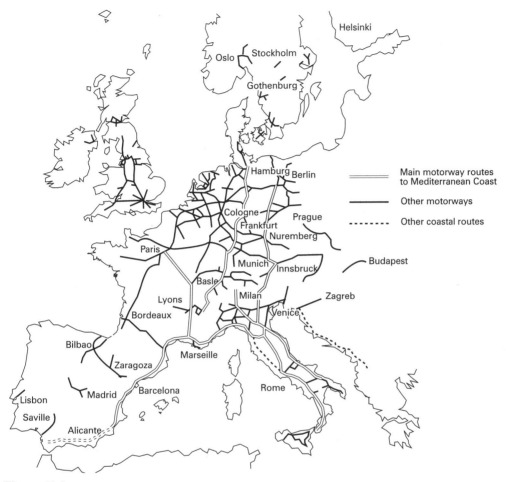

Figure 11.3

Case Study—The development of new motorway links

The Baltic states, led by Denmark, are already taking steps to put themselves in the mainstream of European trade routes. The government in Copenhagen is determined to achieve two things: first, it wants to end its status as the most northerly capital of the EU; second, it has ambitions to be the centre of a new economic area reaching from Esbjerg to Estonia and from Helsinki to Hamburg. Around 100 million people live in the area, almost 20 per cent of Europe's total population.

To promote this, Denmark is committed to spending DKr100bn ($14bn) by the end of the century in high-profile infrastructure projects. These will include new motorways, the electrification and upgrading of the rail network, and the investment of DKr3bn a year in rolling stock and locomotives for DSB, the state railway.

The most ambitious plan, however, will make the country a link between northern Scandinavia and the continental mainland. It involves the building of three huge road–rail bridges. The first, already under construction, is 20 km long and will join the island of Zealand to the Danish mainland. The second, across the Oresund strait, will link Copenhagen with the Swedish city of Malmö. The third is still under discussion with Bonn but is intended to connect Zealand with the north-east coast of Germany.

Questions

1. By using a map, can you identify the area from Esbjerg to Estonia and from Helsinki to Hamburg?
2. Can you identify the proposed locations for the three road–rail bridges?
3. Why is it important for Denmark to build these new communication links?
4. What will be the likely impact of these developments for (a) the Danish economy, (b) the economies of neighbouring regions and states and (c) regions of the EU on the southern periphery?
5. How might the EU as a whole want to balance these new developments?

Case Study—Transport networks 1990

Table 11.1 shows the length of different transport networks in EC member states in 1990. Study the table, then answer the questions that follow.

Table 11.1   Length of transport networks (km) in EC member states in 1990

	Motorways	Other roads	Railways	Inland waterways
Total EC	31 666	2 562 599	123 468	20 696
Belgium	1631	131 810	3513	1514
Denmark	601	70 173	2344	0
Germany	8822	490 039	27 045	4572
Greece	91	40 827	2479	0
Spain	2286	153 410	12 565	0
France	6680	801 192	34 469	6409
Ireland	8	92 295	1944	0
Italy	6091	296 312	16 016	1366
Luxembourg	75	5085	272	37
Netherlands	2045	95 233	2828	5043
Poland	243	9330	3061	124
United Kingdom	3093	376 893	16 932	1631

Questions

1. Which countries appear to have the most extensive major transport links? Why do you think this is so?
2. Which countries appear to have the least extensive major transport links? Why do you think this is so?
3. To what extent do you think that: (a) the economic development of a region depends on its tranport links?; (b) the transport links in a region depend on its economic development?
4. What does the pattern of transport links shown by Table 11.1 tell us about which countries were (a) at the heart of the economic area of the EC, and (b) at the periphery of the economic area of the EC.

Road Transport

Forty per cent of the total tonnage of goods transported between EU countries goes by road. This means that road networks can be very busy. Road transport accounts for 86 per cent of traffic carried by land, and 94 per cent of this is national traffic. It is important to bear in mind that road transport is usually only for a relatively short distance. Over two-thirds of national goods traffic is for distances under 50 km.

In France, Italy and Spain over 90 per cent of motorways are *toll roads*. Drivers entering a particular stretch of motorway pass through a toll gate where they receive a ticket. On leaving the motorway the ticket is fed into a machine which shows how far the driver has travelled and how much is to be paid.

In France every motorway must have an alternative road running close to it so that drivers have a choice. However, the motorway route will be much quicker. The private companies that operate the toll systems are responsible for the maintenance and servicing of the motorway.

In the UK motorways are funded by the central government, but the present government is keen to develop toll roads and has recently given a contract to a private firm to produce a toll road to the north of Birmingham. However, it seems unlikely that toll roads will form a significant part of the UK's road network as there are so many alternative routes that motorists can take.

When making a road journey in other European countries you will need to buy an up-to-date road map or atlas. You can then start to plan a journey.

 Tasks

1. You have been asked to plan a journey for a van driver travelling from Dover to Grenoble in France. The driver will need to take a one-hour break every four hours,

and should not drive for more than eight hours in the same day. Plan a route for the driver with stop-off points for the night.

2. You have been asked to plan a route for a family that is going on holiday by car to Luxembourg from Manchester. They want to get there quickly regardless of cost. Which routes should they take?

Route planning

Organizations such as the RAC and the AA in this country help motorists to plan routes and can warn you of any delays. A similar organization in Germany is the ADAC.

The time of day is always important in route planning. Most urban areas in European states become very congested during the morning and evening rush-hour periods. For example, motorways leading into and around London and Birmingham are extremely congested during the morning and evening rush hours. The same is true of other major cities such as Madrid, Athens and Paris. Today many major towns and cities are by-passed by ring roads, but this is not always the case.

In the summer holiday periods many major routes in Europe can become blocked, particularly from Friday evenings over the week-end period. France, for example, is notorious for its '*bouchons*' at this time. Many French people take their holidays between late July and late August, at which time there tends to be a huge migration of holidaymakers from the cities (particularly Paris) to the sea and mountain areas. In particular, many people take the Autoroute du Soleil, which runs all the way down through France to the Mediterranean coastal resorts. Holidaymakers and other travellers can expect delays of several hours in such congestion. Many of the major roads are notorious for relatively high accident rates as drivers habitually travel at speeds that exceed the safety regulations.

Rail transport

European railways have the ability to join together people and places at great speeds. In recent years a *Transport Infrastructure Fund* has been developed in the EU. One of its main functions has been to help to finance new railway lines which can bring benefits to the EU as a whole.

Clearly, building new rail lines involves huge capital costs so that the venture is best tackled on a Union-wide basis. Such a policy has the ability to join up the periphery with the centre of Europe. Figure 11.4 illustrates the possible shape of the EU's main rail links by the year 2005.

 Tasks

1. Which cities appear to have the best rail links with other parts of Europe?
2. Which parts of the EU appear to have the fewest links with other major EU centres?
3. Why do you think this is?

Figure 11.4   Europe's high-speed rail network (Source: Community of European railways)

4. Do you think that the EU should work collaboratively to ensure that all states are joined to the central railway network?

The Community of European Railways

This is an organization that represents all railway authorities in the states of the EU as well as those in Austria and Switzerland. It has the aim of introducing new lines to strengthen the existing network, e.g. routes through the Pyrenees joining Spain and France. It also sets out to create common standards, e.g. the width and size of track used and type of rolling stock. Clearly, if you are to have an integrated system then trains need to move freely across borders.

France was the first country to develop high-speed train links. Today its TGV, or *train à grande vitesse*, is famous throughout the world with its links through Paris to the north and south of France. In Germany, two fast lines link cities in the north with cities in the south. Italy has also begun to develop fast speed links and Spain has recently opened up new lines.

The Channel Tunnel

The opening up of the Channel Tunnel will be of tremendous importance to people in the United Kingdom, northern France, Belgium and the Netherlands. It will also help to bring Ireland closer in road and rail time to other parts of Europe.

The Channel Tunnel service will involve two kinds of train: shuttle trains and through trains. Shuttle trains will go between the British and French terminals (one near Folkestone and the other near Calais). These will carry passenger vehicles and freight vehicles in special wagons. Through trains for passengers travelling without vehicles and freight will be operated by British Rail (or its privatized equivalent) and SNCF (French railways). Passengers will travel between various destinations on trains that go through the tunnel.

Case Study—Le Shuttle

Figure 11.5 is a transcript of an advert that appeared in a number of major British newspapers in November 1993.

Folkestone to Calais in 35 minutes ... hardly a snail's pace!

Next year heralds the much-awaited opening of Eurotunnel's le Shuttle. From thereon, crossing the Channel will be a quicker, not to say calmer, affair than ever.

Here's the drill.

Simply take the M20, following the signs to 'Channel Tunnel', turn off at junction 11a just before Folkestone and coast into the terminal. Here you can visit the shops for last-minute essentials, sample one of our restaurants or head for the ticket booth.

You don't even need to have booked, though you can pay in advance through a travel agent of Le Shuttle Customer Service Centre.

Next comes customs, not one but two.

Well, anything to speed you on your way; French and English customs being conveniently combined, saving your clearance on the other side. And so straight to Le Shuttle, with up to 4 departures an hour at peak times.

Once underway, you stay with your vehicle.

A repack of the boot, a stretch of the legs, a trip to the loo and voilà, Calais already.

Minutes later, the terminal's behind you and you're on the fastest route South.

Total journey time from English motorway to French autoroute? No more than an hour.

C'est vrai. We don't hover about!

Figure 11.5

Questions

1. What aspects of travel between France and the United Kingdom does this advert focus on? Why?
2. In what way does the advert suggest that the Tunnel route has the edge over other alternatives?

 Tasks

1. Map out the route from your home across the Channel using the Tunnel route. How long would it take you to arrive in France assuming that the times given in the above advert are accurate?
2. In a survey carried out in November 1993 only one-quarter of the people questioned said they would use the Tunnel route. A number of people argued that they did not like the idea of going underground and were worried about accidents in the tunnel and even of terrorist attacks. Carry out your own survey to find out what people's attitudes are in your locality to travelling to France by alternative means of transport, e.g. tunnel, ferry, plane, etc.
3. The following table shows the passenger times between London and Paris using alternative modes of transport:

Channel Tunnel (Le Shuttle)	3 hours
Ferry	7 hours
Hovercraft	5 hours 30 minutes
Aircraft	3 hours

Find out, by enquiring at a travel agent, the relative costs of using each of these methods on a particular day. What would be (a) the advantages and (b) the disadvantages of using these different methods for (i) a family going on holiday to central France and (ii) a business person with an urgent meeting to attend in Paris?

Case Study—Eurotunnel update

With construction and installation equipment virtually complete, tests with fast trains are underway (Fig. 11.6). Half of the HGV carrier wagons have been delivered and 12 single-deck carrier wagons have been completed. Four electric locomotives have been delivered and are being tested on the French terminal.

On 20 June 1993, the first Eurostar test train was hauled through the Channel Tunnel from France to Britain to undergo testing on the British Rail network. The test train is the first example of this purpose-built rolling stock to make a crossing through the Tunnel. Its journey from the Eurotunnel terminal near Calais in France to the Folkestone portal took around two hours. In normal operation the transit time will be under 30 minutes. The passenger through-trains of BR, SNCF and SNCB are one of the four types of service that will operate through the Tunnel from 1994. In addition to Eurostar, there will be international freight trains and Eurotunnel's own Le Shuttle services for both tourist traffic and heavy goods vehicles.

Eurotunnel's Le Shuttle service is quite separate from the services using the rail link and will centre on its two terminals on either side of the Channel. Eurostar services using the tunnel will 'fly' from Paris and Brussels to London in three hours.

On 18 May 1993 the Paris–Arras section of France's high-speed Channel link was officially opened by the French President, François Mitterand. The link, which will be extended to Calais and the Eurotunnel terminal will eventually be used by the new Eurostar service betwen Paris and London.

Along with the opening of the high-speed line a new commercial centre and station were opened at Lille to cater for the new TGV service from Paris. The new complex, called Euralille, is a £620 million international business development in the centre of Lille. It was built to attract international companies to the town, which will be a major crossroads in European communications once the Channel Tunnel is open. The TGV service from Paris to Lille was extended to Calais for the opening of the Tunnel.

Figure 11.6   Eurostar at Waterloo International *European Passenger Services*

Air travel

Air traffic is particularly dense in the London–Paris–Frankfurt triangle (identify this area on a map and draw in the triangle). France, Italy and the United Kingdom have about 20 airports each. Germany and Greece have each about 15 airports while other states (e.g. Ireland) have fewer than 10.

Air transport is becoming increasingly popular in the EU and markets are becoming increasingly competitive. Until recently a country's airline has tended to have a national monopoly over routes. However, the EU has thrown open markets to price competition and by 1996 airlines will no longer have the monopoly on domestic air space. Some commentators argue that increasing competition should lead to falling prices; however, there is a fear that the market may be dominated by a few large-scale airlines who will then develop Europe-wide monopoly positions. There is also a danger that increased competition could lead to falling standards.

If more and more planes fly on the same routes it may become increasingly difficult to organize and control the use of air space. Perhaps at some stage in the future we may need centralized air traffic control.

Inland waterways

Inland waterways are an important method of transporting goods and people in several European states. The River Rhine is the backbone of the inland waterway network and is used to transport vast quantities of heavy goods and materials. It is important to remember that there are over 20 000 km of inland waterways. These help to form an integrated system linking France, Belgium, Luxembourg and the Netherlands in particular.

Sea transport

The sea is still a very important trading route, joining together parts of the European Union and joining the Union to the rest of the world. The bulk of sea transport is concentrated in about 50 ports (see Fig. 11.7). Rotterdam is the major port in the world, handling nearly 300 million tonnes of goods a year. Other major ports include Antwerp, Naples, Hamburg and Marseilles.

Most of the major ports are located on the North Sea or Atlantic coasts. European Union-wide regulations have been established for registering ships so that they must meet particular safety standards. However, many large companies register their ships under flags of convenience, e.g. using the Liberian flag to avoid having to maintain such high standards.

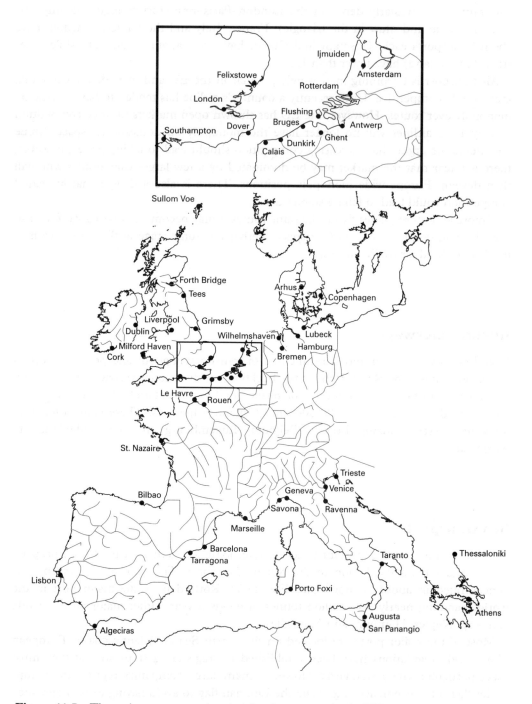

Figure 11.7   The major seaports and main inland waterways in the EU

12

Working in Europe

How flexible are you about where you work? Are you prepared to travel 10 miles, 100 miles, 200 miles or even to another country either to find employment or to make the most of job opportunities with the organization for which you may eventually work? Undoubtedly some of you will stay in the home town or city in which you were born or educated. However, some of you will at some time not only work in other parts of the country but also in other parts of the world.

So why might you make such a move? Perhaps you may find that, as part of your education, even this course, you have to take part in an exchange. Having taken part in an exchange you might make friends, build contacts or develop relationships that open up new horizons and offer you opportunities that you feel you might like to pursue. Alternatively, you might want to work abroad either before or after going into higher education. This might give you a chance to travel before you start your career. Another reason that many people work abroad, particularly in the EU is that in many countries salaries will be higher than in the UK. Working abroad may help you to develop financial opportunities and, at the same time, allow you to explore new places, consider new lifestyle possibilities and open up options that may enable you to have a more varied life. For many of you, career development may be an important reason for working abroad, particularly if you work for a foreign company or a multinational organization with large markets overseas.

Despite all these reasons for working abroad, going overseas may cause many problems, particularly for a family, and social influences will often have to be balanced against such motives.

The European job market

It is important not to presume that in other countries there will be more jobs and that these jobs will pay higher incomes. The EC was badly hit by the recession of the 1990s, after a period during the 1980s when average rates of unemployment across the EC doubled.

Table 12.1.   Different rates of unemployment in EC countries, 1991

Country	% unemployment rates	Country	% unemployment rates
Belgium	8.3	Italy	10.9
Denmark	10.5	Luxembourg	1.6*
France	9.4	Netherlands	4.4
Germany	6.3	Portugal	4.6*
Greece	4.6	Spain	16.3
Ireland	19.1	UK	8.1

* 1990 figures

Table 12.1 identifies the various unemployment rates across the EC in 1991. Though rates in some countries are clearly lower, when looking for a job it is difficult to draw too many conclusions from the figures. Vacancies and rates of pay vary widely throughout the EU, not just according to country but also according to region. For example, in the north of Italy university graduates are getting work for the first time, though it has not been easy, whereas in the south graduates have been waiting an average of two years before gaining employment. By 1993 the average rate of unemployment in the EC had risen to 11 per cent with over 17 million people out of work. All types of jobs and professions had been hit by the recession and forecasts of economic growth lacked optimism.

Case Study—No vacancies in Vlissingen

Many British and Irish people who fail to find jobs at home have headed for the Dutch port of Vlissingen (Flushing) in search of work. The town has a ferry connection with Sheerness in Kent. Early in 1993 employment bureaux in the town reported a 70 per cent rise in the numbers of unemployed arriving in the town. One employment bureau consultant said that some arrive with just a few pounds and only the clothes they are wearing. Many arrive from UK employment blackspots such as Liverpool and Belfast.

Leon Dalley and John Kendall, just out of their teens, scraped together about £200 to try their luck on the Dutch labour market. The pair from Bolton were looking for a job on the docks and signed on with more than a dozen bureaux. They were shocked to find no vacancies and dozens of other teenagers also looking for casual dockside work.

ASB employment bureau consultant Marcel Passenier said:

It's very sad. Those who are arriving daily from Britain and Ireland and signing on with us seem to think Holland is some kind of Eldorado, but it is not. Unemployment has been creeping up here. There has been a huge rise since January. The minute the Single Market opened up they got on the boat and came over, and they have been coming ever since.

According to the bureau, which hires labour directly, many jobs require a working knowledge of Dutch which most of the new arrivals do not have. Some arrivals move on to Rotterdam or to other cities in search of jobs.

Edward Geskes of the Rotterdam regional division of the Dutch central employment service, suggests that 'people check with their local employment office before they come'.

Questions

1. Describe what many young people have hoped to find in Vlissingen.
2. Why should young people research the job market before they make a decision to go to another country?
3. The cast study mentions the problem of language. What other factors might make it more difficult for them to obtain a job.

Finding a job

In the Single Market nationals of member states have the right to go to other member states either to look for work or to take up work as long as they have a valid passport or identity card and comply with laws and regulations on employment. They are then entitled to the same treatment as the nationals of the host state in matters of pay, working conditions, vocational training, income tax, social security and trade union rights.

There are, however, many practical problems associated with the full freedom of movement to gain work. Many jobs in EU countries may require the job holder to have specialist skills such as a language or specific vocational qualifications. Qualifications obtained in one member state may not be accepted as appropriate in another. There are many other practical aspects that may cause problems, such as the transfer of pensions and the availability of housing.

There are a number of different ways of finding work overseas. First, many organizations within the UK look for employees to work abroad, particularly within the EU. This always has a major advantage of being able to return to the UK company to take up a post after overseas work and so avoid a period of unemployment. The other advantage is that it helps overseas work to fit into a career plan. One of the questions to ask when being interviewed for work is 'What are the opportunites for work abroad?'

Opportunities to work abroad often exist with government bodies such as embassies, overseas development aid programmes such as VSO (but not within the EU), the United Nations and the World Bank. It is also possible to apply to work for EU institutions such as those in Brussels.

Case Study—Who gets the jobs in Brussels?

Italian and Spanish university graduates have emerged as the winners of changes to EU recruitment policy. In the most recent EU recruitment policy to find high-flying administrators for the European Commission, more than 40 per cent of the successful candidates came from Spain and Italy. Ironically, the changes to recruitment policy and the recruitment drive to find European civil servants tried to increase the chances of British graduates winning well-paid and influential jobs in Brussels and Luxembourg, but Britons only hold 12 per cent of the 3800 senior administrative posts in the Commission, far fewer than the 15 per cent which the UK's demographic weight should merit.

In theory the nationality of EU officials is irrelevant as they are supposed to be independent of patriotic pressures. In practice, however, governments fiercely compete to place their nationals in key positions. Germany, the most populated country in the EU, has 14 per cent of the EU top staff; France fares better with 17 per cent; and Belgium with only a population of 10 million has 13 per cent, but this is undoubtedly because of the Brussels location.

The campaign to recruit more Britons has been spearheaded by the Regional Affairs Commissioner. Previously recruitment relied upon success in legal and economic exams, which tended to give the French and Germans an advantage with their more specialized university courses. The EU now uses more wide-ranging exams and interviews to recruit staff. Despite these changes they believe that the numbers recruited from the UK are still disappointingly low and that further changes are needed. They fell that there are not enough women applying for posts and that recruitment should include a better geographical spread of employees.

Questions

1. What sort of background, qualifications, skills and abilities would you expect of UK graduates who apply to work for the EU in Brussels?
2. What number of UK graduates currently work for the EU in Brussels?
3. What number should this be if the number of employees properly reflect demographic weights?
4. How many more UK graduates should, therefore, be employed?

Employment in EU member states

Another way of finding out about work in EU member states is to visit the jobcentre offices of the Employment Service. The Employment Service will bring details of UK jobseekers to the attention of employers in other member states and provides information on a range of issues, such as: finding work, health and social security, taxation, education, culture, and employment issues.

Employment offices throughout the EU use the 'Sedoc network' which allows employment services to exchange information on jobs to enable those wishing to work overseas to find details of posts available. The Employment Service also provides a mechanism whereby UK companies may contact them if they wish to employ workers from other member states.

Major newspapers, periodicals and professional journals frequently advertise abroad. Sometimes it is useful to look at such advertising, not just for the job you may be looking for, but also to find out about the range of salaries and benefits being provided in various parts of Europe for different types of profession. Some countries have developed specific career publications. For example, two monthly publications containing a directory of jobs in Germany are *Markt* and *Chance*.

Newspapers and features about Europe may also provide 'leads' that may be possible to pursue—for example, a new factory opening up in a town or a new industry that is developing. Reading EU newspapers will also help to identify the best places to go and where the greatest likelihood of achieving a positive result is likely to be.

Other than keeping in touch with the press, another useful source of information may be professional associations or trade associations. Though these may not have specific lists of jobs, they may provide a list of members to whom it would be possible to write for details.

Some young people go abroad and undertake a range of temporary jobs. Working as an *au pair*, living with a family and looking after children has often been a popular activity and provides some useful experience. Others go to holiday regions and look for jobs in hotels and bars at or near tourist resorts. It may be possible from having undertaken such a period of employment to find something more secure.

Going abroad, however, and looking for jobs when you are there, is not always a good idea. Many overseas job seekers who try this have had unhappy experiences.

When jobs for the EU are advertised in the UK, interviews are often held in London. If applicants are called to travel abroad for interview, expenses are usually paid. Rules for applying for jobs are similar to those within the UK. Letters of application, application forms and CVs should be developed to ensure that the applicants show that they have the essential requirements for the job.

When applying for jobs, one of the most important parts of an application is the applicant's list of qualifications. Before the Single Market there was no system for mutual recognition of qualifications across member states and often professionals who wished to move had to requalify. Since the establishment of the Single Market, those who have applied for jobs have had their qualifications and experience recognized or taken into account in other member states. By establishing specific levels of competence, GNVQs and NVQs have helped to develop recognition of qualifications across national boundaries. Holders of such qualifications now find it easier to achieve recognition of their knowledge and skills.

Employment conditions check-list

Sometimes a job can sound too attractive to refuse. However, when working in another country, there may be a host of other expenses that have not been taken into account and these have to be assessed in relation to the job offer and put into perspective. The following list of questions would be useful to ask and many help to clarify these areas:

1. Will the employer meet the cost of travel out of the UK?
2. Will the employer provide help with accommodation?
3. What is the cost of utilities such as gas, electricity and water?
4. Are other costs in this country a lot higher?
5. Will the employer help with the cost of trips home?
6. Are your personal effects at home going to have to be stored and what will this cost?
7. Is a car provided with the job?
8. What family arrangements might have to be made?
9. Is help going to be provided for:
   — medical expenses?
   — any additional insurance required?
10. What clothes might you require for a different climate?
11. In what form is your salary to be paid, and how might its value be affected by changes in exchange rates?
12. Is any of your salary paid into a UK bank? What other banking arrangements should you make?
13. Has the job offer been confirmed in writing?
14. What working conditions are attached to the job? To what extent do these differ from your existing post?
15. What arrangements are there for sick pay?
16. Have you checked out the reputation of your prospective employer?
17. What risks are you taking by working in another country?
18. What training in areas such as languages will you require either before or after you take up the post?
19. How much will it cost to send your possessions overseas?
20. What benefits do you derive from working overseas?

Taxation

Different methods of collection and assessment of *income tax* appear throughout the EU. If you work in another EU country full time for a period which includes at least one full tax year (6 April to 5 April) in which all duties are performed outside the UK, you will be regarded as no longer resident in the UK as long as your visits to the UK do not exceed 182 days in any one tax year. A *non-resident* is not liable to pay UK income tax on any income derived outside the UK, even if this money is paid or sent to the UK. If you fail to become a non-resident and remain a resident or you do not complete a full tax year abroad, you could be liable for UK tax on your overseas earnings and may even have to pay tax in both countries.

Income tax rates vary throughout the EU. For example, in Germany it is levied on a graduated scale ranging from 19 to a maximum of 53 per cent, and in the Netherlands, after deduction of allowances, rates of tax range from 35 to 60 per cent.

VAT rates and systems also vary throughout the EU. It has been the intention to harmonize VAT rates, but this has not yet happened because of the effects such measures might have on the economies of member states.

Liability to pay inheritance tax still exists while you are in residence abroad unless you become *domiciled* abroad. This means that you take out a permanent home in that country by becoming a citizen and severing all ties with the UK.

National insurance

While working in the UK you will have made compulsory National Insurance contributions and will be entitled to a range of benefits. If, while working abroad, you fail to keep up your contributions, you could lose your entitlement to benefits. For example, in order to qualify for benefits at the standard rate, there must be a record of having made a certain level of contributions during the tax year in which benefits are claimed.

If your employer sends you abroad to another EU country, you will be expected to pay National Insurance contributions as if you were in the UK, as long as your period abroad is less than 6 months in any one tax year (6 April to 5 April). If you are abroad for more than 12 months, you would not be liable to pay UK contributions but will be expected to pay into the scheme of the country in which you are working. It is possible to pay voluntary contributions to protect UK retirement/widow's pension entitlement.

It is possible to receive retirement and widow's pensions abroad, though there are exceptions in some EU countries. UK benefits tend to be lower than many of the benefits provided by EU countries.

Under EU law you can now go job seeking for up to three months in most EU countries. Provided that you are registered unemployed for up to four weeks before departure, it is possible to receive Unemployment Benefit on the day of departure, and while in another EU country it is possible to draw this benefit via the employment services of that country. Some EU countries have put obstacles in the way of this measure with residence permits.

Medical care

One great benefit of living in the UK is the National Health Service (NHS). Medical expenses abroad are not refundable by the NHS and once permanently abroad you are no longer entitled to NHS treatment. Some countries do have health agreements with the NHS but often their services are not comparable.

It is always advisable to take out private health insurance to cover eventualities where free treatment is only partially available in the country in which you take up residence. It is also important to register with a general practitioner when taking up residence abroad. Not all doctors will speak English and one of the most common problems is describing symptoms (Fig. 12.1).

Figure 12.1

Housing

What do you do with your home while abroad?

It is usual for most home owners going abroad to let their houses or flats to a tenant while they are away. There are a variety of types of tenancies and legal advice is usually necessary. Selling the home is sometimes easier, but then there is often the problem of storing bulky items of furniture, and on returning to the country the person also has nowhere to live. Leaving a home empty is often considered hazardous and may result in some form of vandalism by squatters.

Many estate egents have a specialized property management service equipped to deal with the letting, rental and management of property. Agents will advise on rents, agreements, insurance as well as other areas such as repairs and maintenance.

Moving and returning

When moving to work abroad you have to organize what to take. For many people this means making a decision about whether to take everything or just bare essentials. This will largely depend on the duration of the work and the type of accommodation expected. For example, some companies supply their overseas employees with fully furnished flats.

Large removal firms have a knowledge of many of the problems involved in moving abroad and will provide advice on a range of issues, including insurance, storage and professional packing.

Cars may be taken from one EU country to another but must conform to the safety standards of that country. There are several factors to consider such as right- or left-hand drive, security (radio and other thefts are common in some countries) and the use of diesel (which is half the price of petrol in Spain). Driving clubs, such as the AA, are affiliated to the International Touring Alliance.

So who do you need to tell when you are going abroad? The following is an action check-list:

- Income Tax Office
- DSS Overseas Branch
- Motor insurance
- Other insurance
- Dentist and doctor
- Gas, electricity, water, telephone
- Council tax
- Solicitor/accountant/financial adviser
- Credit card companies
- Bank
- National Health Service
- Pension schemes
- Post Office
- Schools.

While living abroad it is possible to retain the right to vote in UK and European parliamentary elections. To do this you have to fill in an Overseas Elector's Declaration form and register every year before the qualifying date.

When returning to the UK it is useful to think about the price differences between the two countries and work out what you want to take back. Beware, however, as you must have the documentation to prove that an article has been owned and used for three months (or six months in some cases) to avoid paying VAT on entry.

Before returning to the UK it is important to inform the letting agents who are looking after your property at least three months before you return to enable them to give notice to the tenants. Another problem may be finding a job, and it might be useful to apply for work before returning.

Education

One of the major problems of going abroad is that of education and the schooling of children. There are often many options such as boarding schools in the UK, expatriate schools abroad, local schools abroad and home teaching. Decisions about the best option to take often have to be based upon wide-ranging considerations.

Education systems throughout Europe vary considerably, often according to different religious beliefs, political considerations and ages for compulsory education, and these factors tend to shape the curriculum of their institutions. Higher education systems are also very different. For example, there are two levels of degree within the UK: bachelors and masters. In many other parts of Europe degrees take longer to achieve and often equate to higher degrees in the UK. There are also many different approaches to technical and vocational education.

Case Study—Education in the Netherlands

The following case study has been adapted from *The Netherlands in Brief*, published by the Foreign Information Service, Ministry of Foreign Affairs, The Hague.

Education

The origins of the present Dutch education system can be traced back to the Batavian Republic, the unitary state which came into being after the French Revolution. Education occupies a central place in the Civil and Constitutional Regulations of 1789 which formed the basis of the first legislation on education in 1801.

In 1848, the Netherlands, which had been a monarchy for 35 years, acquired a constitution which, among other things, enshrined the freedom to provide education. Thinking at the time was that central government should become less involved in governing and managing schools. It was therefore decided that the state should not have a monopoly of schools or education as a whole. Since that time, the municipalities have been closely involved in managing and governing schools, although the necessary funds have always been provided by the state. Schools set up by private organisations were not originally supported financially by the government. In 1917, after an educational debate which dominated political life in the Netherlands for 70 years (1848–1917), private and state schools were placed on an equal footing for financial purposes. Freedom of education became a basic right guaranteed by the constitution. Approximately 75 per cent of all existing Dutch schools were set up by private bodies and associations, many of them of a Protestant or Catholic persuasion.

The Dutch educational system comprises:

- primary schools
- special schools
- secondary schools
- institutes of higher education
- institutes of international education.

Primary education

Primary schools are for children aged 4–12. There are no schools in the Netherlands for children below the age of 4. There are play groups and creches for young children but they do not come under the Ministry of Education and Science. Children may attend primary school from the age of 4; from the age of 5, school attendance becomes compulsory. Primary schools prepare children for secondary education. In their first two years at primary school, they are taught the basic skills of reading, writing and arithmetic and manual skills, using play and learn methods. The curriculum for the remaining 6 years consists of lessons in Dutch, mathematics, writing, history, geography, science and social studies. Religion is also taught at private schools. In their final year at primary school children also learn English.

Primary education is not final, nor do pupils receive a school-leaving certificate when they leave. They go on to secondary school, the type of which depends on their results, intelligence and aptitude and is often chosen in collaboration with teachers.

Secondary education

There are three types of secondary school:

- general secondary schools
- pre-university schools
- vocational secondary schools.

There are two types of general secondary school: junior general secondary schools (MAVO) which offer a 4-year course, and senior general secondary schools (HAVO) which offer a 5-year course. Pre-university secondary schools (VWO) also consist of two types, the atheneum and the gymnasium, both of which offer children 6-year courses to prepare them for higher or university education. There are three levels of vocational education: junior (LBO), senior (MBO) and higher (HBO). All of these secondary school courses culminate in written state examinations. The number of subjects varies as do the levels.

After passing MAVO examinations, students can transfer to an MBO course, while those who pass their HAVO examinations may be admitted to a HBO course. Students with a VWO school-leaving certificate may apply for admission to a university or institute of higher education.

Vocational education courses are available in the following:

- agricultural education
- commercial education
- technical education
- social services and health care education
- home economics education
- tradespeople's education
- nautical education.

Most of these types of vocational education consist of three levels: junior, senior and higher. Students with an LBO or MAVO school-leaving certificate may also take short senior secondary vocational courses, enrol in apprenticeship schemes or follow a senior secondary vocational course for laboratory staff.

Many VWO, HAVO, MAVO and LBO schools have joined forces to form combined schools, each with a single board. Within these combined schools all pupils receive the same education for an initial or transitional period. After which they are required to make a definite choice of the type of course they wish to take.

Full-time education is compulsory up to the age of 16. Children who leave school at the minimum age are then required by law to attend courses of continued training or education for one or two days a week, depending on the type of education. For the remainder of the week they may have a paid job.

Special education

Special education exists for children with a physical, mental or social handicap or a combination of any of the three and consists of primary and secondary schools catering for children aged 3–21. The aim of special education is to enable children to take part in normal primary or secondary education as quickly as possible.

Higher education

Higher education comprises higher vocational and university education. The latter is provided at eight universities and five 'hogescholen' (equivalent to universities). Leiden University, founded in 1575 by Prince William of Orange, is the oldest. All the Dutch universities and 'hogescholen' are financed entirely from government funds, irrespective of whether they are state or private foundations. An additional 7 theological colleges are partly financed from state funds.

Courses at universities are divided into two phases. The first phase takes 4 years (students may be enrolled for a maximum of 6 years) and concludes with the 'doctoraal' examination. The second phase, to which a relatively limited number of students are admitted, consists of specialised study or research leading to a doctorate. To be admitted to a university or equivalent establishment, students must have obtained a VWO or HBO certificate.

Higher vocational education courses are available in the following:

- higher commercial education
- higher home economics education
- higher agricultural education
- higher tradespeople's education

- higher social work education
- higher health care education
- higher technical education
- education in the arts
- teacher training.

In principle, students with certificates from VWO, HAVO, and MBO schools can be admitted to higher vocational education courses which takes 4 years.

International education

A number of educational establishments exist to provide courses for graduates from foreign countries. They are in special subject areas and many of them are in English. A degree from a foreign university is usually required for admission to these courses.

Statistics

Of the 14.9 million people who live in the Netherlands, about 4 million are in full-time education. Education is free during the compulsory period, although some schools ask parents to make a financial contribution.

All teaching and ancillary staff at publicly-run schools are paid by the state. As a result, the Ministry of Education and Science has the highest budget of any government ministry. The Netherlands spends more than 29.6 billion guilders a year on education or roughly 17 per cent of the national budget.

Adult education

Adults, including many housewives, are increasingly interested in courses which were not previously available to them. Special facilities have been or will be created in a large number of municipalities for such people, including the Open School and the Open University.

Questions

1. In what ways is the Dutch education system (a) similar and (b) different to the UK education system?
2. What might the benefits be of going abroad to undertake your higher education?

Rights of workers

When travelling across Europe EU nationals should be treated as equally as the residents of the host country and have statutory protection in areas such as dismissal.

The main exception is military service, which we do not have in the UK. Even though EU nationals may be working in another country, they have to return to their own country to undertake such service.

When working in another country you would have the same rights as everyone else to borrow money, own your property, pay taxes and enter into contractual agreements. Working conditions and benefits at present, however, vary considerably from one country to another. For example, the following are some of the conditions enforced in Portugal:

- a working week cannot exceed 44 hours
- canteen facilities must be provided if there are more than 50 employees in a location
- insurance cover must be taken out against accidents at work
- a company with more than 200 employees must have a clinic staffed by a doctor
- additional leave of 11 days must be granted to a worker for marriage.

Throughout the EU women have often been associated with less-well-remunerated sections of employment. As a vulnerable group they have frequently suffered from occupational discrimination. Despite Article 119 of the Treaty of Rome, stating that pay differentials should be abolished by the end of 1961, the deadline was not achieved and in 1976 member states were given two and a half years to provide equal treatment, protection and working conditions to men and women in employment and vocational training. There still remained areas of unequal treatment and in 1987 member states were given six years to introduce equality of treatment that would abolish discrimination in respect of sex, marital or family status, social security schemes, benefits and allowances.

After the Single European Act in 1986 it was realized that the removal of barriers to trade ought to be matched by progress to improve social and working conditions throughout the EC. This led to the drawing up of the Social Charter, which was accepted by 11 members of The European Council at Strasbourg in December 1989. The UK refused to adopt it despite changes made during the discussions.

The Social Charter has 12 main themes or rights:

1. Free movement of workers with equal treatment in access to employment and social protection.
2. Employment based upon a fair working wage and fair treatment for part-time workers.
3. Improvements in living and working conditions, e.g. working hours, holidays, shift allowances, rest periods, etc.
4. Social protection. (This part of the Charter makes a reference to the guaranteed minimum wage.)
5. Freedom of association and collective bargaining.
6. Vocational training.
7. Equal treatment for men and women.

8. Information, consultation and participation of workers.
9. Standards of health and safety in the workplace.
10. Protection of young people in areas such as working ages, youth employment and training.
11. The elderly and pensions.
12. Benefits for the disabled in areas such as training, rehabilitation and occupational integration.

The Social Charter and the Social Chapter

As stated above, the Social *Charter* was accepted in principle by 11 of the 12 EC European council members at Strasbourg in 1989. With the drawing up of the Maastricht Treaty the Social Charter then became the Social *Chapter*. The UK opted out of the Social Chapter on the grounds that the areas involved were the responsibility of individual member governments. The Social Chapter put the Social Charter into a new treaty context and during the Maastricht negotiations the UK insisted on the Social Chapter being removed from the Union Treaty. As a result, it was put into a separate protocol which enabled the 11 countries to continue with the proposals.

By not signing the Social Chapter the British government has constantly stated that it has increased labour flexibility in the UK. One of the dangers of this, however, is that of 'social dumping' with employers moving to the UK because of lower employment costs and standards.

Case Study—Second-class treatment in Italy

An investigation is currently under way over claims that Italy treats its 1500 foreign language teachers as second-class citizens and denies them the rights given to Italian teachers. The inquiry was launched after a 50-strong delegation of foreign teachers and Italian students travelled from the University of Verona to Strasbourg to lobby MEPs.

A Scottish lecturer, David Petrie, at the University of Verona is coordinator of the campaign. He says: 'We have won every case we have fought in Italy, yet despite that the government refuses to put EC directives into practice. We want the EC to put pressure on Italy and for the Commission in Brussels to raise a legal action against the Italian state on our behalf.'

Matters reached a crisis recently at the University of Verona when foreign teachers were told that the payment of their salaries could no longer be guaranteed. No Italian lecturer received a similar notice.

Mr Petrie said: 'We have been fighting this discrimination since 1986. If we have to keep going through the Italian courts it would last until the next century. How are we going to do that if we are not being paid and have no money?'

The language teachers, who come from at least six EU countries, argue that their second-class status violates Article 48 of the Treaty of Rome, which outlaws any discrimination over pay and working conditions between EU nationals.

Questions

1. Explain why, particularly in the Single Market, nationals from all EU countries ought to be treated equally.
2. How might the Social Chapter help to remove discrimination across national boundaries?
3. Explain, briefly, why the UK opted out of the Social Chapter. What are the dangers of doing this?

Employment opportunities across the EU

Belgium: EU nationals can come and go, but they must register at a local town hall within a month of arrival. A temporary identity card, valid for three months, will be issued and can be extended if employment is obtained. Belgium is so near that visits from the UK to look for jobs are easily made. A knowledge of French is useful and Dutch can be very helpful. Often the best opportunities are with Belgian-based British firms in areas such as insurance, banking and construction.

Denmark: Despite the provisions for the free movement of labour, it is not easy to find work in Denmark. English is spoken by most Danes. Foreigners must apply for a residence permit to stay in Denmark for more than three months, and rented accommodation is scarce. Denmark has a good record in areas such as industrial relations and has one of the lowest strike records in Europe.

France: British citizens may freely enter France to seek work. After three months they must apply for residence permits from the Town Hall or police. The 39-hour week is standard and French workers are entitled to five weeks' annual leave. Equal pay is obligatory and the gap between men's and women's pay is narrower in France than in other EU countries. Many French employees have fringe benefits such as housing and welfare.

Germany: EU nationals require a residence permit. The standard working week is 38–40 hours and wages and salaries are negotiated by collective bargains which have the force of the law. Employers often provide performance bonuses and fringe benefits such as housing, meals, transport and recreation facilities.

Greece: EU nationals can freely take up employment or enter the country to look for work. However, job prospects for foreigners are very slim unless they work for British firms with activities in Greece. Working hours frequently take into consideration a siesta in the afternoon.

Ireland: British and EU citizens do not require work permits. Agencies and Jobcentres are commonly used to look for work. The Irish language is not usually needed for many jobs. Tourism and services are particularly important industries.

Italy: Citizens of EU countries can enter Italy freely without work permits but require residence permits if they stay for more than three months. The main problem with finding work in Italy are the high level of unemployment and the language difficulties.

Luxembourg: A good knowledge of French and German is important in business in this country. All salaries and wages are tied to the cost of living index. The 40-hour week is standard.

The Netherlands: This is often a preferred location overseas for British people as most people speak English, it is close to home and the Dutch way of life is similar to the British. However, it is not easy to get a job and unemployment is high. There is a legal minimum wage for all workers aged 23 to 65.

Portugal: Though Portugal has little unemployment, rates of pay are low. Public administration and services account for over 40 per cent of the working population. Portugal has become an increasingly popular destination for tourists over recent years.

Spain: Spain has a low growth rate and high unemployment. Employment opportunities are limited unless working for a UK company. Tourism and the car industry have expanded over recent years. Working conditions in Spain are similar to those in other EU countries.

13

Living in Europe

What must it be like to live in another country or another part of Europe? Many of you might have already done this and may be able to comment upon what has probably been a very interesting part of your life. However, for those of you who have not lived overseas, it may be difficult to imagine what it would be like. Most of us think about the more physical differences such as heat and humidity and may find it difficult to assess how other changes in the way in which we would have to live might affect our everyday lives.

When you arrive in another country you will probably have to go through a lengthy period of adjustment. So much that you will come across will be new to you and coping with all these adjustments at the same time may be overpowering. Some of the differences in other countries are ones that you might not have even thought about. In the UK we have grown up with similar expectations and values which influence how we do things and how we perceive situations. In other countries people may have different beliefs and concepts of normal behaviour.

So how would you react to all this different stimuli? Would you try to create a 'mini-UK' and live and do things in the same way as you do at home, such as eating fish and chips and speaking in English, or would you accept the new environment and culture, try to understand it and make an effort to learn and adjust to the ways in which others live? In this chapter we are going to look at all the information it would be useful to have if you were intending to live in any of the countries in the EU. In order to provide some structure for our analysis, in each country in turn we shall look at:

- social patterns
- the climate
- finding somewhere to live
- living conditions, shopping and prices
- getting around
- post and telephone
- national holidays
- eating out and tipping.

In this chapter we provide a 'guidebook' view of countries. In reality there are many regions and ways of life in each country covered. So beware of stereotypes!

Belgium

Social patterns: Belgium has the distinction of being the world's most heavily industrialized country and only 5 per cent of the population is involved with agriculture. Many Belgians are natural entrepreneurs and work very hard. Some Belgians are great believers in the quality of life and for the wealthy this often means large houses and cars, lots of meals out and engaging in many social activities.

The climate: Temperatures range from about 40–45°F in winter to around 73°F in July and August. Snow is unusual except in the mountains of the Ardennes.

Finding somewhere to live: There is no shortage of accommodation in Belgium. Flats and houses can be found either through agents or in the press. Though rents have recently risen, they are still comparable with parts of the UK such as London.

Living conditions, shopping and prices: Though food is dearer in Belgium than it is in Britain, it is cheaper than parts of France and Germany. Bread (loaf, 1kg) is BF74 and milk (1 litre) BF35. The Belgians are great beer drinkers and beer is cheap. Cars are also a lot cheaper than in the UK. However, petrol costs more than the UK and household goods and clothes are also more expensive. Despite Brussels' central role in EU administration, prices have not rocketed and are generally less expensive than in many other large European cities.

Getting around: Fast and frequent trains connect all main towns and cities. A Tourrail ticket allows unlimited travel for 5 days over a 17-day period. The Benelux Tourrail Ticket can be used throughout Belgium, Luxembourg and the Netherlands. There is a wide network of local and regional buses throughout the country. It is possible to rent a bicycle from Belgian Railways at 48 stations throughout the country and this is a particularly popular activity in the flat northern and coastal areas.

Post and telephone: Payphones can be used with coins or Telecards which can be purchased at post offices and news-stands. The least expensive way to make an international phone call is to buy a Telecard and make a call from a telephone booth. Airmail letters to the UK are BF14 for the first 20g.

National holidays: 1 January; Easter Monday; 1 May (May Day); Ascension Day; Pentecost Monday; 21 July; 15 August (Assumption); 1 November (All Saints' Day); 11 November (Armistice) and 25–6 December.

Eating out and tipping: Belgians take eating out seriously and are concerned about fresh produce and new recipes. Menus and prices are posted outside restaurants. Specialities include *lapin à la bière* (rabbit in beer) and *faisan à la brabanconne* (pheasant with chicory). Dogs are often allowed in restaurants. Belgians usually have lunch between 1 and 3 p.m. and often make this a long and lavish meal; however, the main meal of the day is dinner which they eat between 7 and 10 p.m. Belgians usually dress conservatively and formally when eating out. Tipping in Belgium has been less favoured in recent years because of a service charge in most restaurant bills. It is usual to tip washroom attendants.

Denmark

Social patterns: Many Danes are helpful and friendly. They use a term 'hyggelig' which describes their feeling of well-being which comes from their hospitality. Denmark is a liberal country with a highly developed social welfare system. Though taxes are high they are proud of their state-funded systems and their high standard of living. They also have a strong sense of community spirit.

The climate: Temperatures vary from 28–36°F in January and February to 57–71°F in July and August.

Finding somewhere to live: Rented accommodation is fairly inexpensive but difficult to find. Over recent years the Danes have experienced a slump in house prices and, as in the UK, buying a property has become more of a buyer's market.

Living conditions, shopping and prices: Danes have a high average income and their standard of living is one of the highest in Europe. However, living costs are also high, particularly in Copenhagen. Bread (0.5 kg) is DKr 6.50 and milk (1 litre) DKr 7.00. Clothes, alcohol and consumer goods are much more expensive than in the UK.

Getting around: Travel by train or bus is easy in Denmark. Danish State Railways (DSB) covers the entire country with a network of railways and this network is supported by bus services in remote areas. The Nordpass provides 21 days of unlimited travel by rail and some sea routes. Denmark also has good ferry services. The Danes are reputed to have more bicycles per head than any other country in the world. As the country has a flat landscape and many uncrowded roads, it is a cycler's paradise.

Post and telephone: Payphones take DKr 1, 5 or 10 coins and letters and postcards cost DKr 3.50 to send to the UK. Stamps can be bought either at post offices or at any shop selling postcards.

National holidays: 1 January; Easter weekend; 7 May (Common Prayer); Ascension Day; Pentecost; 5 June (Constitution Day); and 24–6 December.

Eating out and tipping: Danish food is simple and contains many fresh ingredients. As an agricultural country, fish and meat are of top quality. Their famous *smorrebrod* contains a mound of fish or meat, together with lots of pickle relish and this is accompanied by rye and wheat bread. Another speciality is the Danish pastry. As with all Scandinavian countries, Denmark has its own version of the cold table, called *det store kolde bord*. The Danes eat lunch at noon, and evening meals are taken early. Dress is usually casual and few restaurants require a tie. Danes do not expect to be tipped, though it is a custom to tip hotel porters and leave a small coin when using a public toilet.

France

Social patterns: Whether eating, drinking, talking, shopping or going through daily routines, the French are famous for how they live. Throughout the day rituals are to be enjoyed. Food, for example, is to be savoured and the French do not like to rush their meals. The French are fiercely patriotic and proud of their country, its culture and all of their achievements.

The climate: The north of France has a northern European climate with cold winters, unpredictable summers and a lot of rain. Southern France has a Mediterranean climate with cold winters and long hot summers.

Finding somewhere to live: Houses or apartments can be found through agents or the press. Prices have risen significantly over recent years. Home ownership is rapidly becoming more widespread in France.

Living conditions, shopping and prices: The French cost of living is similar to that in the UK. Paris tends to be more expensive but prices tend to be lower outside the tourist regions. Bread (250g) is FF3.00 and milk (1 litre) FF5.95. Household goods, such as refrigerators and TV sets, are usually expensive. Petrol prices are also above the European average and there are tolls on major roads.

Getting around: The French national railway company, SNCF, is regarded as fast, comfortable and comprehensive and is recognized as Europe's best train service. Long-distance buses are rare because of the quality of the train service. France has a domestic internal air service caled Air Inter. It also has Europe's biggest waterway system.

Post and telephone: The telephone system is modern and efficient. Booths are plentiful and nearly always at post offices and cafés. Stamps can be bought in post offices and cafés sporting a red 'Tabac' sign outside.

National holidays: 1 January; Easter Monday; 1 May (Labour Day); 8 May (VE Day); Ascension Day; Pentecost; 14 July (Bastille Day); 15 August (Assumption); 1 November (All Saints' Day); 11 November (Armistice); and 25 December.

Eating out and tipping: Eating in France is taken very seriously. A *brasserie* with steak and french fries remains a classic, as does the picnic of a baguette with ham, cheese or paté. Lunch is normally taken betwen 12.00 and 1 p.m. and dinner usually begins at 8 p.m. Jacket and tie are usually expected at more expensive restaurants. It is customary to leave some small change as a tip in a bar or restaurant. It is also expected to tip cloakroom attendants, taxi drivers, hairdressers, bellhops and porters.

Germany

Social patterns: Germany is Europe's powerhouse and this is reflected in the way Germans work. They rise early and are often at work by 7 or 8 a.m. Their leisure time is taken just as seriously and they have long annual vacations. Festivals also occupy another 12 days. The outdoors is very important for many Germans.

The climate: Germany's climate is mainly temperate. Winters vary from being very mild and damp to being cold and bright. Though summers are usually sunny and warm there may be some cloudy and wet days.

Finding somewhere to live: House prices and rent costs vary from region to region. For example, a family home of average residential value would sell for DM120 000 in Meiningen and DM950 000 in Munich. In the cities Germans tend to live in flats in preference to houses. West German flats tend to have more space than those in the new federal states.

Living conditions, shopping and prices: Germany is a high-cost country with a high standard of living. Bread (1 kg) is DM3.50 and milk (1 litre) is DM1.35. Though clothes are more expensive, other household goods such as TVs and fridges are about the same price as in the UK. In the former GDR people earn considerably less than their Western colleagues. The 1990s have seen rising inflation in Germany primarily because of the integration of East Germany. For example, a 'reunification tax' has been levied on a number of basic commodities.

Getting around: Despite reunification, the two publicly owned train networks from the former two Germanies operate separately. All major cities in Germany are linked by fast Intercity services. Long-distance bus services are part of the Europe-wide Europabus network. Germany's national airline is Lufthansa and serves all major cities. Germany has many rivers and it is possible to cruise lakes and rivers throughout the country (Fig. 13.1). Bicycles can be rented at railway stations throughout the country.

Post and telephone: Telephone lines between the western and eastern parts of Germany are now much improved and nearly all the eastern regions can now be reached by direct dialling. If you have no change or wish to make a lengthy call, you can go to the post

Figure 13.1   Cruisers on the Rhine at St Goarshausen

office where the counter clerk will get you a line and charge you for the call after it has been made. Airmail letters to the UK cost DM1.

National holidays: 1 January; 6 January (Epiphany); Good Friday; Easter Monday; 1 May; Ascension Day; Pentecost Monday; Corpus Christi, (south Germany only); 3 October (Germany Unity Day); 1 November (All Saints' Day); 17 November (Day of Prayer and Repentance); and 24–6 December.

Eating out and tipping: The quality of German food is good and portions are ample. Hot sausages, spicy meatballs (*fleischpflanzerl*), meatloaf topped with a fried egg and sauerkraut are always popular. The most famous German dish is the sausage. Lunch is served from around 11.30 a.m. until 2 p.m. and dinner is from 6 to 9.30 p.m. Though the Germans are punctilious about tipping, overtipping is disapproved.

Case Study—Reducing inequalities

There are significant differences in the standards of living among the countries of the EU. In countries such as Denmark and Germany the per capita income is a full quarter above the EU average, while Portugal and Greece barely manage to achieve one half of this average. Distinguishing between member states is only a rough measure of differences in standards of living. By looking at the 166 different regions within the EU it is possible to identify many regions where prosperity is six times higher than in the poorer regions.

The economic strength of the EU is confined to a number of relatively small areas which dot the map in an imaginary quadrangle between London, Paris, Milan and Copenhagen. These economic zones comprise about one-third of the population but account for more than half the income. On the other hand, one-quarter of the EU's population account for barely an eighth of the income and live in peripheral regions from Ireland to Portugal and from southern Italy to Greece.

One question that is frequently asked is whether these differences in income will increase or decrease in the Single Market. The view from the EU is that sometimes it is necessary to help certain regions to catch up. To do this the EU has a structural policy which undertakes action to alter the structures in a region. Such action may include contributions to the social sphere to raise the standard of living, transport policy, vocational training, agricultural policy and numerous other fields. The aim is to promote the development of regions that are not as well advanced.

Questions

1. Look through this chapter to identify (a) the two most prosperous and (b) the two least prosperous countries in the EU.
2. Explain the importance of vocational training. How might improvements in such training help a region to improve its standards of living?

Greece

Social patterns: About one-third of Greeks live in the Greater Athens area, which includes the capital, the port of Piraeus and a number of suburbs. This area accounts for about 50 per cent of Greece's industry. There are more than 2000 islands around Greece, and all areas of Greece seem to be close to the sea. Its people are kind and generous. In the past many Greek workers emigrated because of low living standards and few employment opportunities, but this has become less pronounced over recent years. Many young people looking for opportunities are absorbed into family businesses.

The climate: Greece is a hot country in the summer, and this can be almost unbearable in July and August, particularly in Athens. On the islands, the brisk north-westerly wind, the *meltemi*, makes life more comfortable. The winter months tend to be damp and cold.

Finding somewhere to live: Despite a lot of building work in towns and cities in recent years, accommodation may be difficult to find. Rents and house prices are both high.

Living conditions, shopping and prices: Wages and salaries are lower than the EU average, and so is the standard of living. Athens, however, is more expensive than the rest of Greece. Bread (1 kg) costs Dr150–200 and milk (1 litre) Dr150. Wine, fresh fruit and vegetables are cheap.

Getting around: A variety of vehicles such as jeeps, buggies and cycles can be rented on the islands. Though trains are slow they are cheap and convenient. Olympic Airways have services between Athens and most towns and islands. Buses are inexpensive. There are frequent ferries between most of the islands.

Post and telephone: Kerbside kiosks can be used for local calls. The easiest way to make international calls is to go to a Telecommunications Office (OTE). Airmail letters within Europe cost Dr80.

National holidays: 1 January; 6 January (Epiphany); Shrove Monday; Clean Monday; 25 March (Independence); Good Friday; Easter Sunday; Easter Monday; 1 May; Pentecost; 15 August (Assumption); 28 October (Ochi Day); and 25–6 December.

Eating out and tipping: Much of Greek food combines vegetables such as eggplants, tomatoes and olives with olive oil, and seasonings such as lemon juice, garlic, basil and oregano. Traditional Greek food includes souvlaki (*shish kebab*) and pastries filled with stuffings such as spinach, cheese or meat. Lunch in Greek restaurants is served from 12.30 to 3 p.m. and dinner begins late at around 9 p.m. Dress is normally informal. Though there are no strong rules about tipping, it is usually expected to tip waiters, porters and taxi drivers.

Ireland

Social patterns: In Ireland many people are friendly and informal and there is a relaxed pace of life. Nightlife for many consists of a visit to a local pub and there are many outdoor activities. Religion plays an important role in the lives of its people and 95 per cent are Roman Catholics.

The climate: The climate of Ireland is influenced by the moderating effects of the seas and, as a result, snow is rare except in the mountain areas in winter.

Finding somewhere to live: Accommodation can be found either through the press or through agents. Rents and property prices are reasonable.

Living conditions, shopping and prices: Though Ireland is roughly comparable to the UK on prices and cost of living, Dublin is more expensive than the rest of the country. Bread (1 kg) is IR£0.77 and milk (1 litre) IR£0.57. There is a high rate of VAT on luxury goods and just 10 per cent on all other items.

Figure 13.2   An Aer Lingus jet at Cork Airport

Getting around: Ianod Eireann (Irish Rail) and Bus Eireann (Irish Bus) are independent companies of the state-owned public transportation company Coras Iompair Eireann (CIE). The network is extensive though speeds are slow. The bus service is more widespread but infrequent in remote area. Aer Lingus is the national airline (Fig. 13.2).

Post and telephone: As well as street booths there are phones in all post offices and most bars and hotels. Letters to the UK cost 32p.

National holidays: 1 January; 17 March (St Patrick's Day); Good Friday; Easter Monday; Whit Monday; first Monday in August; and 25–6 December.

Eating out and tipping: Some people say that Ireland has some of the best food ingredients in the world. Specialities are boiled bacon and cabbage, Irish stew and colcannon (cooked potatoes diced and fried in butter with onions and either cabbage or leeks and covered in thick cream). Guinness is an Irish national drink. Lunch is taken between 12.30 and 2 p.m. Dinner is between 7 and 9.30 p.m. Other than in up-market hotels and restaurants, tipping is not expected.

○ Case Study—Ireland's trading partners

Tables 13.1–13.3, adapted from a fact sheet issued by the Department of Foreign Affairs, Dublin, give the value of imports and exports between Ireland and its main trading partners.

Questions

1. What percentage of Ireland's trade (both imports and exports) is with the EU?
2. Describe what has happened to Ireland's exports over recent years.
3. Name *two* disadvantages of Ireland being at the far west of the EU.

Table 13.1   Ireland's main trading partners 1991 (IR£m)

		Imports	Exports	Total	% of trade
1	United Kingdom	5320	4798	10 118	36.3
2	United States	1922	1309	3231	11.6
3	Germany	1058	1910	2968	10.6
4	France	559	1426	1985	7.1
5	Netherlands	563	997	1560	5.6
6	Belgium/Luxembourg	271	737	1008	3.6
7	Japan	640	342	982	3.5
8	Italy	321	647	968	3.5
9	Spain	134	343	477	1.7
10	Sweden	200	251	451	1.6

Table 13.2   A comparison of export values (IR£m), 1981 and 1991

Exports	1981	%	1991	%
Agriculture	1177.0	24.6	2046.0	13.6
Forestry and Fishing	59.4	1.2	204.9	1.4
Industrial	3490.0	73.11	12 592.3	1.2
Unclassified	51.2	1.1	181.3	1.2
Total	4777.6	100.0	15 024.6	100.0

Table 13.3   Value of Ireland's foreign trade (IR£m), 1984–91

	Exports	Imports	Trade balance	Exports as % of imports
1984	8898	8912	−14	100
1985	9743	9428	315	103
1986	9374	8621	753	109
1987	10 724	9155	1568	117
1988	12 305	10 215	2090	120
1989	14 597	12 284	2313	119
1990	14 336	12 468	1868	114
1991	15 024	12 853	2171	116

Italy

Social patterns: Italian lifestyle rarely runs smoothly and this may mean delays or complications. Italians are friendly and many Italians have flair and style. Italy has a number of non-Italian speaking minorities and a variety of regional cultures.

The climate: Italy is a hot country with temperatures ranging from 40 to 52°F in January and from 67 to 86°F in August.

Finding somewhere to live: Most people live in apartments, and housing is very difficult to find in cities.

Living conditions, shopping and prices: Though the cost of living is higher in cities, on the whole Italian prices are slightly lower than those of northern Europe. Bread (1 kg) is 2800 lire and milk (1 litre) is 1500 lire. Pasta is the stable diet of Italians and is cheap, as are wines and spirits. Clothing and household goods are about the same price as those in the UK.

Getting around: Ferrovie dello Stato (FS) is the state-owned railway. There are often long queues at railway stations and trains can be crowded, particularly in the holiday season. By air, Alitalia and ATI provide services throughout Italy. An extensive bus network also provides services throughout the country.

Post and telephone: Pay phones take coins, tokens or cards. To make long-distance calls it is sometimes best to go to 'Telefoni' exchanges to make calls, where payment is made after the call. The Italian mail system is erratic and slow.

National holidays: 1 January; 6 January (Epiphany); Easter Monday; 25 April (Liberation Day); 1 May (May Day); 2 June (Republic Day); 15 August; 1 November (All Saints' Day); 8 December (Immaculate Conception); and 25–6 December.

Eating out and tipping: The cost of eating out varies enormously between reasonable prices at a family run *trattoria* and prices at a *ristorante*. There are usually service charges. Lunch is eaten from 1 to 3 p.m. and dinner from 8 to 10 p.m. It is usual to tip waiters, porters and taxi drivers.

Luxembourg

Social patterns: Luxembourg is a prosperous country and there are many visible signs of such prosperity. Of the population of 390 000 around 25 per cent are foreigners. Though Luxembourgers have their own dialect, French and German are the national languages. Luxembourg seems besieged by bankers and Eurocrats.

The climate: Temperatures tend to be moderate and it drizzles frequently.

Finding somewhere to live: Rents are high in Luxembourg City but lower in country areas. Letting agencies are recommended by the Luxembourg National Trade and Tourist Office.

Living conditions, shopping and prices: Living costs are similar to Belgium. However, prices of food tend to be lower while lodging is more expensive. Bread (500 g) is LF50 and milk (1 litre) LF36. Luxembourgers are among the most wealthy communities in Europe and have more cars per 1000 people than any other country.

Getting around: Luxembourg is served by frequent trains from Paris, Brussels and Amsterdam. Bus services are highly efficient in Luxembourg City and also serve other parts of the country. One of the best transport options is the Oeko-Carnet, a block of five one-day tickets for unlimited transport on trains and buses.

Post and telephone: Public phones are on the street and in Post Offices. It costs LF14 to send letters to the UK.

National holidays: 1 January; 22–3 February (Carnival); Easter Monday; 1 May (May Day); Ascension Day; Pentecost Monday; 23 June (National Day); 15 August (Assumption); 1 November (All Saints' Day); and 25–6 December.

Eating out and tipping: Restaurants at lunchtime often offer a *plat du jour* as a one-course special. Pizzerias also offer an excellent choice of food. There are many chic pastry shops offering a variety of dishes. Lunch is from noon to 2 p.m. and dinner is between 7 and 10 p.m. Tipping is not always necessary though it is sometimes usual to round upwards.

The Netherlands

Social patterns: The Netherlands has a tradition as a land of traders. Its history has also been characterized by resistance to invasion. The Dutch are determined and independent, yet also tolerant. They have many liberal ideas and attitudes. Religious and political freedom are an important part of Dutch life. They are hospitable to strangers and also firm about their own ideas if challenged.

The climate: Summers are generally warm though they can be wet. Winters are chilly and wet.

Finding somewhere to live: Despite a massive house-building programme houses and flats are difficult to get. There are few detached houses in the country and those that exist are very expensive.

Living conditions, shopping and prices: On the whole the cost of living is similar to that of the UK. Bread (a large loaf) is Fl.2.50 and milk (1 litre) is Fl.0.80. Wine and some spirits are a little cheaper than in the UK. The prices of consumer goods, clothes and personal services is higher.

Getting around: Trains operate throughout the country and are fast and comfortable. A rail pass provides unlimited travel either for one or seven days. There are also excellent bus networks between towns. The Netherlands is a 'cycle-friendly' country and there are many cycle paths, signs and picnic areas. Bicycles can often be rented at stations.

Post and telephone: The telephone system is reliable. Many booths have been converted to credit card systems. The post service is reliable, and it costs 75 cents to send letters to the UK.

National holidays: 1 January; Easter weekend; 30 April (Queen's Day); 5 May (Liberation); Ascension Day; Pentecost; and 25–6 December.

Eating out and tipping: There are a variety of cuisines which range from traditional Dutch to Indonesian. Specialities include *erwtensoep*, which is a rich, thick pea soup with pieces of tangy sausage or pigs' knuckles, and *hutspot*, which is a meat, carrot and potato stew. Dinner is normally between 6 and 7 p.m. Casual dress is acceptable. It is usual to tip porters and washroom attendants.

Portugal

Social patterns: Portugal has been a maritime nation for most of its history. There are differences between Portugal's northern and southern peoples. The northern character is more Celtic and in the south Moorish ancestry is noticeable. Portuguese people are often welcoming.

The climate: Portugal is temperate all year round and does not suffer from the extremes of heat felt by Mediterranean countries.

Finding somewhere to live: Buying a house in Portugal is a complex process full of legal pitfalls. Rents vary considerably throughout the country.

Living conditions, shopping and prices: Prices in Portugal are about 20 per cent less than in the UK. Transportation, dining and rents remain around the lowest in Europe. Bread (1 kg) costs 250$00 and milk (1 litre) 123$00. Meat and dairy foods tend to be expensive but fruit and vegetables tend to be cheap.

Getting around: The Portuguese railway system is extensive. Trains are clean and reliable but slow. The national state-owned bus company, Rodoviaria Nacional, run regular bus services throughout the country.

Post and telephone: Pay phones take a variety of coins. International calls from hotels can be expensive and it is usually wiser to make such calls from a post office. Postal rates increase twice a year.

National holidays: 1 January; Carnival/Shrove Tuesday; Good Friday; 25 April (Anniversary of the Revolution); 1 May; 10 June (National Day); Corpus Christi; 15 August (Assumption); 5 October (Day of the Republic); 1 November (All Saints' Day); 1 December (Independence Day); 8 December (Immaculate Conception); and 25 December.

Eating out and tipping: Seafood is an important part of the diet in Portugal. Lobster, crab, squid, tuna and sole are prepared in many different ways. *Caldeirada* is a stew made from food fresh from the sea. Lunch usually begins around 1 p.m. and dinner is served around 8 p.m. Modest tips are usually expected by those who render services.

Case Study—Comparing Portugal with the UK

The following details have been adapted from *Portugal in Figures,* published by the National Institute for statistics.

Visitors' visas
Visitors to Portugal who are residents of other EU countries need only present their national identity card or passport to enter and leave. Visitors from countries outside the European Union may require, in addition to a passport, a visa obtained from the Portuguese consulate in their country.

Currency
The Portuguese unit of currency is the escudo, which is subdivided into 100 centavos. Reference is frequently made in Portugal to a further unit called the 'conto' which represents 1000 escudos. The symbol used internally is Esc.

Thousands and fractions of monetary units can be denoted 55 000$00; 55 contos; or Esc 55 000.00.

Business hours
Banks are open weekdays from 8.30 a.m. to 2.45 p.m. Most government departments are open to the public on weekdays from 9 a.m. to 12 noon and from 2 to 3.30 p.m. Stores are generally open from 9 a.m. to 1 p.m. and from 3 to 7 p.m. during the week and from 9 a.m. to 1 p.m. on Saturdays. In addition, there are growing numbers of shopping centres

(*centros comerciais*) in urban areas, which remain open at lunchtime and have more flexible hours on weekday evenings and weekends.

Office hours in industry and commerce are usually from 9 a.m. to 1 p.m. and from 2 to 6 p.m., Monday to Friday. It is, however, common for work in factories to start at 8 a.m. and finish at 5 p.m.

Weights and measures
Portugal uses the metric system.

Dates and numbers
Portuguese generally write the date in full (day, month, year), e.g. 30 of September of 1992, abbreviated to 30/9/1992. In business the year/month/day abbreviation adopted within the European Union, e.g. 1992/9/30, is becoming generally used.

The Portuguese economy is very open, total trade in goods and services amounting to some 75 per cent of GDP. The country has consistently run a trade deficit. The main net export sectors are shoes, forest products, textiles, clothing, and wine; the main imports are leather, transport material, minerals and metals, chemicals, machinery, plastics and rubber, and food.

The continuing devaluation of the Portuguese currency and the country's low labor costs have been the key factors in maintaining a competitive position.

Local customs
There are no local customs, other than normal courtesy, that business visitors should feel compelled to observe *vis-à-vis* their Portuguese counterparts.

Questions

In what way is living in Portugal (a) similar to and (b) different from living in the UK?

Spain

Social patterns: Spain, which is a large and varied country, has some interesting cities, hilltop villages and a Moorish legacy.

The climate: Temperatures range from 35–47°F in January to 63–87°F in July.

Finding somewhere to live: Spanish property tenure is complicated and it is advisable to appoint an agent to deal with legal matters. There are more than a quarter of a million British residents in Spain.

Living conditions, shopping and prices: Prices in Spain are now similar to those of the UK. Bread (1 kg) is 167.70 Ptas and milk (1 litre) is 78.20 Ptas. Hotels are now expensive.

Getting around: The Spanish railway system is the RENFE. It has been much improved in recent years. The RENFE Tourist Card is an unlimited pass valid for 8, 15 or 22 days' travel. Iberia and its subsidiary Aviaco operate a widespread network of internal flights. Spain has an excellent bus network.

Post and telephone: Pay phones take a variety of coins but calling overseas is best done from a telephone office. Airmail letters to the UK cost 45 Ptas.

National holidays: 1 January; 6 January (Epiphany); 19 March (St Joseph); Holy Thursday; Good Friday; 1 May; Corpus Christi; 25 July (St James); 15 August (Assumption); 12 October (National Day); 1 November (All Saints' Day); 6 December (Constitution); 8 December (Immaculate Conception); and 25 December.

Eating out and tipping: There is a wide selection of bars, restaurants and cafès. Drinks are often accompanied by *tapas* (savoury bites). The national dish is *paella*, a mixture of saffron rice with seafood, chicken and vegetables. Lunch begins at 1 p.m. until 2.30 p.m. and dinner is usually available from 8.30 p.m. onwards. Tipping is appreciated though the practice is now less widespread.

 Task

Using a currency converter and the latest exchange rates, work out the countries in Europe in which bread and milk is (a) cheaper and (b) more expensive.

14

Assignment work

1. Database package

Load a database package and set up a file containing the following information about countries in the European Union. The information will be entered under the following headings: Country, Capital, Date of entry, Population at 1991 ('000s).

Country	Capital	Date of entry	Population at 1991 ('000)s
Spain	Madrid	1976	39 000
Greece	Athens	1981	10 000
France	Paris	1957	56 000
Portugal	Lisbon	1986	11 000
Germany	Berlin	1957	80 000
Luxembourg	Luxembourg	1957	400
UK	London	1973	60 000
Belgium	Brussels	1957	10 000
Ireland	Dublin	1973	3500
Denmark	Copenhagen	1973	5200
Netherlands	Amsterdam	1957	15 000
Italy	Rome	1957	60 000

(a) Save and print all of the file, record by record.
(b) Sort the file into alphabetical order. Print this list.
(c) Who were the founder members of the EU?
(d) Which countries joined most recently?
(e) Which two countries have (i) the largest population? (ii) the smallest population? Sort the file in descending order of population size.
(f) Other European countries would now like to join the EU. These include: Poland, with a population of 40 million and Czechoslovakia with a population of 16 million. Assuming that these countries join the EU in the year 2000, add them to your file.
(g) Assuming that Norway, Sweden, Austria and Liechtenstein join the EU in 1996, add them to your file. You will need to research details of the populations and capitals of these countries. Also research and add the following information to your

database: (i) the currencies of these countries; (ii) the current national income of these countries; and (iii) the current level of unemployment in these countries.

2. Spreadsheet package

Locate the most recent annual abstract of statistics in your college library or local library.

(a) Find the pages showing the UK's most recent exports to and imports from other EU countries.
(b) Design a spreadsheet to contain these data. Enter the data.
(c) Convert these data into charts and tables showing the UK's trade with other members of the EU. Analyse the results showing Britain's major trading partners in the EU.

3. The opportunities and threats posed by the Single European Market

From 1 January 1993 the Single Market was completed between members of what is now the European Union. The creation of the Single Market involved:

1. The removal of internal tariffs.
2. A common external tariff.
3. The free movement of labour, capital, goods and services between member states.
4. Common policies for transport, energy, industry and agriculture.

Brief

In this assignment you will need to produce a leaflet and carry out a 15-minute presentation.

You work for a government department with responsiblity for developing exports to other EU states. You have been asked to produce a leaflet highlighting the benefits of trading with other member states. The leaflet will need to show that we already trade with other EU countries in a big way. The leaflet should highlight the opportunities that a Single European Market provides. You will also need to highlight the importance of the EEA. Your leaflet will outline briefly the reasons for the Single Market and how this creates new opportunities for British business. You will also need to prepare a 15-minute presentation that will be used to 'launch' your new leaflet. At the launch you will need to answer questions from an invited panel. This questioning session may bring to light some of the threats to British business posed by the creation of the Single Market. Research some of the potential threats posed by the Single Market and possible ways of limiting or overcoming these potential threats.

4. Who makes the decisions in the European Union?

The EU today has increasing responsibilities for making decisions that affect our everyday lives. The EU is comprised of a number of institutions with powers to make particular decisions.

Brief

Your local newspaper has asked you to produce a short article with clear diagrams to illustrate the powers of the various institutions in the EU. The editor has asked you to focus on the roles of the Commission, the Parliament, the Council of Ministers and the Court of Justice. The editor would like you to illustrate the roles and responsibilities of each of these bodies by giving actual examples of decisions they have made. The editor would also like you to mention some of the clashes that currently exist between institutions and member states. The editor has given you the following article from a national newspaper which she feels may be helpful.

EU power struggle brewing

European Union states are heading for clashes with the European Commission and Parliament, following attempts by both to increase their influence. They are trying to push the powers granted by the Maastricht Treaty as far as possible.

The Parliament is still working out the implications of the new powers it won in the Maastricht Treaty. An official told journalists last week that it might have the right to vote on a GATT agreement once it was negotiated and added that 200 pieces of legislation would have to be reconsidered.

The Parliament is now asking for new Commission proposals on some Directives and demanding the right to reconsider others.

The Treaty was supposed to halt the move towards a single federal structure by dividing policy areas into three separate 'pillars'. All the EU institutions are involved in one set of decisions, broadly those concerning social and economic issues which the EU inherited from the European Community. In the other two—security and defence issues on the one hand, and home and justice affairs on the other—action was largely to be the preserve of member states.

5. Creating a Eurobrand

It is no longer possible to buy a Marathon chocolate bar since the UK's fourth favourite chocolate bar has been renamed 'Snickers'. The reason for the name change is to bring it into line with Mars's global branding strategy—every individual product has one brand name, worldwide. As Snickers was known in every market except the UK, 'Marathon' became 'Snickers'.

Many other companies are harmonizing brands across Europe. For example,

Unilever's Radion is now identical in most European markets. Such global branding allows economies of scale, enables production to be standardized and saves on advertising costs because the same images can be used with different captions and voice-overs.

With this in mind, greater care now needs to be taken when naming and establishing new brands, to ensure that they have the potential to be successful on a Europe-wide basis. Denmark's Plopp chocolate would probably not be well received in the UK; neither would France's Pschitt lemonade. Irish Mist liqueur has a problem in Germany where 'mist' translates to 'manure'!

Brief

You are a member of a group of consultants who are specialists in European marketing. You have been approached by a chocolate manufacturer to promote its chocolates on a Europe-wide basis. The name of the chocolate manufacturer is Merdons. It currently produces a range of chocolates called Merdons Fancies.

You have been asked to devise a name that would have Europe-wide appeal. In addition, you have been asked to design a logo for the company that would appeal throughout Europe. The chocolates are aimed at the up-market segment of the chocolate market. You have also been asked to design a set of storyboards which would support an advertising campaign for the product.

6. Researching one of the European Union's policy measures

The EU is responsible for many policies, ranging from the new technologies, the Common Agricultural Policy, educational exchanges, fishing policy, etc. These policies will be altered regularly in the light of changing conditions in the world at large and different priorities given to measures by individual member states.

Brief

You are employed by the European Affairs section of a major public company. The job of the European Affairs section is to keep other sections of the company up-to-date on current changes in European policy.

Your task is to research one particular policy area.

You must present your findings on a specific policy in the form of a short report. Included in your report should be:

- The aims of the policy.
- What the policy covers.
- The origins of the policy.
- The main features of the policy.

- The effects and potential effects of the policy.
- The most recent changes in the policy.

As part of your report you need to show the impact that the policy has (or may have in the future) on individuals and business organizations.

7. Changes in the European Union's budget

The final EU budget comes about in the following way: The budgetary procedure requires the Commission to draw up a draft budget for the following year before 1 September. It takes the form of two sections:

- commitments
- payments.

The commitments part is based on estimates for individual items of spending in a particular year, while the payments section covers the actual expenditure to be incurred.

This is then sent to Council, which has until 5 October to reach an agreement on a draft text by qualified majority. The draft then goes to Parliament, which has 45 days to vote (a) amendments, which require the approval of an absolute majority of members, and (b) 'modifications', which concern agricultural spending and require the support of just a majority of the votes cast.

After the vote on the first reading the amended draft budget is then sent to Council. Council then has 15 days in which to react by qualified majority to Parliament's

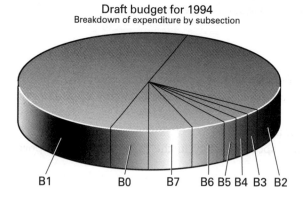

Draft budget for 1994
Breakdown of expenditure by subsection

Subsection		Amount (ECU million)
B1	Agriculture (including 1 billion ECU reserve)	37 465
B2	Regional and social	23 428
B3	Education, health and culture	387
B4	Energy and environment	292
B5	Consumer protection, industry and trans-European networks	424
B6	Research	2283
B7	Foreign aid	4231
B0	Administration and reserves	3896
	Total	72 406

Figure 14.1

amendments and proposed modifications. In practice it usually trims back the sums voted in the amendments and rejects the modifications. This draft is then sent back to Parliament for a second reading, which takes place in December. It is at this stage that Parliament usually reinstates cut-backs made by Council to non-compulsory spending, only this time it needs the support of a majority of members and three-fifths of the votes cast.

It is then up to Parliament's President to decide that the procedure has been completed and declare the budget adopted.

Figure 14.1 highlights the EU's draft budget for 1994.

Brief

You work for a public relations agency and have been asked by your local MEP to produce a short leaflet highlighting the major items of expenditure for the 1994 budget. The leaflet needs to use simple and easy to understand language so that householders who receive it can understand how EU money is being spent. You also need to highlight ways in which EU expenditure patterns have changed from what they typically would have been in the mid-1980s (in general terms).

8. Taking advantage of the Single European Market: exporting lingerie to France

Outline was a highly successful producer of women's quality underwear in the 1980s, producing a range of knickers, bras and teddies. In 1988 the sales department of the company mounted a highly successful exhibition in Paris where they received orders equalling their current annual production level. In response, the company expanded the size of its existing factory and doubled its workforce.

However, Outline soon ran into difficulties. Costs began to rise because of the expense involved in transporting the goods, the need to translate information into French, and the extra paperwork involved in exporting. The company also needed to produce a slightly smaller bra and this involved altering existing patterns and designs.

In 1992 the company ran into further difficulties due to the falling value of the pound therefore the goods sold to France were not worth as much as expected when the francs received in payment were converted into pounds sterling.

Brief

You have been employed as a consultant by Outline to set out proposals for counteracting some of the difficulties they have encountered in the early 1990s. You must produce a short report supported by a 15-minute presentation setting out:

1. The main problems encountered by Outline in selling to France.

2. The benefits of selling to France.
3. The benefits of the Single European Market.
4. Ways in which Outline could counteract the problems encountered in selling to France.
5. Suggestions for future planning for success.

9. Preparing to visit another country

Brief

You are the training officer for a firm producing soft drinks. A group of your colleagues will shortly be visiting Calais with a view to setting up a joint venture with a French company. Your task is to prepare a briefing pack to prepare your colleagues forthe visit.
  The briefing pack will need to contain the following items.

* Information on how to reach Calais.
* Details of how to book a hotel once they reach Calais.
* Information on changing currency before they leave on the trip.
* Details about Calais and the surrounding region.
* A list of about 50 key phrases that may be useful to your colleagues on the trip.

In addition to the briefing pack you should prepare a 10-minute presentation containing at least three overhead transparencies that can be presented to colleagues before the trip takes place.

15

Useful information sources for tutors and learners

European initiatives in the field of education

Most European Union initiatives in the field of education apply to the post-16 age group. Many of these initiatives are relevant to young people on vocational training courses or entering higher education. Some are open only through the youth service. In this chapter we present some of the most important initiatives.

1. Lingua

Lingua is a project to promote foreign language capability in the EU. It provides grants and assistance for:

- training of teachers and trainers of European languages
- helping people to gain knowledge of foreign languages used in work and other aspects of economic life
- exchanges of young people aged 16-25 in professional, vocational and technical education.

2. Youth for Europe

Youth for Europe offers information on EU youth exchange programmes in order to encourage youth exchange and youth mobility. It seeks to increase the numbers and quality of experience of those involved in youth exchanges. It particularly seeks to help those who are disadvantaged through personal, socio-economic or geographical circumstances. It particularly seeks to help students to make exchanges who live in areas on the periphery or in areas whose language is not widely used in the EU.

Three types of project can be supported by Youth for Europe ll (1992-4):

(a) Voluntary service activities in the educational, social, cultural or environmental fields in another member state.

(b) Study visits for youth workers.

(c) Bi-, tri- or multilateral youth exchanges for those between the ages of 15 and 25 and lasting for more than a week.

3. Petra

Petra is the EU programme for the vocational training of young people and their preparation for adult working life. It sets out to ensure that all young people who so desire are entitled to two or more years' initial vocational training. In addition Petra seeks to:

- complement and support member states' activities in developing the range, quality and relevance of initial vocational training
- add a European dimension to vocational training and guidance
- create training or work experience placements abroad
- develop trans-national training partnerships.

Grants are available for:

- initial training placements abroad
- young worker and advanced training placements
- the joint development of training modules and the joint training of trainers
- youth initiatives managed and controlled by young people in the areas of training, information or job creation
- the development and up-dating of data for use by guidance services in other member states
- co-operative research on important issues within the field of vocational education and training.

4. Force

Force sets out to develop continuing vocational training of employees in companies and to achieve a Union-wide impact on improving continuing training provision. It supports innovation in continuing vocational training by programmes to:

- set up and develop, with regional bodies, a continuing training network within the Union
- encourage exchange programmes
- promote trans-national and trans-frontier pilot schemes
- forecast trends and changes in qualifications and occupations
- co-operate in analysing and comparing current policy.

5. Iris

This is the network of training programmes for women. It seeks to stimulate better quality vocational training for women to help them to enter or re-enter the workforce, improve their qualifications and gain career promotion. The network offers:

- contact with other EU women's training projects
- trans-national partnerships and exchanges
- grants for model women's training projects
- seminars on training needs
- publications and information services.

6. Erasmus

Erasmus is the programme for the mobility of university students. It sets out to encourage student mobility and co-operation within higher education and aims to achieve academic recognition and credit transfer between educational establishments in the European Economic Area. The objectives of Erasmus are to:

- help everyone to reach the highest possible level of vocational training needed for their professional activity
- broaden vocational training to meet the new needs created by technical progress
- link vocational training to economic and social developments.

Erasmus provides financial support to higher education to encourage:

- student mobility (fully recognized periods of study in another institution as a part of their academic qualifications)
- teaching staff mobility
- the joint development of new curricula
- intensive teaching programmes involving students and staff from several member states.

7. Tempus

This is the Trans-Europe Mobility Programme for University Students, which aims to promote the quality and support the development of higher education system in the countries of Central and Eastern Europe and to encourage their growing interaction with partners in the European Union through joint activities and relevant mobility.

8. Comett

Comett is the European programme on co-operation between universities and industry regarding training in the field of new technologies.

The objectives of Comett are to:

- improve the contribution of technology training to economic and social developments
- foster joint university–industry training efforts
- respond to the training needs of small and medium-sized enterprises
- promote equal training for men and women
- promote the European dimension of the co-operation.

9. Eurotecnet

Eurotecnet stands for the EUROpean TEChnology NETwork for training. It is a programme which seeks to promote innovative actions in the areas of vocational training in order to deal with technological changes, and to identify new skills needed by the workforce as a result. To do this, Eurotecnet promotes the exchange of good practice and expertise by means of a network of innovative projects throughout the 12 member states and provides support to these projects via research and analysis.

Sources of information on individual countries

The Austrian Embassy, 18 Belgrave Mews West, London SW1X 8HU.
The Belgian Embassy, 103 Eaton Square, London SW1W 9AB
CIS, 13 Kensington Palace Gardens, London S8
The Royal Danish Embassy, 55 Sloane Street, London SW1X 9SR
The Finnish Embassy, 38 Chesham Place, London SW1X 8HW
The French Embassy, 58 Knightsbridge, London SW1X 7JT
The German Embassy, 23 Belgrave Square, London SW1 8PZ
The Greek Embassy, 1a Holland Park, London W2
The Irish Embassy, 17 Grosvenor Place, London SW1 7HR
The Italian Embassy, 14 Three Kings Yard, Davis Street, London W1
The Luxembourg Embassy, 27 Wilson Crescent, London SW1X 8SD
The Netherlands Embassy, 38 Hyde Park Gate, London SW7 5DP
The Norwegian Embassy, 25 Belgrave Square, London SW1X 8PJ
The Polish Cultural Institute, 34 Portland Place, London W1N 4HQ
The Portuguese Embassy, 11 Belgrave Square, London SW1X 8PP
The Spanish Embassy, 24 Belgrave Square, London SW1X 8QA
The Swedish Embassy, 11 Montague Place, London W1H 2AL
The Swiss Embassy, 16-18 Montague Place, London W1H 2BQ

UK-Based travel organizations

North Sea Ferries, King George Dock, Hull, HU9 5QA
Hoverspeed, International Hoverport, Ramsgate CT12 5HS
Brittany Ferries, 84 Baker Street, London W1
Sealink UK Ltd, Eversholt House, Evershold Street, London W1
P&O Company, 220 Tottenham Court Road, London W1P 9AF
Sabina Belgium World Airlines, 36 Piccadilly, London W1
Air France, 158 New Bond Street, London W1
British Airways, Terminal House, 52 Grosvenor Gardens, London W1
Lufthansa German Airlines, 38 Gillingham Street, London W1
Alitalia Italian Airlines, 251 Regent Street, London W1
Air Portugal, 38 Gillingham Street, London W1
Netherlands Railways, 4 Burlington Street, London W1

EU Institutions

Commission of the European Union, 200 Rue de la Loi, B–1049 Brussels
European Parliament, Avenue de L'Europe, F 67006 Strasbourg Cedex
Economic and Social Committee, 2 Rue Ravenstein, B–1000 Brussels
Statistical Office of the European community, Bâtiment Jean-Monnet, Rue Alcide-de-Gasperi, L2920 Luxembourg
Office of Publications for the European Union, 2 Rue Mercier, L–2985 Luxembourg
Official Journal of the European Union, 26 Rue Desaix, F–75732 Paris Cedex 15
European Centre for Young Farmers, 23-5 Rue de la Science, B–1040 Brussels
European Environment Bureau, 29 Rue Vautier, B–1040 Brussels
Equal Opportunities in Europe, Director Générale X-Service Information Femmes, 20 Rue de la Loi, B-1049 Brussels

Educational Organizations

COMETT, 71 Avenue de Cortenbergh, B–1040 Brussels
ERASMUS, 70 Rue Montoyer, B–1040 Brussels
LINGUA, 10 Rue du Commerce, B–1040 Brussels
PETRA, 32 Square Ambiorix, B–1040 Brussels
EUROTECNET, 37 Rue des Deux Eglises, B–1040 Brussels
Youth for Europe, 2–3 Place du Luxembourg, B–1040 Brussels

Index